Maastricht School of Management Series in
Leadership, Change an.

Maastricht School of Management Series in Intercultural and Global Management

LEADERSHIP, CHANGE AND RESPONSIBILITY

Edited by:
Joop Remmé
Stephanie Jones
Beatrice van der Heijden
Silvio De Bono

Meyer & Meyer Media

Maastricht School of Management Series in Intercultural and Global Management
Series Editors: Ronald Tuninga & Fred Phillips

British Library Cataloguing in Publication Data
A catalogue record for this book is available from the British Library

Remmé, Jones, van der Heijden & De Bono
Leadership, Change and Responsibility
Oxford: Meyer & Meyer (UK) Ltd., 2008
ISBN: 978-1-84126-238-3

© 2008 by Meyer & Meyer (UK) Ltd.
Adelaide, Auckland, Budapest, Cape Town, Graz, Indianapolis,
Maidenhead, New York, Olten (CH), Singapore, Toronto
Cover Design: Mana co, The Netherlands
Printed and bound in the Netherlands by: Koninklijke Wöhrmann bv, Zutphen
ISBN: 978-1-84126-238-3
E-Mail: verlag@m-m-sports.com
www.m-m-sports.com

CONTENTS

MAASTRICHT SCHOOL OF MANAGEMENT

Series in Intercultural and Global Management

Series Editors Ronald Tuninga and Fred Phillips

Volumes To Date

Stephanie Jones, Khaled Wahba, and Beatrice I.J.M. van der Heijden
How To Write Your MBA Thesis: A Comprehensive Guide for All Masters'
Students Required to Write a Research-Based Thesis or Dissertation (2007)

Joop Remmé, Stephanie Jones, Beatrice I.J.M. van der Heijden and Silvio De Bono
Leadership, Change and Responsibility (2008)

Stephanie Jones and Silvio De Bono
Managing Cultural Diversity (in press)

Introduction to the Series

This series makes excellent, affordable textbooks available to students in emerging and developing countries. By emphasizing the international, multicultural, sustainability, and social responsibility dimensions of management, and by giving special attention to change issues in transitional economies, these volumes aim to define the way management subjects can be taught to multicultural audiences. Our goal as editors is to have the series seen as the imprimatur of the best textbooks in the field, and thereby influence the future of teaching international business.

Targeted readers include MBA students in MSM's overseas outreach programs, students enrolled in other universities, and practicing managers in many countries. Our authors write for readers who wish to be world-class managers, whether in their home countries or abroad, whether for indigenous companies or for multi-nationals.

We nonetheless believe it is not fair to such readers to frame all content in terms of problems and persons representing only business in the OECD nations. Volumes in the series therefore depict business situations drawn from many of the countries where MSM is active. We have chosen authors with broad experience on multiple continents, and specifically in emerging economies and developing countries.

We do not assume readers have access to the books, periodicals, databases, research journals, and fast reliable Internet connections that are taken for granted by MBA students in the OECD countries. Thus, each textbook in the series is a self-contained course on its topic. Each book is suitable for a condensed course format, but also allows teachers the flexibility to use the book for online or face-to-face courses in other formats. For more than a half century Maastricht School of Management (MSM) has focused on international cooperation. As a key player in the global education field, MSM is one of the few management schools that systematically combine education, technical assistance and research in its professional services. Offering high-quality management degree programs (MSc, MBA, DBA and PhD) and executive programs, MSM also implements management development research and international projects. With more than 2000 students graduating each year in nearly thirty countries, MSM is the largest and most international business school of the Netherlands.

MSM has worked for years at the interface of public- and private-sector management of transition processes in culturally diverse environments. Our guiding principle is the enhancement of performance of the private and public sectors to support balanced economic development. MSM provides technical assistance and specific training to government agencies, semi-government agencies, NGOs, post-secondary education institutions and the private sector, including small and medium enterprises. MSM offers graduate programs at campuses in China, Egypt, Germany, Indonesia, Jordan, Kazakhstan, Kenya, Kuwait, Malawi, Malaysia, Mongolia, Russia, Namibia, the Netherlands, Peru, Rwanda, Saudi Arabia, Suriname, Tanzania, Uganda, Vietnam, Yemen, Zambia, and Zimbabwe.

Ronald Tuninga and Fred Phillips

CHAPTER ONE

LEADERSHIP, CHANGE AND RESPONSIBILITY IN ORGANIZATIONS

ROBERT FLOOD

LEARNING OBJECTIVES

- To highlight the main issues dealt with in the book and their relevance to modern day management.
- To introduce the purpose, structure and contents of the book.
- To introduce the four main themes Leadership, Organizational Design, Change Management, and Corporate Social Responsibility.
- To emphasize interrelatedness between the four main themes and the need for a systemic approach to Leading Change in Organizations.

CONTENT

- An introduction to contemporary issues/problems of Leading Change in Organizations.
- An overview of what is required to tackle issues/problems of Leading Change in Organizations.
- An overview of four key approaches to Leading Change in Organizations:
- Leadership
- Organizational Design
- Change Management
- Corporate Social Responsibility.
- A systemic approach to Leading Change in Organizations (a stakeholder approach).
- The structure and content of the book and how the book will realize a systemic approach to Leading Change in Organizations.

INTRODUCTION

The industrial revolution in the mid 18th to the mid 19th centuries changed the nature of industry and society. Prior to the industrial revolution organizations were small tightly knit groups of people serving their local communities. Such small enterprises were an important driver behind the development of local and national economies. A typical enterprise of the pre-industrial revolution era is one built upon a craft, like furniture making, weaving, and blacksmithing. There was also the family enterprise, for example a provision store, a locksmith, and a farm. Such organizations were small, employing just a handful of people, and thus were easy to lead, had simple structures like master craftsman and apprentice, and were easy to control in terms of managing people and maintaining quality. So effective were these organizations that in some cases their products are still available today and are highly prized. Some furniture from the pre-industrial era is robust and attractive and sells at incredible prices in modern day auctions.

All this changed with the Industrial Revolution. All of a sudden a new kind of organization emerged – the factory. What was effective in small enterprises was barely relevant to this new form of economic activity. Factories enabled mass manufacturing of products but to do this many people were employed in one organization and vast amounts of materials had to be handled. How could the mass of people and materials be organized into an efficient and effective force rather than collapse into an anarchistic maelstrom? The answer was found in leadership and design.

An organizational design was needed to structure people and their work. Two main issues surfaced. First was the task of designing operational processes and making them efficient. The second was designing administrative systems by which to manage and control all factors of operational processes so that the enterprise was effective at achieving strategy and goals.

EARLIEST IDEAS

The earliest ideas on efficiency are found in works like Frederick Taylor's scientific management followed by Henry Ford's version called Fordism. The central idea was to split up processes into parts and train people to become specialists in one activity. It was believed that specialization that aligned workers to a specific or limited task would lead the workers to become most proficient and ultra-efficient in the work they performed because they would perform the tasks many times leading to perfection or, from a capitalists perspective, greater efficiency and profit.

Earliest ideas on effectiveness are found in organizational design and the seminal design solution, the hierarchical tree. In this structure there would be workers, supervisors and managers. The three-tiered hierarchy put in place clear lines of authority. Hierarchy quickly evolved into a functional structure and over time spawned specialist management activities including finance and accounting, personnel and human resources, and sales and marketing. Effectiveness would come through management setting and implementing policy and goals and supervisors watching closely over the workers to ensure goals were achieved. Workers would be motivated by financial rewards – 'the economic man theory'.

SOLUTION

This solution remains the dominant one in modern day management and that it survives today in a post-industrial revolution era, sometimes called the information revolution era, is surely testament to strengths inherent in hierarchical management and specialization in job design. The solution also has hit very many serious problems. Here are a few of them:

- Hierarchical decision-making is the basis of bureaucracy that combined make for long and convoluted decision-making processes that slow down organizational activities rather than deliver quick and effective support to operational activities.
- Hierarchy led to functional silos out of touch with each other and consequently poorly coordinated organizations.

- Workers felt alienated and more like a cog in a machine rather than a human being in a social activity. Supervisors and managers treated workers as cogs. This caused conflict and strife that in extreme circumstances resulted in the formation of unions to protect workers and strikes as their main defense weapon.
- Routine repetitive work for workers led to boredom and inefficiency rather than perfection and high efficiency in performing tasks. Human needs had been neglected.
- Lines of authority originated from a few senior managers at the top of the hierarchy and this became understood as a power structure resulting in centralized management. Centralized management further alienated the workforce and made life at the top extremely stressful because top managers became overwhelmed with information, requests and demands that flowed upwards only stopping when reaching the top.

In the early to mid 1900s management attained a foothold as a main topic studied by professional researchers in academia and soon these points and many others fuelled heated debate. Emerging out of the storm was a better understanding of the organization as both an economic and social activity, although there were strong disagreements between contrasting and sometimes contradicting schools of thought. Hot topics were those of leadership, organizational design, change and change management, and corporate social responsibility and ethics.

THE MODERN ERA

The modern era in which we live has spawned many different types of organizations that are far removed from small craft enterprises and factories, from small, to medium-sized, to large organizations and, the 'monster amongst all beasts', the multinational. In addition to the challenges of operating in a domestic environment the multinational poses unique challenges involved in 'doing business' across national boundaries. There are brand new problems relating to for example legislation, culture, local and global knowledge, organizational structure, maintaining high integrity across political and economic boundaries, and, of course leadership. This book aims to explore the multinational in the 21st Century in these terms, developing an in-depth understanding of the multinational in the modern era. Our book has been thoughtfully structured to achieve this aim. We start by developing an understanding of effective leadership in modern day management.

THE CONTENTS OF THE BOOK

Chapter 2 We begin by introducing the key topic 'Leadership'. Our aim is to unmask the origins and evolution of leadership. Competencies emphasized include how well a leader affects and influences people, the integrity that is key to attaining trust, and leaders' abilities related to making effective decisions. To gain deeper insight we investigate the work of early leadership theories including: 'Great Man Theories' where leaders are born with innate qualities, 'Trait Theories' that lists traits in people associated with leadership, 'Behaviorist Theories' that concentrates on what people do rather than their qualities, 'Situational Leadership' that sees leadership as specific to the situation in which it is exercised, 'Contingency Theory' that goes one step further saying appropriate leadership is contingent upon the context, and 'Transformational and Transactional Theory' that emphasizes the relationship between leader and followers. The next chapter brings leadership theory up-to-date by highlighting new challenges and realities and leadership theories relevant to them. 'Seven leadership action logic roles' focuses on how a leader might act, compared to his or her philosophy.

Chapter 3 In this chapter we aim to present important aspects of new thinking on leadership, focusing on work of contemporary leadership theorists that especially emphasizes the contextual nature of leadership. We see two new competencies emerging; results-orientated leadership and innovative leadership. There are very many new theories and we have chosen four that provide a good insight into directions leadership theory has moved. 'Soft management' says the strength of leadership is in inviting candid feedback and acknowledging that one person at the top cannot know everything. This idea is contra the old one that leaders must be tough and rough and must be experts on all matters. 'Five minds of a manager' emphasizes the close relationship of leadership and management, and that they are two sides of one coin. 'Eight questions of leadership' are distilled from the life and times of Lord Admiral Nelson and his success as a leader. Why reinvent the wheel when the answers are there for the taking. 'Ten roles of a manager' places heavy emphasis on context like some theories in Chapter 2, but states it is what managers do to fulfill the tasks and roles needed in their organizations that matters, not what managers are. With a sound appreciation of leadership now in place we are well set to investigate the relationship between strategist leaders and the structure of the organizations in which they operate.

Chapter 4 The emphasis now switches to the relationship between strategy and structure. We will study the organization's mission for improvement to enhance overall efficiency and effectiveness and attain competitive advantage. In particular we examine the current need for adaptation of organizations to the global arena. Conventional thinking in this area focuses on either diversification or on divisionalization, but we go beyond this first by examining several 'complex strategic and structural configurations' and raise debates about organizations in an environment and about mechanistic versus organic organizations. We then explore the organization's mission for improvement and keys to attain excellent levels of efficiency and effectiveness. We wind up the chapter by exploring issues pertaining to organizational adaptation to globalization and implications that arise for developing and emerging countries/economies. The next chapter identifies organizational design as central to understanding the relationship between strategy and structure.

Chapter 5 We switch the emphasis of our exploration from strategy to structure since effectiveness of all strategy will depend on the strengths and weaknesses of the very design within which work is carried out. We begin by defining organizational structure in terms of key questions and design options, then examine key elements of organizational structure like span of control and work specialization, and lastly explain how environmental, strategic, and technological factors affect the design of organizations. These topics offer the background by which we may understand in the next chapter, a presentation of actual organizational structures recommended by different philosophical orientations.

Chapter 6 Herein we define organizational structure and then describe and analyze traditional design alternatives. Common approaches to structural design are investigated in an activity versus group debate. The traditional forms of structural design are introduced that are often found in literature on strategic management and business policy; simple, product, geographical, hybrid, matrix structures (including context plus advantages and disadvantages). This is followed by bringing to the fore critical ideas about contemporary organizational design for better integration and coordination. We place this in the context of the multinational with additional discussion of network and virtual organizations. Perhaps the single most important fact that emerges in the first six chapters is that the only thing that does not change is that things are always changing. That is why leaders must be flexible and adaptive, why designs must be under continual review and open to change, and why strategy is better understood as a continual process of learning and adaptation. What we are saying here points us immediately to issues of organizational development and change, the topic of the next chapter.

Chapter 7 In this chapter on organizational development and change we aim to facilitate understanding about the forces for change experienced by organizations including financial ones, and those from employees, from competitors and from customers. We also raise awareness of pressures relating to technology and globalization. All in all we want to make abundantly clear that since change is inevitable successful modern day leaders will know this and respond accordingly. The contemporary management strategy relevant here is the 'learning organization' that appreciates three levels in the organization; the individual, the group, and the organization itself. To succeed learning must be an integral part of the functioning and activity at all three levels. In short, all must recognize change, be ready for change and be responsive to changing circumstances. This is not always straightforward because not everyone recognizes the inevitability of change and indeed may even feel threatened by change. So, in this chapter we also explore problems of resistance to changes and how to cope with this. The next chapter works on the idea of the need for change.

Chapter 8 This chapter addresses the question "why do we need organizational change?" We aim to develop awareness of change processes and how these are managed in different companies. Accordingly, we introduce the differences between interpersonal methods, team methods and organizational methods in the change process and the importance of creating a simple road map for change, with milestones and goals. We achieve this by providing an introduction to initiatives that contribute to an effective change process, exploring the process of promoting change in organizations (through interpersonal, team and organizational methods), and highlighting the importance of goal-setting and documenting the change process as essential stages in the change process. In this chapter we ask "why change?" whereas in the next chapter we address the question "how do we change?"

Chapter 9 The main aim in this chapter is to appreciate the importance and nature of planned and managed change. We present these ideas hoping to raise awareness that intuitive leadership and management is insufficient in the local and global business worlds that are characterized by great complexity. So, it is key that we understand basic approaches to managing change and the role of change agents (as leaders). To this end we examine a number of change approaches namely the economic approach and the organizational development approach, and thereto the use of surveys, consultation, and teamwork. We place importance on measurement and the establishment of indicators that provide information about how well the change process is proceeding. However, many leaders/strategists do not have to live with the consequences of change that they facilitate. They change other people's working lives and the lives of other stakeholders who may not be employees of the firm, but may be victims of the firm's strategy and related activities. This has all sorts of implications in terms of fairness that we raise in terms of ethical issues in organizational change. The next chapter firmly grasps this prickly topic raising the hoary old problems of ethics and corporate social responsibility.

Chapter 10 This chapter is about ethics and corporate social responsibility. The topic is a tricky one but we hope to reveal the critical issues in terms of ethics in society and in management and by explaining what is meant by corporate social responsibility and how issues of corporate social responsibility can be addressed. Whilst we are not delivering a course on philosophy, it is important we grasp the importance of the debates about ethics and morality in the work place. Traditions of ethics are discussed as they are relevant to management. Corporate Social Responsibility is discussed as a managerial reality. This chapter nurtures a basic understanding of the issues. The next chapter looks in much more detail at issues within corporate social responsibility.

Chapter 11 In this chapter we aim to provide a working insight into some of the most important challenges in corporate social responsibility. We wish to give the students some practical ideas about how to deal with those challenges. We identify four key issue areas; corruption, discrimination, finance, and health. The last chapter discusses the issue of social responsibility in the context of sustainability.

Chapter 12 Herein we think about leadership, organizational design and organizational change in terms of stakeholders and stakeholder management. The stakeholders of an organization are understood to comprise all those people and groups of people inside and those outside of the organization who will be involved in or affected by the implementation of current or recently formulated strategy. In many senses this notion of stakeholder obliterates old-fashioned ideas about the organization and its boundaries by recognizing people and groups of people that are not employed by the organization but may be affected by an organization's plans for the future and in this way have a stake in them and should be given a voice in the process. Any solution ultimately will be some kind of compromise since it is utterly impossible to fully meet all of the demands of the stakeholder group. Finally, sustainability is discussed as a societal and managerial challenge and that arguably an organization must behave in a socially responsible manner as part of fostering sustainable activities.

Questions:
- *What were the main ideas behind organizing in the era of the industrial revolution?*
- *What were the main ideas behind organizing within 'scientific management'?*
- *What are the problems that can be associated with 'the information revolution era'?*
- *Where do you find those persisting problems addressed in the case-studies in the chapters that follow this chapter? (A question to keep in mind as you read the rest of the book)*

SUMMARY

In summary, this book offers an introduction to contemporary issues/problems of Leadership, Change and Responsibility. It provides an overview of what is required to tackle issues/problems of leading change in organizations. To achieve this, the book offers an overview of four key approaches to leading change in organizations: (1) Leadership, (2) Organizational Design (3) Change Management, and (4) Corporate Social Responsibility. In so doing the book develops a systemic approach to leading change in multinationals through a stakeholder approach. This approach encourages the involvement of everyone who is involved in and affected by the strategic developments of an organization. The structure and content of this book thus realize a systemic approach to Leadership, Change and Responsibility.

CHAPTER TWO
LEADERSHIP – EVOLUTION AND TRADITION
STEPHANIE JONES

OPENING CASE: ALEXANDER THE GREAT

John Adair, in his study *Great Leaders* (1989: 231) pointed out that "physical height was deeply associated with superiority in the ancient mind, possibly because tall men had an advantage in hand-to-hand fighting and tended to be chosen as war-leaders". Alexander was less than middle height for the era, but he did have physical features which suggested to others his genius for leadership (especially if we relate these observations to the trait theory of leadership). His portraits emphasized his large, staring, luminous eyes. He could speak effectively and move men's emotions with his words, and his enthusiasm and energy seemed unlimited. His royal birth and successes in battle gave him an aura of divinity. If a leader had traits like Alexander, maybe he could achieve Alexander's successes too.

As an inspirer or motivator of soldiers few have exceeded Alexander. He shared in the men's dangers, as the scars of his wounds testified. Alexander would eat the same food as they did. He was highly visible, giving instructions, but he also encouraged his men, backed up by rewards. He always fought hard himself but he was on the watch for any acts of conspicuous courage. He could sum up the inevitably confused situations on battlefields and then take the appropriate action in an effective way. He had clear intuition – a feeling for the real situation long before it becomes plain to others. These attributes were an important part of his leadership style – sharing and rewarding, seeing clearly and knowing what to do, which all added to his ability to inspire.

What went wrong with Alexander? The source of his army's troubles lay in its success, as victory succeeded victory and went to Alexander's head. A group of obsequious courtiers around the young king (Alexander was only twenty-two years old when he crossed the Hellespont in Greece) flattered him. They tried to convince him that his successes and conquests were due to his own courage and brilliance, and not the army's superb qualities as a fighting team. Alexander was being encouraged to take the credit rather than give it, and see himself as having God-like qualities. His mother, a priestess, also convinced him of this.

This led to disaster when, six years after the expedition had set out from Greece, Alexander and some of his officers were resting after battle and had been drinking heavily. He was flattered to the extent that he started to believe he was superior to the Gods to whom he had been sacrificing that day. Only the envy of his officers deprived him of the divine honors due, the courtiers told him. Alexander's officers denounced such insults to the Gods, and pointed out that the achievements were the work of Macedonians as a whole. The young king lost his temper and in the ensuing brawl he speared his best friend and favorite officer to death. As a young and immature leader, he allowed himself to be manipulated, and was driven to the destruction of those and the organization he loved best. And it continued: as Alexander reached Persia, the subjects of his new eastern domains deemed it inconceivable that a great conqueror such as Alexander was not a God in human form.

15

At last the trail of conquests came to an end when Alexander finally heard the truth that the army wanted to return home. He was told the army was departing, "no longer in poverty and obscurity, but famous and enriched by the treasure you have enabled it to win. Do not try to lead men who are unwilling to follow you; if their heart is not in it, you will never find the old spirit or courage. . . Sir, if there is one thing above all others a successful man should know, it is when to stop. Assuredly for a commander like yourself, with an army like ours, there is nothing to fear from any army; but luck, remember, is an unpredictable thing, and against what it may bring no man has any defense" (Adair, 1989: 233). By this stage he was out of touch, and obsessed with continuing his advance, surrounded by his personal guard.

This can be compared with one of the issues of modern rulers: the demands of personal security compel them to distance themselves from their subjects, even to the stage of being out of touch with their needs. At the same time the call for democracy and participative leadership asks for a greater closeness between leaders and the led. Alexander started off as a close and in-touch leader, but became estranged from his men through his willingness to buy in to his own legend. This can be a highly dangerous development for a leader.

Case Questions:
- *How and why was Alexander such an influence on early theorists of leadership?*
- *Do you believe that Alexander fulfilled the ideals of a leader of his era – or not?*
- *Why was Alexander's tendency to stay close to his men and share their hardships so powerful in his role as their leader? What was the more usual practice at that time?*
- *Why did Alexander eventually fail as a leader?*
- *Can you think of any present-day leaders like Alexander?*
- *Why do most leaders find it hard to stop being leaders?*

LEARNING OBJECTIVES:

This chapter aims to help you to examine how the concept of leadership has emerged and evolved, and the theories and reflections of some of the early writers on leadership. Many authors initially described leadership in simple terms – the characteristics of leaders, the behaviors of leaders, and the situations leaders found themselves in. We start off by introducing you to leadership competencies, then the heroic tradition of leadership, and a summary of leadership theories down the ages. This chapter aims to lead into the next chapter, on new perspectives of leadership, introducing you to some of the 'captains of industry' around the world demonstrating these.

LEADERSHIP COMPETENCIES

The traditional way of seeing what a leader does is summarized by these three main competencies – the leader is either good or bad at impacting and influencing what people do; he or she has to exhibit integrity, in order to attract trust and committed followers; and he or she has to make decisions and solve problems. In less complicated times, this was often seen as enough. Now, more is expected of the leader, as discussed in the next chapter.

IMPACT AND INFLUENCE: NEGATIVE BEHAVIORAL INDICTORS

- Is not sure if views will be listened to, has no confidence in own opinions
- Arguments are not convincing, contradictory, even changes his/her mind in the middle of a sentence
- Spends too much time on small matters and gets easily side-tracked and off the point
- Does not think of ways in which his/her suggestions could be of benefit and interest to the customer and thus is not able to persuade them
- Is not sure of the point of the whole discussion and therefore cannot influence others, as is himself/herself confused and unclear

POSITIVE BEHAVIORAL INDICATORS

- Helps customers to come to a decision which is acceptable to them, making them think they thought of it themselves
- Is very clear on own understanding, has confidence and is able to inspire confidence in others
- Uses rational arguments and logic, facts and figures, not just subjective arguments
- Makes friends easily – people want to work with him/her
- Is modest, mild and reasonable in approach, assertive but not passive or aggressive

INTEGRITY: NEGATIVE BEHAVIORAL INDICATORS

- Is willing to sacrifice the company's values (quality, customer service standards etc.) in exchange for a short-term solution to an immediate problem, in order to save time, effort and for a quick fix
- Criticizes team-mates and the company and its policies in front of outsiders (dealers, customers, principals) to make self look better, regardless of others
- Looks for personal gain rather than company gain – especially if these are conflicting – asking "what's in it for me?"
- Is quick to offer large discounts and inducements in order to get the business
- Can allow fear to damage and compromise integrity

POSITIVE BEHAVIORAL INDICATORS

- Insists on company values being uppermost from the beginning of the negotiations and they should be upheld, whatever the principals, dealers, customers are suggesting
- Even if privately disagrees with the company's policies and colleagues, does not express it in public; shows loyalty
- Does not make rash promises – says "I can't promise this because I don't know if I can keep my promise"

- Sells on quality, customer service, company values – not just on price
- Does not 'sell stones for eggs' – does not seek 'win/lose'; no short term solutions
- Shows flexibility within a certain range but will not compromise values
- Puts cards on the table – does not try to make private deals – shares with his team-mates openly his plan – transparent, open, no hidden agendas

PROBLEM-SOLVING: NEGATIVE BEHAVIORAL INDICATORS

- Makes the assumption from the beginning that "this will be difficult" – seeing complexities and hurdles where they may not exist
- Sees difficulties as insurmountable without thinking of ways around them
- Procrastinates – I don't have to decide now, if I keep putting off making a decision maybe the issue will just go away
- Takes avoiding behavior – refuses to recognize the problem or the need to make a decision
- Waits to hear what everyone else says first, tries to avoid making an opinion, but if forced will agree with everyone else

POSITIVE BEHAVIORAL INDICATORS

- Thinks around the problem, not just considering obvious solutions, and challenges all suggested solutions – which could be better?
- Can make a decision which covers several areas – such as a broad policy decision, not just on a small matter – and uses it to apply to a number of decision-making requirements at the same time
- Quickly makes decisions where possible – does not ponder too long
- Is confident and assured in decision-making, sticking to his/her decisions and not changing his/her mind later
- Has several suggestions in solving problems and making decisions – not just one or two
- Able to be 'sensing' and 'intuitive' – can make judgments based on facts and on hunches – does not ignore the data or subjective feelings

EXERCISE: How can you measure yourself using these behavioral indicators? How do you measure up as a leader on these basic, traditional leadership competencies? Where would you pin-point your strengths and weaknesses as a leader based on these indicators? Do you think these offer a limited perspective of leadership, and that there must be more than this? Or do you feel that these are still of crucial importance?

THE HEROIC TRADITION OF LEADERSHIP

Where does the concept of 'Heroic Leadership' come from, and what does it mean? 'Hero', a Greek word, refers to a person of superhuman strength, fearlessness and integrity, favored by the Gods, with "extraordinary courage, firmness or greatness of soul, in the course of some journey or enterprise. We, as humans, have a tendency to admire and venerate... [such a person] ...for their achievements and noble qualities", explains John Adair in his study *Great Leaders* (1989: 227).

The concept was more recently discussed in quite a different way in a *Harvard Business Review* article (Gosling & Mintzberg, 2003) including a comparison between 'heroic management, based on self' and 'engaging management, based on collaboration'. This takes a more negative view of 'Heroic Leadership'. Heroes can be self-centered, selfish, and make assumptions that followers will follow, more or less reluctantly, with few inputs. Heroes are strong, clever and responsible, making the necessary decisions based on the strategy they have developed. But they don't necessarily consider collaboration with the rest of the team. 'Heroic Management' is described as "thrust upon those who thrust their will upon others" (2003: 61) by contrast with 'Engaging Management' where "leadership is a sacred trust earned through the respect of others" (2003: 61). Note the contrast between 'thrust' and 'trust'!

Yet whilst 'Heroic Leadership' is still popular, the concept of 'Post-Heroic Leadership' has also attracted interest (Jones & Eicher, 1999) and, inevitably, the Heroic Follower. The debate continues with articles on heroic leadership and the role of gender (Fletcher, 2003), suggesting that heroic leadership is masculine and post-heroic leadership emphasizes feminine values and approaches. Meanwhile quiet leadership is sometimes seen as the opposite of heroic leadership (Badaracco, 2004).

However, in his popular 'Moral Leader' class at Harvard, Badaracco "discovered that students like their leaders cut from heroic cloth; that is, with high principles, noble behavior, and acts of self-sacrifice that inspire a legion of followers...even today, though its stories of human triumph and tragedy, the [heroic leadership] model provides people with momentary escape from the routines of everyday life and, on occasion, the inspiration necessary to transcend circumstances and perform unexpected acts of greatness"(2004). Here, moral leadership can include heroic leadership – depending on its direction, focus and circumstances. Thus the Mahatma Gandhi, Martin Luther King and Mother Teresa are at the top of the list for Badaracco's students – but it can be argued that they are both moral and heroic leaders. However, it is important to make the warning that heroic leadership can conflict with empowerment – the heroic leader is too busy being a leader to allow room for others.

And historical biographies with specific leadership lessons have emerged, of which an early instance was of Shackleton (Morrell & Capparell, 2003). Another example is of the famous British Admiral, Lord Nelson, whose bicentennial was recently celebrated. Of the more than 30 books on his life published to celebrate the event, one in particular focused on the leadership lessons suggested by Nelson's career and the relevance to modern-day leaders (Jones & Gosling, 2005).

Nelson can be seen as an archetypal heroic leader, who committed to heroism as a teenager: "I will be a hero, and confiding in providence, I will brave every danger" (Jones & Gosling, 2005: 13). Heroism was the way that Nelson defined leadership, as a "transcendent sense of purpose and a level of ambition that can only be described as obsessive" (Jones & Gosling, 2005: 16). If you want to be a heroic leader, the authors ask, "have you got the energy and commitment for it?" They also suggest that you should "spread the word about your achievements with stories that will be repeated, to inspire others and remind them of the values they most admire" (Jones & Gosling, 2005: 20). As

UK leadership guru Sir John Harvey-Jones argued, "the lessons from Nelson's leadership are even more appropriate today than they were two centuries ago" and "people want leaders they can respect, on whom they can model themselves. Heroes are examples of people from whom you can go on learning" (Jones & Gosling, 2005: 195).

Thus, 'Heroic Leadership' can encompass many concepts. It includes the leader as hero, with heroism defined as courage, strength, firmness and greatness of soul, and thus as a role model. It also features the pull factor - the addressing of the need for hero worship on the part of the populace. Then there is the anti-hero, the manipulative and unscrupulous leader who can pull the strings for good or evil, given the need for heroes and the lack of discernment on the part of the populace. Next is the 'Heroic Management' concept, where strategy and decision-making is passed down from on-high to the un-consulted and largely resisting workers below.

'Post-heroic leadership' tends to argue for the reverse, of leaders and managers seeking engagement and collaboration, seen by some as a form of 'quiet leadership'. Yet 'heroic leadership' is also seen as playing a part in 'moral leadership', but in a selective way. Finally, 'heroic leadership' stays with us through the heroes around us, both historical and contemporary, which suit this early 21st century celebrity-watching age we live in (Jones, 2008).

EXERCISE: Do you think that 'heroic leadership' still has a part to play in the modern era? Or is it 'consigned to the dustbin of history', as the Russian revolutionary leader Trotsky liked to say? Which kind of heroes might still be admired – and are they still heroes? Do you see a connection between heroic leadership and moral leadership? Who is your favorite heroic leader, and why?

LEADERSHIP THEORIES – THE EVOLUTION OF A WAY OF THINKING

The 'great man' notion of heroic leaders was one of the first ways of thinking about leadership, which developed into an exploration of trait theories, behaviorist theories, the idea of situational leadership, and then contingency theories. Transactional and transformational leadership theories take us into the modern era. Whilst early theories tend to focus upon the characteristics and behaviors of successful leaders, later theories begin to consider the role of followers and the contextual nature of leadership.

Great Man Theories	Based on the belief that leaders are exceptional people, born with innate qualities, destined to lead. The use of the term 'man' was intentional since until the latter part of the twentieth century leadership was thought of as a concept which is primarily male, military and Western. This led to the next school, that of Trait Theories

Trait Theories	The lists of traits or qualities associated with leadership exist in abundance and continue to be produced. They draw on virtually all the adjectives in the dictionary which describe some positive or virtuous human attribute, from ambition to zest for life, seen as defining a leader. Maturity, breadth of interest, intelligence and honesty were frequently quoted
Behaviorist Theories	These concentrate on what leaders actually do rather than on their qualities. Different patterns of behavior are observed and categorized as 'styles of leadership'. This area has probably attracted most attention from practicing managers, and still attracts current interest
Situational Leadership	This approach sees leadership as specific to the situation in which it is being exercised. For example, whilst some situations may require an autocratic style, others may need a more participative approach. It also proposes that there may be differences in required leadership styles at different levels in the same organization, depending on follower readiness
Contingency Theory	This is a refinement of the situational viewpoint and focuses on identifying the situational variables which best predict the most appropriate or effective leadership style to fit the particular circumstances
Transactional Theory	This approach emphasizes the importance of the relationship between leader and followers, focusing on the mutual benefits derived from a form of 'contract' through which the leader delivers such things as rewards or recognition in return for the commitment or loyalty of the followers
Transformational Theory	The central concept here is change and the role of leadership in envisioning and implementing the transformation of organizational performance of his or her followers, through influences which impact on the growth and development of the followers

Each of these theories (summarized in general terms above from several sources) takes a rather individualistic perspective of the leader, although a school of thought gaining increasing recognition is that of 'dispersed' leadership. This approach, with its foundations in sociology, psychology and politics rather than management science, views leadership as a process that is diffuse throughout an organization rather than lying solely with the formally designated 'leader'. The emphasis thus shifts from developing 'leaders' to developing 'leaderful' organizations with a collective responsibility for leadership.

THE TRAIT APPROACH TO LEADERSHIP

The trait approach arose from the 'Great Man' theory as a way of identifying the key characteristics of successful leaders (based on the belief that leaders are exceptional people, born with innate qualities, destined to lead). It was believed that through this approach critical leadership traits could be isolated and that people with such traits could then be recruited, selected, and installed into leadership positions. This approach was common in the military and is still used as a set of criteria to select candidates for commissions. The problem with the trait approach lies in the fact that almost as many traits as studies undertaken were identified. Although there was little consistency in the results of the various trait studies, however, some traits did appear more frequently than others, including: technical skill, friendliness, task motivation, application to task, group task supportiveness, social skills, emotional control, administrative skills, general charisma, and intelligence. Of these, the most widely explored has tended to be 'charisma'. The table below lists the main leadership traits and skills identified by Stogdill in 1974.

Traits	Skills
• Adaptable to situations • Alert to social environment • Ambitious and achievement-orientated • Assertive • Cooperative • Decisive • Dependable • Dominant (desire to influence others) • Energetic (high activity level) • Persistent • Self-confident • Tolerant of stress • Willing to assume responsibility	• Clever (intelligent) • Conceptually skilled • Creative • Diplomatic and tactful • Fluent in speaking • Knowledgeable about group task • Organized (administrative ability) • Persuasive • Socially skilled

THE BEHAVIORAL SCHOOL

The results of the trait studies were inconclusive. Traits, amongst other things, were hard to measure. How, for example, do we measure traits such as honesty, integrity, loyalty, or diligence? Another approach in the study of leadership had to be found. The Behavioral theories concentrate on what leaders actually do rather than on their qualities. Different patterns of behavior are observed and categorized as 'styles of leadership'. After the publication of McGregor's classic book *The Human Side of Enterprise* in 1960, attention shifted to 'behavioral theories'.

McGregor was a teacher, researcher, and consultant whose work was considered to be 'on the cutting edge' of managing people at that time. He influenced many behavioral theories, emphasizing the nature of human relationships and the results of output and performance.

MCGREGOR'S THEORY X AND THEORY Y MANAGERS

Although not strictly speaking a theory of leadership, the leadership strategy of participative management proposed in Douglas McGregor's book has had a tremendous impact on managers. The most publicized concept is McGregor's thesis that leadership strategies are influenced by a leader's assumptions about human nature and the attitude of workers to their work. As a result of his experience as a consultant, McGregor summarized two contrasting sets of assumptions made by managers in the workplace:

Theory X managers believe that:	Theory Y managers believe that:
• The average human being has an inherent dislike of work and will avoid it if possible. • Because of this human characteristic, most people must be coerced, controlled, directed, or threatened with punishment to get them to put forth adequate effort to achieve organizational objectives. • The average human being prefers to be directed, wishes to avoid responsibility, has relatively little ambition, and wants security above all else.	• The expenditure of physical and mental effort in work is as natural as play or rest, and the average human being, under proper conditions, learns not only to accept but to seek responsibility. • People will exercise self-direction and self-control to achieve objectives to which they are committed. • The capacity to exercise a high level of imagination, ingenuity, and creativity in the solution of organizational problems is widely distributed in the population, and the intellectual potentialities of the average human being are only partially utilized under the conditions of modern industrial life.

It can therefore be seen that a leader holding Theory X assumptions would prefer an autocratic style, whereas one holding Theory Y assumptions would prefer a more participative style.

BLAKE AND MOUTON'S MANAGERIAL GRID

The Managerial Grid developed by Robert Blake and Jane Mouton in 1964 focuses on task (production) and employee (people) orientations of managers, as well as combinations of concerns between the two extremes. The grid features concern for production on the horizontal axis, and concern for people on the vertical axis, and plots five basic leadership styles. The first number refers to a leader's production or task orientation; the second, to people or employee orientation. In the centre is 'Middle of the Road', referring to an equal balance between the concern for people and the concern for production. Blake and Mouton's Managerial Grid is as a useful way of conceptualizing various management or leadership styles. In this grid system, styles are classified according to a rating on these two key dimensions of leadership behavior. In effect these two dimensions are extensions and popularization of the concepts on initiating structure and consideration, stemming from a series of studies conducted at Ohio State University. The grid identifies two extremes, rates them on a nine point scale and plots them on a horizontal and vertical axis respectively. Among the eighty one possible combinations, five main styles of management/leadership emerge.

Team Management (9,9): concern for production and needs of people are integrated in the team direction. The skills involved in achieving this position are difficult to attain. The theory for integrating effective production with sound human relationship is complex both in concept and in application. This style is not absolute and is not applicable for all occasions.

Task Management (9,1): this is more concerned with the production or attainment of goals rather than with empowering people to deliver the required tasks. This case is more applicable in crisis situations.

Impoverished Management (1,1): in this particular case attention is neither given to the task nor to the people. The result of this style of leadership and management is chaotic and rarely are positive results attained. There is lack of confidence and trust in the group and in the task.

Country Club Management (1,9): in this particular case a lot of importance is given to people and not to task. This situation is very rare and is only applicable in social clubs. People who come from a task-oriented organization find difficulty in communicating in such an environment.

Middle of the Road (5,5): this is generally the case in the majority of organizations. In some instances more attention is given to the tasks to be attained and in other instances more importance is given to people. There is no hard and fast rule of when to give more attention to task and people. It all depends upon the leader and his/her aptitude to read and comprehend the situation.

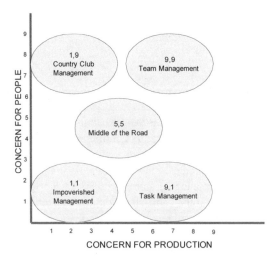

Blake and Mouton propose that 'Team Management'- a high concern for both employees and production - is the most effective type of leadership behavior.

THE CONTINGENCY OR SITUATIONAL SCHOOL

Whilst behavioral theories may help managers develop particular leadership behaviors, they give little guidance as to what constitutes effective leadership in different situations. Indeed, most researchers today conclude that no one leadership style is right for every manager under all circumstances. Instead, contingency-situational theories were developed to indicate that the style to be used is contingent upon such factors as the situation, the people, the task, the organization, and other environmental variables. Some of the major theories contributing towards this school of thought are described below.

FIEDLER'S CONTINGENCY MODEL

Fiedler's contingency theory postulates that there is no single best way for managers to lead. Situations will create different leadership style requirements for a manager. The solution to a managerial situation is contingent on the factors that impinge on the situation. For example, in a highly routine (mechanistic) environment where repetitive tasks are the norm, a relatively directive leadership style may result in the best performance; however, in a dynamic environment a more flexible, participative style may be required.
Fiedler looked at three situations that could define the conditions of a managerial task:
1. Leader-member relations: How well do the manager and the employees get along?
2. Task structure: Is the job highly structured, fairly unstructured, or somewhere in between?
3. Position power: How much authority does the manager possess?

Managers were rated as to whether they were relationship-oriented or task-oriented. Task-oriented managers tend to do better in situations that have good leader-member relationships, structured tasks, and either weak or strong position power. They do well when the task is unstructured but position power is strong. Also, they did well at the other end of the spectrum when the leader-member relations were moderate to poor and the task was unstructured.

Relationship-oriented managers do better in other situations. Thus, a given situation might call for a manager with a different style or a manager who could take on a different style for a different situation. These environmental variables are combined in a weighted sum that is termed 'favorable' at one end and 'unfavorable' at the other. Task-oriented style is preferable at the clearly defined extremes of 'favorable' and 'unfavorable' environments, but relationship-orientation excels in the middle ground. Managers could attempt to reshape the environment variables to match their style.

Another aspect of the contingency theory is that the leader-member relations, task structure, and position power dictate a leader's situational control. Leader-member relations are the amount of loyalty, dependability, and support that the leader receives from employees. It is a measure of how the manager perceives how he or she and the group of employees are getting along together. In a favorable relationship the manager has a high task structure and is able to reward and or punish employees without any problems. In an unfavorable relationship the task is usually unstructured and the leader possesses limited authority.

Position power measures the amount of power or authority the manager perceives the organization has given him or her for the purpose of directing, rewarding, and punishing subordinates. Position power of managers depends on the taking away (unfavorable) or increasing (favorable) the decision-making power of employees. The task-motivated style leader experiences pride and satisfaction in the task accomplishment for the organization, while the relationship-motivated style seeks to build interpersonal relations and extend extra help for the team development in the organization. There is no good or bad leadership style. Each person has his or her own preferences for leadership. Task-motivated leaders are at their best when the group performs successfully such as achieving a new sales record or outperforming the major competitor. Relationship-oriented leaders are at their best when greater customer satisfaction is gained and a positive company image is established.

THE HERSEY AND BLANCHARD MODEL OF LEADERSHIP

The Hersey and Blanchard Leadership Model takes a situational perspective of leadership. This model posits that the developmental levels of a leader's subordinates play the greatest role in determining which leadership styles (leader behaviors) are most appropriate. Their theory is based on the amount of direction (task behavior) and socio-emotional support (relationship behavior) a leader must provide given the situation and the 'level of maturity' of the followers.

- *Task behavior* is the extent to which the leader engages in spelling out the duties and responsibilities to an individual or group. This behavior includes telling people what to do, how to do it, when to do it, where to do it, and who's to do it. In task behavior the leader engages in one-way communication.

- *Relationship behavior* is the extent to which the leader engages in two-way or multi-way communications. This includes listening, facilitating, and supportive behaviors. In relationship behavior the leader engages in two-way communication by providing socio-emotional support.

- *Maturity* is the willingness and ability of a person to take responsibility for directing his or her own behavior. People tend to have varying degrees of maturity, depending on the specific task, function, or objective that a leader is attempting to accomplish through their efforts. In summary therefore leader behaviors fall along two continua:

Directive Behavior	Supportive Behavior
• One-Way Communication • Followers' Roles Clearly Communicated	• Close Supervision of Performance • Two-Way Communication • Listening, providing support and encouragement • Facilitating interaction • Involve follower in decision-making

For Hersey and Blanchard the key situational variable, when determining the appropriate leadership style, is the readiness or developmental level of the subordinate(s). As a result, four leadership styles result:

- *Directing:* The leader provides clear instructions and specific direction. This style is best matched with a low follower readiness level.

- *Coaching:* The leader encourages two-way communication and helps build confidence and motivation on the part of the employee, although the leader still has responsibility and controls decision-making. Selling style is best matched with a moderate follower readiness level.

- *Supporting:* With this style, the leader and followers share decision-making and no longer need or expect the relationship to be directive. Participating style is best matched with a moderate follower readiness level.

- *Delegating:* This style is appropriate for leaders whose followers are ready to accomplish a particular task and are both competent and motivated to take full responsibility. Delegating style is best matched with a high follower readiness level.

To determine the appropriate leadership style to use in a given situation, the leader must first determine the maturity level of the followers in relation to the specific task that the leader is attempting to accomplish through the effort of the followers. As the level of followers' maturity increases, the leader should begin to reduce his or her task behavior and increase relationship behavior until the followers reach a moderate level of maturity. As the followers begin to move into an above average level of maturity, the leader should decrease not only task behavior but also relationship behavior. Once the maturity level is identified, the appropriate leadership style can be determined.

ADAIR'S ACTION-CENTERED LEADERSHIP MODEL

The Adair model (1973) states that the action-centered leader gets the job done through the work team, and through relationships with fellow managers and staff.
According to Adair's explanation an action-centered leader must:
- direct the job to be done (task structuring)
- support and review the individual people doing it and co-ordinate and foster the work team as a whole

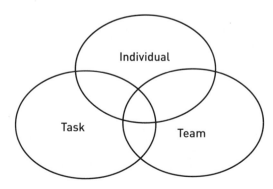

Adair's famous three circle diagram is a simplification of the variability of human interaction, but is a useful tool for thinking about what constitutes an effective leader/manager in relation to the job he/she has to do. The effective leader/manager carries out the functions and exhibits the behaviors depicted by the three circles.

Situational and contingent elements call for different responses by the leader. Hence imagine that the various circles may be bigger or smaller as the situation varies, i.e. the leader will give more or less emphasis to the functionally-oriented behaviors according to what the actual situation involves. The challenge for the leader is to manage all sectors activities mentioned in the diagram below:

Task	
	• define the task
	• make the plan
	• allocate work and resources
	• control quality and rate of work
	• adjust the plan

Team	
	• maintain discipline
	• build team spirit
	• encourage, motivate, give a sense of purpose
	• appoint sub-leaders
	• ensure communication within group
	• develop the group

Individual	
	• attend to personal problems
	• praise individuals
	• give status
	• recognize and use individual abilities
	• develop the individual

LEADERS AND FOLLOWERS

The models discussed so far have dwelt on the leader as some frontal figure who stands out from the rest as being somehow different and 'leading' the rest of the people. The discussion now moves to recognition of the importance of the leaders' relationship with his/her followers and an interdependency of roles. This is the case of no longer the hero or solo leader, but the team leader. Not the leader always out in front but the leader who has the capacity to follow. Not the master, but the servant.

SERVANT LEADERSHIP

The notion of 'Servant Leadership' emphasizes the leader's duty to serve his/her followers - leadership thus arises out of a desire to serve rather than a desire to lead. Robert Greenleaf, founder of the Center for Servant Leadership describes it as follows (1970) and reproduced on the center's website:

"The servant-leader is servant first... It begins with the natural feeling that one wants to serve, to serve first. Then conscious choice brings one to aspire to lead. He or she is sharply different from the person who is leader first, perhaps because of the need to assuage an unusual power drive or to acquire material possessions. For such it will be a later choice to serve – after leadership is established. The leader-first and the servant-first are two extreme types. Between them there are shadings and blends that are part of the infinite variety of human nature.

The difference manifests itself in the care taken by the servant-first to make sure that other people's highest priority needs are being served. The best test, and difficult to administer , is: do those served grow as persons; do they, while being served, become healthier, wiser, freer, more autonomous, more likely themselves to become servants? And, what is the effect on the least privileged in society; will they benefit, or, at least, will they not be further deprived?"

Characteristics of Servant Leaders are as follows:
"Servant-Leadership is a practical philosophy which supports people who choose to serve first, and then lead as a way of expanding service to individuals and institutions. Servant leaders may or may not hold formal leadership positions. Servant-leadership encourages collaboration, trust, foresight, listening, and the ethical use of power and empowerment". The emphasis on serving a higher purpose has made this model popular within the Church and other religious institutions.

THE FOLLOWING PART OF LEADING

Katzenbach and Smith, authors of 'The Wisdom of Teams' (1994) talk of the 'following part of leading' suggesting that the critical behaviors of leaders are:
They go on to say that the indicators of when a leader must follow are:

Asking questions instead of giving answers	By asking such questions such as "What do you think we should do?" or "How do you suggest we proceed?" you take a step behind another person. Whether you stay behind, of course, depends on your intention to actually follow the suggestion or answer of that other person.
Providing opportunities for others to lead you	This goes beyond the traditional notion of looking for growth opportunities for other people. Unless the opportunity in question bears a real risk for your personal performance outcome, you are not actually positioning yourself as a follower.
Doing real work in support of others instead of only the reverse	Rolling up your sleeves and contributing 'sweat equity' to the efforts and outcomes of other people earns you their appreciation as someone upon whom they can depend, regardless of the relative hierarchical or functional position each of you holds.

Becoming a matchmaker instead of a 'central switch'	In addition to following other people yourself, you must learn to help them follow each other. This requires you to get beyond considering yourself the 'central switch' through which all decisions flow. Instead, you need to look for every possible chance to help people find their best collaborators. "Have you asked them what they think?" is often the only input required to facilitate the effort at hand, although you then must submit your effort and support to whatever the people in question suggest.
Seeking common understanding instead of consensus	The pejorative meaning associated with consensus management has nothing to do with either effective leading or effective following. Leaders are those who know when and how to follow, and to build deep common understanding, not superficial consensus, around the purpose, goals, and approach at hand. They submit themselves and others to the discipline of ensuring that all sides to any disagreement are fully understood by everyone, recognizing that mutual understanding is far more powerful than any particular decision to choose path A over path B. All people will follow strong, commonly understood purposes and goals more easily than the 'put-up jobs' associated with consensus.

Individual performance	As a leader, you must follow another individual, regardless of hierarchy, if: • That individual, through experience, skill, and judgment, knows best. • That individual's growth demands that you invest more in his or her skill and self-confidence than in your own. • Only that individual, not you, has the capacity (the time and opportunity) to 'get it done'.
Team performance	As a leader, you must follow the team if: • The team's purpose and performance goals demand it. • The team, not you, must develop skills and self-confidence. • The team's agreed-upon working approach requires you, like all the others, to do real work.
Team performance	As a leader, you must follow the team if: • The team's purpose and performance goals demand it. • The team, not you, must develop skills and self-confidence. • The team's agreed-upon working approach requires you, like all the others, to do real work
Organizational performance	As a leader, you must follow others, regardless of hierarchy, if: • The organization's purpose and performance goals demand it. • The need for expanding the leadership capacity of others in the organization requires it. • 'Living' the vision and values enjoins you to do so.

TRANSFORMATIONAL AND TRANSACTIONAL LEADERSHIP

James MacGregor Burns writing in his book 'Leadership' was the first to put forward the concept of 'transformational leadership'. To Burns, transformational leadership is a relationship of mutual help and support that helps followers become leaders, and may help leaders to care more about their people. Burns went on to also further define it by suggesting that transformational leadership took place when one or more people work with others in such a way that leaders and followers help improve each others' motivation levels. Bass, however, deals with the transformational style of executive leadership that incorporates social change, a facet missing from Burns' work. For Bass 'transformational leaders' may:
• expand a follower's portfolio of needs
• transform a follower's self-interest
• increase the confidence of followers
• elevate followers' expectations
• heighten the value of the leader's intended outcomes for the follower
• encourage behavioral change
• motivate others to higher levels of personal achievement (Maslow's 'self-actualization').
Tichy and Devanna in their book 'The Transformational Leader' (1986) built further on the work of Burns and Bass in organizational and work contexts. They described the hybrid nature of transformational leadership as not necessarily about the presence of charisma, but a style of leadership which could be learned. Bass and Avolio suggested that transformational leadership is about an ideal kind of leader, able to act as a role model, and with whom followers actively want to relate.

Transactional leadership has been the traditional model of leadership with its roots from an organizational or business perspective in the 'bottom line'. Stephen Covey writing in 'Principle-Centered Leadership' (1992) suggests that transformational leadership "focuses on the 'top line'" and offers contrast between the two (a selection being):

Transactional Leadership	Transformational Leadership
Builds on the employee's need to get a job done and make a living • Is preoccupied with power and position, politics and perks • Is mired in daily affairs • Is short-term and hard data orientated • Focuses on tactical issues • Relies on human relations to lubricate human interactions • Follows and fulfils role expectations by striving to work effectively within current systems • Supports structures and systems that reinforce the bottom line, maximize efficiency, and guarantee short-term profits	*Builds on an employee's need for meaning* • Is preoccupied with purposes and values, morals, and ethics • Transcends daily affairs • Is orientated toward long-term goals without compromising human values and principles • Focuses more on missions and strategies • Releases human potential – identifying and developing new talent • Designs and redesigns jobs to make them meaningful and challenging • Aligns internal structures and systems to reinforce overarching values and goals

Arguably, both kinds of leadership are necessary. Transactional leadership has remained the organizational model for many people and organizations that have not moved into or encouraged the transformational role needed to meet the challenges of our changing times. How do we recognize transactional leadership in action? It is associated with these behaviors:

Provides you with assistance in exchange for your efforts – Contingent Reward
Fails to interfere until problems become serious – Management by Exception – Passive
Focuses attention on irregularities, mistakes, exceptions and deviations from standards – Management by Exception – Active
Discusses in specific terms who is responsible for achieving performance targets – Contingent Reward
Waits until things go wrong to take action – Management by Exception – Passive
Concentrates full attention on correcting unanticipated mistakes, complaints and failures – Management by Exception – Active

EXERCISE: How do we recognize transformational leadership practices? These include Inspirational Motivation, Intellectual Stimulation, Individualized Consideration and Idealized Influence. When our manager or leader... he/she is showing (see answers below)
1. *Re-examines critical assumptions to question whether they are appropriate*
2. *Provides an exciting image of what is essential to consider*
3. *Instills pride in being associated with the concept*
4. *Treats you as an individual rather than just a member of a group*
5. *Seeks differing perspectives when solving problems*
6. *Talks optimistically about the future*
7. *Goes beyond his self-interest for the good of the group*
8. *Spends time on individual teaching and coaching*

ANSWERS:
1. *Intellectual Stimulation*
2. *Inspirational Motivation*
3. *Idealized Influence*
4. *Individualized Consideration*
5. *Intellectual Stimulation*
6. *Inspirational Motivation*
7. *Idealized Influence*
8. *Individualized Consideration*

DISPERSED LEADERSHIP

The importance of social relations in the leadership contract, the need for a leader to be accepted by their followers and a realization that no one individual is the ideal leader in all circumstances have given rise to a new school of leadership thought. Referred to as 'informal', 'emergent' or 'dispersed' leadership, this approach argues a less formalized model of leadership where the leaders' role is dissociated from the organizational hierarchy. It is proposed that individuals at all levels in the organization and in all roles (not simply those with an overt management dimension) can exert leadership influence over their colleagues and thus influence the overall leadership of the organization.

Heifetz (1994) distinguishes between the exercise of 'leadership' and the exercise of 'authority' – thus dissociating leadership from formal organizational power roles whilst Raelin (2003) talks of developing 'leaderful' organizations through concurrent, collective and compassionate leadership. The key to this is a distinction between the notions of 'leader' and 'leadership'. 'Leadership' is regarded as a process of sense-making and direction-giving within a group and the 'leader' can only be identified on the basis of his/her relationship with others in the social group who are behaving as followers. In this manner, it is quite possible to conceive of the leader as emergent rather than predefined and that their ('their' is in the plural, but it refers back to 'leader', which is in the singular) role can only be understood through examining the relationships within the group (rather than by focusing on his/her personal characteristics or traits).

The origins of such an approach have their foundations more in the fields of sociology and politics than the more traditional management literature and draw on concepts such as organizational culture and climate to highlight the contextual nature of leadership. It is a more collective concept, and would argue for a move from an analysis and development of individual leader qualities to an identification of what constitutes an effective (or more appropriate) leadership process within an organization. This suggests a move in focus from the individuals to the relationships themselves.

QUESTIONS ON THE LEADERSHIP THEORIES:

- *How do the traits theories explain the characteristics and skills required for successful leaders?*
- *Do these theories suggest that you are born with these traits?*
- *Or that the job of acquiring them is relatively easy?*
- *Do you think that some traits such as 'desire for power' or being 'controlling' would definitely hinder a manager's ability to ever become a true leader?*
- *Do people with a love for power forget about people as 'individuals' and are they weak at building teams?*
- *How do Behavioral Theories, such as the X and Y theory, help identify between different leader behaviors?*
- *Do you believe that in some industries, and depending on the maturity level of the employees and educational level and cultural background, this X leadership style is necessary?*
- *Is Y leadership now more appropriate in this increasingly competitive world, where talent and skills are now required in all jobs?*
- *How can situational theories help explain and guide managers to be effective leaders?*
- *Leaders that are action-centered and can combine their care for individuals, team building, and task management are most likely to be successful - please discuss.*
- *Why are followers and their roles attracting more and more attention in the search for new ways of explaining successful leadership?*
- *Is both transformational and transactional leadership needed in a typical organization?*

- *Is the transformational approach necessarily more effective?*
- *Contrast leaders with whom you have worked in terms of how much you admired them and enjoyed working with them, and the extent to which they were transformational or transactional.*

CLOSING CASE: SUN TZU, PLATO, MACHIAVELLI, IBN ZFAR AL-SIQILLI

The study of leadership is as old as civilization. As far back as 350 BC, Sun Tzu wrote 'The Art of War', his treatise to morality, power, and doctrine in the service of victory. What are the leadership implications of Sun Tzu's work, particularly as it applies to business practices? Given that, "today, 'The Art of War' is read by business leaders throughout Asia" (Rarick, 1996: 38).

The main characteristics of a leader were of great importance to Master Sun. Without suitable leadership the troops would lack discipline, direction and esprit. Sun wrote: "the traits of the true commander are: wisdom, humanity, respect, integrity, courage, and dignity. With his wisdom he humbles the enemy, with his humanity he draws the people near to him, with his respect he recruits men of talent and character, with his integrity he makes good on his rewards (and his punishments), with his courage he raises the morale of his men, and with his dignity he unifies his command". Sun differentiates the leadership behavior to be employed between the 'king' and the 'commander.' The effectiveness of a very charismatic chief executive officer may not be able to be duplicated by the first level supervisor in every detail. Different situations require different styles of leadership. "A confused army predicts victory for the enemy." "The side that has superiors and subordinates united in purpose will take the victory." When all members of the organization share the same values, know the mission of the organization, and know their part in that mission, the chance of organizational success is enhanced. This, according to Sun, is the task of the leader.

In 400 BC Plato wrote 'The Republic', an exploration of leadership and justice in the State. In The Republic, Plato emphasizes leadership as qualities of legitimate leadership coupled with a radical rethinking of what is involved in the notion of political constitutions. Plato identified leadership as a function of a series of qualities among which emerges wisdom seen as a combination or fusion of ethical character and intellectual/cognitive qualities (especially knowledge of the good). Plato's philosophy is revealed in answer to the question "Who should lead us?" He responded that it should be the wisest among us, the individual with the most knowledge, skill, power and variety of resources, and the person closest to ultimate wisdom and insight.

In the 16th century, Machiavelli offered up his formula for manipulation and deceit in 'The Prince'. "Of course, Machiavelli was a marvelous person on organizational material" (Blackwell, Gibson and Hannon, 1998: 143) and he was the "first person to highlight and explore the dark side of leadership, and notions of expediency and ruthless power" (Thomas, 2006: 94). Machiavelli was consumed with power, how to achieve it and how to hold on to it, and he felt that leaders should know how to enter into evil when necessity commanded. One of Machiavelli's most famous quotes was, "it is best for leaders to be loved but if they can not be loved they must be feared". Machiavelli argued that a leader must always exhibit mercy, honesty, humaneness, uprightness and religiousness and how to be deceitful when it suits his purpose and not appear that way." Machiavelli exposed the dark side of leadership, the side that stands in marked contrast to many of the works of today's human centered leadership studies (Thomas, 2006: 95). Machiavelli's contribution to leadership seems to be very relevant to today's business, with the scandals and Machiavellian leadership tactics that are going on in businesses around the world. A study entitled 'Machiavelli on Leadership' by conservative foreign policy expert Michael Ledeen argues that Machiavelli's observations on leadership ring true five centuries later (Rust, 1999). It is widely debated, whether Machiavelli advocated a particular style of leadership or mainly described, in admiration, the leadership of the condottieri.

In the Twelfth century Ibn Zfar al-Siqilli, a distinguished Arab philosopher and political activist, wrote a classic work on leadership, strategy and power, Sulwan al-Muta. "Ibn Zafar was considered a worthy precursor to Machiavelli by Gaetano Mosca", claim Dekmejian and Thabit, (2000: 125). His work can be summarized in the formula: planning (tadbair) + artifice (hila) + force (quwwa) in a flexible manner = Victory. Thus, in choosing alternative plans of action, the leader should be engaged in a phased process of decision-making: planning is the first step which includes strategy and collecting internal and external information. Secondly, the employment of ruse or artifice is a stratagem based on guile and trickery, as a possible option to the use of force. For Ibn Zafar, who so often preached truth and morality, the use of artifice is a contradiction. But he resolves it by stating that the end justifies the means. When all else fails, then the leader should resort to force, to the fullest extent and not to attack the enemy unless knowing the enemy is weaker.

EXERCISE: Thus leadership in the historical context can be seen to have evolved from the value of leadership in war, in raising the morale of a leader's people; from the leader as a wise politician, a thinker; to the leader as a manipulator in business, using leadership to gain power; and the leader as ultimately relying on force, according to the justification of the outcome. All these elements of leadership can be seen as still relevant today. Give a present-day example from your own experience of each style of leader.

CONCLUSION

This chapter has aimed to introduce you to the historical antecedents to leadership theories, and the ways of thinking and contemporary examples which gave rise to theorizing about leadership in the pre-modern era, right up to today. The theoretical views of leadership range from the focus on the leader as a person to the contextual factors of situation and contingency, and how these issues can impact on leadership style. But can a leader change his or her style to fit his or her followers? Is a mix and match approach to leadership realistic? The next chapter takes the issue further, with more ideas about the ongoing "what is leadership?" debate.

REFERENCES

Adair, John. 1989. *Great Leaders*. Guildford: Talbot Adair Press.

Adair, John. 1973. *Action-Centred Leadership*. New York: McGraw Hill.

Badaracco, J. L. Jr. 2004. Beyond Heroic Moral Leadership. *Conversations on Leadership of the Center for Public Leadership*., Conversations on Leadership, 2000-2001, Rountable 4. Boston: Harvard College Publications.

http://www.ksg.harvard.edu/leadership/beyond_heroic_moral_leadership.html

Blackwell, C.W., Gibson, J.W. and Hannon, J.C. 1998. Charismatic Leadership: the Hidden Controversy. *Journal of Leadership Studies*. 5

Blake, R.R.and Mouton, J.S. 1964. The managerial grid. Houston TX: Gulf Publications.

Burns, J. M. 1978. *Leadership*. New York: Harper & Row.

Dekmejian, R. and Thabit, A. 2000. Machiavelli's Arab Precursor: Ibn Zafar al-Siqilli. *British Journal of Middle Eastern Studies*. 125-137.

Fletcher, J. K. 2003. The Greatly Exaggerated Demise of Heroic Leadership: Gender, Power and the Myth of the Female Advantage. In Ely, R, Foldy, E, Scully, M and the Centre for Gender in Organizations, Simmons School of Management (eds.). *Reader in Gender, Work and Organization*. Oxford: Blackwell. 204-210.

Gosling, J. and Mintzberg, H. 2003. The Five Minds of a Manager. *Harvard Business Review*. *81* (11): 54-63.

Greenleaf, R. 1970. *The Servant as Leader*. New York: Center for Applied Leadership Studies.

Jones, S. 2008. Heroic Leadership. In Marturano, A. and Gosling J. *Key Concepts in Leadership*. London: Routledge.

Jones, S. and Gosling, J. 2005. *Nelson's Way: leadership lessons from the great commander.* London. Nicholas Brealey.

Jones, J. and Eicher, J. 1999. *Post-heroic Leadership Leaders Guide*. New York: Human Resource Development Partners.

Heifetz, G. 1994. *Leadership Without Easy Answers*. Cambridge: Belknap Press.

Hersey, P. and Blanchard, K H. 1977. *Management of Organizational Behaviour*. Englewood Cliffs, NJ: Prentice Hall.

Katzenbach, J.and Smith, D. 1994. *The Wisdom of Teams*. New York: Harper Business.

McGregor, D. 1960. *The Human Side of Enterprise*. New York: McGraw Hill.

Morrell, M. and Capparell, S. 2003. *Shackleton's Way*. London: Nicholas Brealey.

Raelin, J. 2003. *Creating Leaderful Organizations*. San Francisco: Berrett-Koehler Publishers.

Rarick, C. 1996. Ancient Chinese Advice for Modern Business Strategists. *SAM Advanced Management Journal. 1* (1): 38+.

Rust, M. 1999. Machiavelli Was Ahead of His Time. *Insight on the News. 15* (34): 24.

Stogdill, R.1974. *Handbook of Leadership*. New York: Free Press.

Thomas, M. 2006. *Gurus on Leadership.* London: Thorogood Publishing.

Tichy, N.M. and Devanna, M.A. 1986. *The Transformational Leader*. New York: Wiley

RECOMMENDED FURTHER READING

Alvesson, M. 1996. Leadership studies: from procedure and abstraction to reflexivity and situation. *Leadership Quarterly*. 7: 455-485.

Antonakis, John, Cianciolo, Anna & Sternberg, Robert. 2004. *The Nature of Leadership*. London: Sage Publications.

Avery, G. 2005. *Understanding Leadership*. London: Sage Publications.

Barbuto, J.E. Jnr. 2005. Motivation and transactional, charismatic, and transformational leadership: a test of antecedents. *Journal of Leadership and Organizational Studies. 11* (4): 26-40.

Bass B.M.1985. *Leadership and Performance Beyond Expectations*. New York Free Press.

Bass B.M. and Avolio B.J. 1990. From Transactional to Transformational Leadership: Learning to Share the Vision. *Organizational Dynamics. 18*: 19-31.

Bass B.M. and Avolio B.J. 1993. Transformational Leadership: A Response to Critiques. in M.M. Chemers and R. Ayman eds. 1993. *Leadership Theory and Research: Perspectives and Directions*. New York: Academic Press.

Bass B.M. and Avolio B.J. 1994. *Improving Organizational Effectiveness Through Transformational Leadership*. Newbury Park, CA: Sage Publications.

Bass. B.M. et. al. .2003. Predicting Unit Performance by Assessing Transformational and Transactional Leadership. *Journal of Applied Psychology. 88*: 207–218.

Beyer. J.M. 1999. Two approaches to studying charismatic leadership: competing or complimentary? *Leadership Quarterly. 10*: 575-588.

Boulden. R. 2004. *What is Leadership? Research Report.* Exeter: Centre for Leadership Studies.

Campbell. D.J. Bommer. W. and Yeo. E. 1993. Perceptions of appropriate leadership style: participation versus consultation across two cultures. *Asia Pacific Journal of Management. 10* (1): 1-19.

Covey. S. 1992. *Principle-Centered Leadership*. New York: Simon and Schuster.

Den Hartog. D. N. House. R. J.. Hanges. P. J. et al. .1999. Culture specific and cross culturally generalizable implicit leadership theories: are attributes of charismatic/ transformational leadership universally endorsed? *Leadership Quarterly. 10* (2) 219-56.

Fiedler. F.E. 1967. *A theory of leadership effectiveness*. New York: McGraw Hill.

George M. and Jones G. 2002. *Organizational Behavior*. Upper Saddle River, NJ: Prentice Hall.

Goffee. R. and Jones. R. 2000. Why Should Anyone Be Led By You? *Harvard Business Review*. 62-70.

Gosling. J. and Mintzberg. H. 2004. *Education of Practicing Managers*. MIT Sloan Management Review. 19-22.

Gregersen. H.B. Morrison. A.J. & J.S. Black. 1998. Developing leaders for the global frontier. *Sloan Management Review*. Fall. 21–32.

Grint. K. 2000. *Arts of Leadership*. Oxford. Oxford University Press.

Hellriegel. D. and Slocum. J. 2004. *Organizational Behavior*. Mason, Ohio: Thomson.

Hersey. P. and Blanchard. K. 1988. *Management of Organizational Behavior*. Upper Saddle River, NJ: Prentice Hall.

House. R.J. and Howell. J.M. .1992. Personality and charismatic leadership. *Leadership Quarterly. 3* (2): 81-108.

House. R.J. Shamir. B. 1993. Toward the integration of charismatic. visionary and transformational leadership theories. *Leadership Theory and Research: Perspectives and Directions*. San Diego, CA: Academic Press.

Hunt J.G. 1999. Transformational/Charismatic Leadership's Transformation of the Field: A Historical Essay. *Leadership Quarterly. 10*(2): 129-144.

Hunt. J. and Larsen. L. H. 1979. *Cross-Currents in Leadership*. Illinois: Southern Illinois University Press.

Jones. Stephanie .2003. On Top of the World: Leadership and Management Lessons from Everest. *Human Assets Middle East*. 16-19.

Judge. T.A. and Piccolo. R.F. 2004. Transformational and transactional leadership: a meta analytic test of their relative validity. *Journal of Applied Psychology. 89* (5): 755-768.

Kotter. J. 2001. What Leaders Really Do. *Harvard Business Review*. 1-12.

Mant. A. 1983. *Leaders We Deserve*. London: Martin Robertson.

Northouse. P. 2004. *Leadership: Theory and Practice*. USA: Sage Publications.

Ozaralli. N. 2003. Effects of transformational leadership on empowerment and team effectiveness. *Leadership and Organization Development Journal. 24* (6): 335-344.

Raelin. J. .2004. Don't bother putting leadership into people. *The Academy of Management Executive. 18*: 131-135.

Shermerhorn. J. Hunt J. and Osborn. R. 2002. *Organizational Behavior*. USA: John Wiley.

Useem. M. 2001. The Leadership Lessons of Mount Everest. *Harvard Business Review*. 51-58.

Vroom. V. H. & Jago. A. G. 1988. *The New Leadership: managing participation in organizations*. Englewood Cliffs, NJ: Prentice Hall.

Yukl. G. 2002. *Leadership in Organizations*. Englewood Cliffs, NJ Prentice Hall.

Zaleznik. A. 2004. Managers and leaders: are they different? *Harvard Business Review*. 105-126.

CHAPTER THREE
LEADERSHIP – NEW CHALLENGES AND REALITIES
STEPHANIE JONES

OPENING CASE: A CONTEMPORARY LEADER

In 1993, when Louis V. Gerstner took over IBM, the company reported a loss of $8 billion dollars, with the share value plummeting from a "decent $43 to a heartbreaking $12" (Gerstner, 2002: 10). Economists and experts hardly expected IBM to survive. Competitors like Oracle publicly commented, "IBM? It's not just dead, it's become irrelevant". Even Lou Gerstner said "it just looked like it was going into a death spiral... I wasn't convinced it was solvable." He accepted the job only after IBM board member James Burke appealed to his sense of civic duty and patriotism: IBM was vital to the American economy, and it must not be allowed to die.

Five years later, in 1998, IBM posted record revenues of $81.7 billion, and a profit of $6.3 billion. Its market capitalization has grown around tenfold since Gerstner took over, and the company continues to perform strongly.

Gerstner began his task by focusing on the customers: "he spent his early days flying around the customers analyzing their needs" (Lundquist, 2002: 5). Armed with this information, he started to restructure the company. From the outset, Gerstner was convinced that it was wrong to divide the company into units. "At the end of the day, in every industry there is an integrator," affirms Gerstner, who saw his job as keeping IBM intact. This was opposed to the views of many top managers, who were contemplating the division of IBM into smaller, supposedly more manageable and potentially profitable units.

So, a conference of the top 200 of IBM's corporate customers was convened and asked: "What kind of IBM do you want?" Gerstner wanted a one-stop shop, offering hardware, software, and services. "Look at what many of our competitors are doing: buying each other, striking deals and alliances so they can offer more pieces of the solution" Gerstner told *Software* magazine in 1997. "In many ways, they're trying to cobble together a lot of what IBM already has." Having made that decision, how to make IBM's units work harmoniously? At that point there was no incentive for IBM employees to think beyond their business unit, developing products without regard to the company's larger goals.

Gerstner recognized that the company was unclear about its culture. Was teamwork or individual ambition rewarded? Employees were apprehensive about issues like risk-taking, consensus building, and corporate protocol. The company was obsessed with internal rules and conflicts. Competition among teams led to lost productivity.

He also observed jealousy among employees, each one protecting his own privileges. Employees stationed in Europe received only selected communication from Gerstner, because the IBM head in Europe intercepted his e-mails. Gerstner confronted him and clarified that these employees were not his personal property, they belonged to IBM.

Gerstner started off by pegging 40% of every employee's bonus pay to the performance of the overall company, as opposed to the business unit. Individual bonuses were tied to performance evaluations, and were determined in part by the 'team,' meaning "how well you leveraged IBM's overall resources in your work," said Jana Weatherbee, a spokesperson for IBM. Gerstner introduced a new mantra at the company: the customer first, IBM second, your business unit third. And he reinforced it by dragging the scientists out of the lab and having them meet with customers.

In order to inspire employees (and customers), Gerstner had to find a vision. He started to position IBM to lead the next wave of 'network-centric' computing. An internal IBM document recalls that the industry 'laughed' at Gerstner's claim that in the future "the Internet will be about business and working, not surfing." It now seems that Gerstner's vision appears to be materializing.

His first task was to change the ingrained attitudes that had prevented IBM from seeing the world around it. He witnessed the 'good news only' syndrome at one of his early meetings, when he attended a presentation from the chip-making division, known to be having problems. Gerstner was told that the problem was that there was no mainframe business, so the division couldn't make money making chips for mainframes. Gerstner stopped him right there and asked why the mainframe guy had just told him his division was doing fine!

"Gerstner made it very clear very quick that you tell the boss the truth," says one IBMer. He spent much of his time in the beginning talking to IBMers, consultants, and customers about the company and making it very clear that he wanted the exact truth. "He was the best listener I have ever seen," says Sam Albert, an IBM analyst who worked for the company from 1959 to 1989 (Worth, 1999: 8).

Meetings were too large and complicated, because people were included based on their rank, whether or not they had anything of substance to add. The most famous ritual at these meetings were the visual-display 'foils' executives used to project charts and graphs onto the wall. "We used to describe talks as a `six-foil talk' or a `four-foil talk`," one expert recalls.

He asked his top 20 executives to write a short paper, answering these questions: What is your business? Who are your customers? What is your marketplace? What are your strengths and weaknesses? Who are your main competitors? He told them to get it done in two weeks, and would meet with each of them one-on-one shortly afterward to discuss it.

Restructuring the company's workforce was another serious challenge. "Unless you did something really bad, they didn't fire you," says Sam Albert. "They'd just move you to another job." John Akers had downsized the company significantly starting in the late 80s, with generous early retirement incentive plans (Worth, 1999). The problem with this method was, as one IBMer put it, that "some of the best people were tempted to take it - because they were the ones who knew they could get work elsewhere. The less talented people were more likely to play it safe and stay, with the same ill effects: the people who should be fired stay on, while those who do real work leave."

How did Gerstner handle this? In order to make sure that IBM downsized effectively, a new evaluation scheme was introduced. He replaced the friendly annual report (with grades on a scale of one through four) to the more challenging method of using 360 degree feedback. Also, the annual performance grades were put on a curve within the division. The new system gave managers the tools to fire poor performers, and it kept everyone up to standards. "The corporate entitlement culture was gone," says Ken Thornton, general manager of IBM's public sector department. "The slogan became happy to be here, but prepared to leave.'"

Gerstner also recruited far more aggressively than IBM had in the past. During its heyday, "we just used to wait for the resumes to come in," recalls one longtime IBMer. "Now the competition for good people is extreme." IBM's stodgy image didn't help: By the early 1990s ambitious young people with computer skills were far more likely to head for hipper, younger companies on the West Coast.

Lessons from Lou Gerstner's leadership included that point that "he simply set out on a course and kept IBM moving in a direction that he felt would find success" (Lundquist, 2002: 6). Then there was 'The Truth Factor'. Just as Lou Gerstner cracked IBM's 'good news only' culture, leaders need to ensure that employees are rewarded, not punished, for sticking their heads up and delivering honest criticisms of their organizations.

'Meaningless meetings' was a further issue: "too many sign-offs, too many reviews, too many task forces, which add up to work but not much value," as Gerstner once put it. No more sectarianism was a further lesson. The transformation Gerstner pulled off at IBM was helped by forcing his people to overcome their notorious internal divisions and work for the good of the company. Measuring performance was another initiative: Gerstner looked to other large companies to find an evaluation scheme that would keep people on their toes and help to identify those who should be fired. Hiring the best made a big difference: IBM recognized quickly that it couldn't get back in the game without drawing on the best people at every rank. Finally, Gerstner was able to see the future and predict opportunities.

QUESTIONS ON THE OPENING CASE

- *How would you describe Gerstner's leadership style?*
- *Did the leadership style shown by Gerstner fit IBM's situation?*
- *Does his way of operating fit in with any of the leadership theories we saw in Chapter 2?*
- *This chapter introduces several new perspectives on leadership – are these more relevant in understanding Gerstner's contribution? (Discuss when you have read the chapter).*
- *Do you need to be an expert in your field to be a leader in your field? (See the 'Eight Questions of Leadership' below).*
- *How did Gerstner start the job of implementing his approach to leadership?*
- *In which areas did he clash with the way that IBM had been led in the past?*
- *How did Gerstner build teamwork in IBM?*
- *How did he go about changing the culture?*
- *What had been the impact of the company's entitlement culture?*
- *How were people at IBM kept busy but not working for the good of the company?*
- *Would your current organization benefit from a leader like Lou Gerstner?*

LEARNING OBJECTIVES:

This chapter continues our examination of the evolution of leadership styles, approaches and theoretical constructs introduced in Chapter 2, touching on some of the modern-day thinking in the field, especially emphasizing the contextual nature of leadership. You will have the opportunity to study how leadership theories are still being created. Here, we will look more at the attributes of an effective leader, the need for a broader spectrum of understanding on the part of the successful leader, and the categories and classifications of leadership styles which have emerged from recent research. In the process, we look at the work of some of the recent thinkers in the field, and challenge some of the long-established theories of the past. As you will discover, leadership continues to be a highly contentious subject.

LEADERSHIP COMPETENCIES

In looking at the competencies of the newer brand of leader, there is a greater need to recognize the characteristics of leaders in specific situations, and to relate these to new thinking in the field of leadership. We saw in Chapter 2 how basic leadership competencies have been traditionally seen as including influencing skills, being a role model as a source of integrity, and problem-solving and making the necessary decisions. These are more isolated, individualistic behaviors, with little consideration for the context. For the future, more competencies have become increasingly important for leaders, especially those of being results-oriented and innovatory:

RESULTS-ORIENTATION IN LEADERS

Firstly, leaders who are not focused on outcomes might tend to exhibit these behaviors: *Negative behavioral indicators*

- Makes suggestions without considering the consequences – does not think through the issues
- Interested only in short-term results without considering long-term, overall results and outcomes
- Will make sacrifices for immediate gain with no future thinking
- Sees things in terms of activities rather than objectives or results
- Day-to-day attitude
- No big-picture thinking; a limited perspective, in time and in scope
- Will use all resources on one quick result without thinking of other requirements in the future

By contrast, leaders driven by the need to show results are likely to show these behaviors: *Positive behavioral indicators*

- Keeps reminding others of long-term objectives during the negotiations, rejecting suggestions which conflict with these
- Talks about long-term, overall objectives at the start of the meeting

- Has strong sense of budgeting, planning and thinking about the future
- Will make short-term sacrifices and is flexible on small matters in order to gain good overall result

INNOVATION

Leaders not concerned with innovation, or seeing it as a low priority, are likely to show these behaviors:
Negative behavioral indicators

- Satisfied with things as they are, avoids change
- Old-fashioned, conservative in outlook – rejects new things which are different
- Plays safe, goes for guaranteed, low-risk options
- Keeps saying "it won't work" or "what if it doesn't work?" or "it's better to stick to the old way we've been doing before"
- Copies others with tried-and-tested solutions rather than 'sticking his/her neck out'
- Suggests ideas, but reluctantly, and has no confidence that they will work

Whilst leaders embracing innovation may show these attributes:
Positive behavioral indicators

- Takes a different view, risk-taking, outspoken
- Individual style in dress, manner
- Suggests ideas off the beaten track
- Understands and embraces newness enthusiastically – "I like this, it's new, it's different"

NEW LEADERSHIP APPROACHES

In the following section we will be looking at only four of very many new recent approaches to studying leadership. These are quite different to what we have been looking at in the previous chapter in terms of creativity, and are challenging to the accepted and traditional approaches. It should be emphasized that this is only a small, selective and highly subjective list of new thinking on leadership, which have been selected to help you to understand how leadership theories continue to evolve. Other approaches recommended and worthy of further research would include the concept of 'Post-heroic leadership' – and 'Quiet Leadership' – with an investigation of examples of new style leaders. For instance, in what ways do Akio Morito, Richard Branson, Anita Roddick, and Rudy Giuliani (whatever you might think of them as leaders) differ in leadership styles from the most highly-regarded, classical leaders of the past? Meanwhile, 'Inspirational leadership' – or leaders with the attributes and ability to win the hearts of others – has become increasingly important, with the war for talent in many business fields. These characteristics include tough empathy, intuition, and allowable weaknesses – discussed in the *Harvard Business Review* case 'Why Should Anyone Be Led By You?' This exemplifies an important aspect of the new brand of a leader – that leadership is not a given, in the sense that followers will always respect the role of the leader. There is a much stronger view than before of the need for a leader to earn and live up to the demands of the role and the context in which he or she operates.

One of the most thoughtful new studies of leadership is provocatively entitled, 'The Hard Work of Being a Soft Manager'. Management has traditionally been thought of as a 'hard' discipline, and the higher a manager rises, the greater his or her power of command and the larger number of people who must obey the orders. CEO William Peace, in his reflective article, challenges the common figure of a leader as a solitary tough guy, certain of his tasks and immune to criticism. Relating to his own experiences, Peace considers that effective leaders should invite candid feedback and admit they do not have the answers to everything.

However, "soft management does not mean weak management" (Peace, 2001: 72). Soft issues can hit you very hard as a leader! Soft management requires great courage and emotional self-control. It means candor, openness, and vulnerability, as well as a willingness to take responsibility for difficult decisions.

Such an approach worked well when Peace was faced with having to lay off fifteen people at US-based Westinghouse's Synthetic Fuels Division in the early 1980s. Meeting with all the people in person, explaining the reasons behind the layoff, giving employees the opportunity to object, criticize, and vent their anger, eased the emotional blow for those laid off and reassured the remaining employees that the division would not face immediate closure.

Peace's action so eased the emotional blow for those laid-off that when the division got the chance to rehire some of them a few months later, they all came back, including those who had found other jobs. Moreover, Peace noticed that the remaining employees had a renewed determination to hold the business together. Clearly, if you are too hard on the people you fire, you effectively de-motivate the people remaining.

The points made by Peace make considerable sense. The article would have been even more revealing if the author had tackled the tricky issue of the limits of soft management, and how different styles might be appropriate in varying cultural contexts, without losing underlying values and integrity.

EXERCISE: *explain an instance in your workplace where a manager (perhaps it was you!) had to make a difficult decision – did he or she (you!) behave in a hard or soft way? How and why? Was this conscious and thought-through? Or spontaneous? What were the outcomes? How would these outcomes have been different if the alternative approach had been chosen? How does this relate to his/her/your personality and culture as a leader?*

GOSLING AND MINTZBERG'S 'FIVE MINDS OF THE MANAGER'

Leadership and the connections and differences between leadership and management are reviewed in a further Harvard Business Review case, 'The Five Minds of the Manager', which considers the reflective, analytical, global, collaborative, and change-oriented aspects of a manager's thinking frames. Jonathan Gosling and Henry Mintzberg argue about the dangers of the separation of management and leadership, that "management without leadership encourages an uninspired style, which deadens activities, whilst leadership without management encourages a disconnected style, which promotes hubris" (Gosling & Mintzberg, 2003: 54). They then point out the contradictory aspects of management: be global and be local. Collaborate and compete. Change perpetually but preserve values...etc. Thus, managers are called on to pursue multiple and apparently conflicting goals.

To help managers reconcile these conflicting demands, the authors urge them to focus not only on goals but on 'how they have to think.' To encourage the synthesis of competing demands, they illustrate that managing involves five tasks, each with its own mind-set:

- managing the self (the reflective mind-set) – thinking through implications, and turning happenings into experiences – how can I learn from successes and mistakes on a daily basis?;

- managing organizations (the analytic mind-set) – organizing logically, seeing the wood for the trees, seeing the context and environment in a broad basis, not missing the main objective for small details;

- managing context (the worldly mind-set) – appreciating national cultural differences rather than global convergence, immersing yourself in a new culture to quickly learn the main differences;

- managing relationships (the collaborative mind-set) – seeking win-win partnerships rather than seeing people as resources, as lemons to be squeezed; and

- managing change (the action mind-set).

These mind-sets, explained in detail by the authors in this article, reveal the multi-dimensional requirements of the leader of today. Multi-tasking alone is not enough: it needs to be combined with multi-thinking and multi-processing. A successful leader is now under much more pressure to understand a wider array of aspects of an organization. The leader no longer stays in conventional, functional management silos, but needs to grasp the whole, balancing contradictions encountered along the way.

EXERCISE: Which of these mindsets is easiest for you? Which is the most challenging? How difficult is it to handle all of these at the same time? Considering a manager of your choice (this could be a classmate you know well) – which are his/her strengths and weaknesses? What are the implications of these?

THE 'SEVEN LEADERSHIP ACTION LOGIC ROLES'

From this chapter so far and from Chapter 2, we are already familiar with analyses of leadership that examine the role of an individual's philosophy of leadership, personality, or leadership style, but not necessarily how he or she might act, especially in order to progress his or her career. Rooke and Torbert have in mind something different from any of the previous leadership commentators when, in their article (2005) they define 'action logic' as the way in which a leader decides what to do when there is an attack on his or her power base. Very few leaders operate on the basis of the two most effective action logics, and most are confined to the less effective styles. According to these authors, in large part, leadership can be learned. They profile seven leader types, based on extensive research on attitudes to leadership:

The **Opportunist** - these leaders see the world in terms of its potential to give them personal gain. People and resources are to be exploited. These leaders may have a place in emergency or tough sales situations, but that might be it. Opportunists constitute 5% of the leaders studied by the authors.

The **Diplomat** - these people are driven by a need to satisfy higher-level managers while avoiding conflict. They follow group norms and rarely 'rock the boat.' They have a role in holding a group together and constitute 12% of the leaders profiled in this article.

The **Expert** - experts believe they influence control through their knowledge. They largely see collaboration as a waste of time as they 'know' the correct answer. They are good as individual contributors and make up the largest proportion of leaders - 38% of those analyzed by the authors of this article.

The **Achiever** - these leaders focus on creating a positive work environment and also on the deliverables. They tend not to think outside the box, but function well in managerial roles. They make up 30% of all the leaders profiled in this study.

The **Individualist** - these people tend to ignore rules with a view to getting things done. They recognize and work on tensions between principles and their actions, or between organizational values and the implementation of those values. They work well in venture capital and consulting roles and constitute 10% of the leaders profiled by Rooke and Torbert.

The **Strategist** - strategists are different from individualists in so far that they recognize organizational constraints which they are prepared to discuss and transform. They have the ability and desire to focus on personal relationships, organizational relationships, and national and international developments. They are characterized by their need for inquiry, vigilance and ability to focus on the short and long term. Effective as transformational leaders, they make up only 4% of the random group of leaders analyzed.

The **Alchemist** - these people differ from strategists in their ability to renew or re-invent themselves and their organizations in historically significant ways. Typically charismatic, they live by high moral standards. They are good at leading society-wide transformations and make up only 1% of the leaders looked at in this study.

The authors argue that leaders can, and do, transform themselves, and to a certain extent these types can be taught, so you do see transitions from one leader type to another. One of the largest bottlenecks within organizations, however, is from the leadership role of

Expert to that of **Achiever**. Because people such as engineers, lawyers and other professionals can often demonstrate **Expert** characteristics, the transition to **Achiever** can be difficult, but it is possible and can be positive for an organization.

The authors propose that the most effective teams are those with a **Strategist** culture where people see challenges as opportunities for business growth and learning. They also report that few organizations operate this way. Most operate with an **Achiever** culture focused on goal achievement. The rarest but most transformational kinds of leaders are **Strategists** and **Alchemists**. The latter can transcend a narrow role in business to take on more truly a national role, becoming a cult figure.

JONES AND GOSLING'S 'EIGHT QUESTIONS OF LEADERSHIP'

Our author of this chapter, Stephanie Jones and her co-author Jonathan Gosling (a co-author with Mintzberg, see above), have looked in detail at the life of Lord Nelson, the British naval hero of the eighteenth and early nineteenth centuries (Jones & Gosling, 2005). Their recent study seeks to explain Nelson's success as a leader in the context of their review of leadership theory and practice. Seeing Nelson as having a dynamic approach to leadership and management, they distilled the lessons of his approach into a series of practical and contemporary insights for today's managers. The 'Eight Questions of Leadership' were developed in the course of this explanatory approach.

The authors suggest that the answers to the questions define a leader's style and context, and argue that this framework can have modern applicability in identifying how leaders see themselves, and why. The 'Eight Questions' ask the leader to reflect on such issues as motivation for leadership, the role of expertise in leadership, visibility in leadership, work/life balance, attitudes to teamwork, the combination of leadership and management, the engagement of followers and the legacy of the leader. Nelson's answers to these questions are identified as the pursuit of Heroism, Vocation, Courage, Passion, Loyalty, Diligence, Inspiration and Glory.

Other leaders interpret their own responses in their own way. The authors propose that every leader, or every person inspired to be leader, should ask him/her self these questions. For example "why you think others should follow you?" The answers will be a mix of reasons, but if a leader hopes to inspire their followers it must be something the followers will recognize as special. The way the questions are answered adds up to an individual's 'leadership style', revealing the cultural context in which that leader operates. Elements of this relate to time frame and to national or organizational context, or can be universal. These 'Eight Questions,' and the leadership lessons which can be derived from them, are explained in more detail at the end of this chapter.

A CLASSIC APPROACH TO LEADERSHIP – WITH A NEW TWIST

Leadership and organizational needs – what leaders and managers actually do day-by-day – is discussed in Mintzberg's classic 'Ten Roles of a Manager.' It is included here rather than in our previous chapter because of its heavy emphasis on context. It is not what managers are which is important – it is what they do to fulfill the tasks and roles needed in their organizations.

How can we understand the demands for these leadership and management roles and practices? One idea is to apply the learning from a live case. Mintzberg himself carried out his research through observation of the daily work of managers in many organizations. Here, as a case study, we examine an extended experiential training event. This was an Everest Base Camp expedition, revealing the need for a leader/manager to fulfill these tasks and roles. Mintzberg's concept of three headings and ten roles can be seen as essential parts of the portfolio of an outstanding leader, and the ability to use one or more of these as required:

(Interpersonal) **Figurehead, Leader and Liaison**
(Informational) **Monitor, Disseminator and Spokesman**
(Decisional) **Entrepreneurial, Disturbance-Handler, Resource-Allocator, Negotiator**

Within these areas would be other characteristics: communication skills, political savvy, getting buy-in and consensus, having vision and keeping focus, goal-setting, planning and organizational skills, logistical and supply-chain management ability, overcoming obstacles, interacting with the group, reporting to the outside world, maintaining a positive outlook, innovation, adaptation, etc.

AN EVEREST BASE CAMP EXPEDITION AND THE 'TEN ROLES OF THE MANAGER' – THEORY IN ACTION IN THE HIMALAYAS IN NEPAL

This event can be seen in a business context as it had a series of specific objectives, not least of these financial. In terms of the background context, the overall objectives of this particular expedition were:

Financial – to secure at least USD 50,000 in funding for the charity being supported (in this case the Mobile Breast Cancer Screening Unit of Tawam Hospital in Al Ain, United Arab Emirates), which required the successful completion of the exercise, i.e. all (or the majority) of the 18 participants, all women, personally making it to Base Camp

Fulfilling sponsor obligations – in return for items donated to the group (sunglasses, altitude watches, tracksuits, trainers, medical kits etc.) to obtain publicity photographs at Base Camp advertising the sponsors, to be subsequently used in press reports

Safety – that all participants' health and safety would be protected at all times, without undue risk, and that any emergency could be dealt with promptly, effectively and appropriately

Within budget – that the whole expedition would be successfully completed within the budgeted expenditure limits

The ten roles in action were clearly identifiable – but unlike Mintzberg's ideal of one person able to carry out all roles, in this case study a number of people took on one or more of the tasks needed to fulfill these roles. Firstly, the role of the **Figurehead** of a group is to act as an ambassador, representing the group with the highest authorities. During the expedition, on arrival in Nepal, there were immediate immigration problems with one of the participants. Three of the other participants successfully argued on behalf of the group, representing the expedition, putting forward the importance of entry being allowed for the group as a whole. This was the highest level of negotiating, almost on a country-to-country level, addressing the whole matter of the admission of expedition groups, the implications for the tourism industry in Nepal, and the politics of decision-making by government agencies. This role was adopted by a group member with the most experience of high-level negotiations.

Secondly, the **Leader's** job is to hold the group together, focus on the group objectives, yet satisfy individual needs. For example, in the expedition, on the morning of the day designated for the Everest Base Camp ascent, the weather posed a significant problem. At 5 am, at wake-up call, at least five inches of snow lay around the tents and it was still snowing heavily. At 6 am it was still a complete white-out. Then a meeting was held – this time led by the official guide – to make a decision on going to Base Camp, just as the snow was beginning to settle and the sun was coming out. Starting later than planned, it was looking difficult to make Base Camp, get back safely to the village where the expedition was currently camped (Gorak Shek) and keep to the very tight itinerary of reaching the lower altitude village of Lobuche before nightfall.

The leader role was focusing on dividing the expedition into groups based on speed and ability, which alienated some of the slower participants who felt that they might be denied the opportunity to go to Base Camp, which threatened to undermine the objectives of the whole expedition. Unlike earlier parts of the trek, the climb up the glacier was seen as presenting new dangers especially in worsening weather conditions, and it was important for people to be close together, at least all groups having their own guide. The possibility of all going as a group altogether or not at all was mooted. All staying together would have, in fact, undermined the team objectives. Logistical arguments were seen by some as an excuse for inaction and indecision. Whose tents and luggage would be carried by the porters down to Lobuche? When should the decision to go on to Lobuche or stay at Gorak Shep after Base Camp be made? What were safe turnaround times? Also, how long would the first group have to wait at Base Camp for the second group and the third group in order to take the photographs of all 18? Teamwork was important – if some wanted to go quickly, they should not then complain of having to wait. This wait was significant, given freezing conditions (-10 to -15°C) the altitude (5,364 m or 17,600 ft) and exposure, with the lack of our own camp there (in the end the expedition used the Everest Base Camp Internet Café for the purpose).

Liaison between participants and sherpas, porters, and staff generally was a vital requirement, and often things went wrong. The 18 participants were supported by a group of 40, carrying tents, sleeping bags, equipment, luggage, cooking utensils and food, including five Dzo or Dzomo (local animals cross-bred between yaks and cows). On occasion, there were groups of participants without guides who then got lost; tents were in the wrong place; meal stops were too early or too late; the porter carrying the medical supplies was not to be found when needed; the departing yak train was causing a traffic jam on the trekking route holding-up the participants, etc. None of these liaison problems proved disastrous but, given higher altitudes on the mountain with the need for oxygen, could potentially have been (and were significant in previous high-altitude ascents such as detailed in *Into Thin Air* and other Everest summit accounts). These roles were adopted by the supervisors of the sherpas.

The role of being a **Monitor**, of measuring the achievement of each milestone, regularly surveying levels of participant morale and health, and readiness for the next challenge, was encouraged among all participants. The daily 'buddy-check' system, altitude readings compared with symptoms of potentially debilitating AMS ('acute mountain sickness') and tolerance of the food made simple enquiries such as "how are you?" more significant than usual. Most participants had to cope with minor illnesses, some more alarming than others, some exaggerated, some played-down. This all had an impact on group chemistry and attitudes to each day's new challenge. Participants learned the value of empathizing, of 'being in the same boat,' of not emphasizing one's own healthiness if others were suffering, especially because the situation could be reversed the next day – and often was. In terms of monitoring morale, some participants rushed out in front, eager to reach the next camp, whilst others chose to slow down to keep company and maintain the morale of those lagging behind. The more successful team players saw it as more important to make others in the group feel good than to prove their personal speed and performance.

The role of **Disseminator**, spreading information about objectives, progress, concerns, and logistics, was especially contentious, with the need to achieve a balance between the most able people with the most expertise making decisions and announcing these, with the need to achieve consensus. On the expedition, there was some dissention with arrangements, especially when timings slipped and promised arrangements were not in place. Despite the dissemination of information – often by the official guide and the team leader – many made their own arrangements. They decided to stay in lodges rather than in the tents supplied, to eat meals in local restaurants rather than those provided by the expedition's own cooks, to negotiate with local providers of showers and other washing services than use the plastic bucket and rather grubby communal towel set up by the porters. A balance had to be made between providing services, yet leaving people with a choice about whether to use them or not, according to their preference. Personal expedition budgets were exceeded in some cases, but according to personal decisions and preference. The provision of equipment had to be adapted as the expedition went along, to accommodate the availability of cheap and good trekking gear at Namche Bazaar 'en route,' and to adapt to more extreme weather conditions than expected, when three participants had to send porters down the mountain for a day's trek and back to purchase the necessary warm gear in freezing and wet conditions. It can be very challenging to envisage the requirements of extreme altitudes and cold for participants living in permanently sunny weather at sea level, despite expert advice.

The **Spokesman** role was also important, as the expedition maintained daily contact with home through 'live-links' with a Dubai radio station. Even after eight hours of trekking in rain, snow and blizzards, whilst suffering from an upset stomach, nausea, headaches, blisters and other ailments, the expedition's 'anchor-woman' had to make an up-beat, innovative and descriptive radio broadcast – and do this every day. This involved commentating on interesting and humorous happenings and surroundings in a positive, motivational way, especially given that sponsors and contributors would be listening, as well as anxious family and friends.

Entrepreneurial skills were required before the event, in developing opportunities for fund-raising, and press coverage, for example. Asking sponsors for equipment, approaching community leaders for sponsorship, and negotiating the use for an evening of 446 ft yacht for a fund-raising bash, were further instances. This was arranged by yet another expedition participant. The difficulties encountered on the expedition encouraged innovation, such as drying wet socks by inserting water bottles containing freshly-boiled hot water in them, for example. Useful trekking tips were freely passed onto other trekkers. Barter practices were used, such as exchanging slices of apple pie for a lecture on avoiding altitude sickness. Amusing songs describing the unfortunate ailments of the expedition participants were composed. The success of the Everest Base Camp Internet Café was widely discussed (a worthwhile venture given the presence of 35 expeditions and up to a thousand people at Base Camp preparing for summit bids during the May summit season; customers were charged USD1 per minute for the satellite phone-based facility).

The role of **Disturbance-Handler** was one of the most significant, especially in dealing with the major crisis of the expedition – the sickness of one of the participants at Base Camp (thankfully after the promotional photographs were successfully taken), necessitating an emergency evacuation by helicopter. Luckily, insurance for such an eventuality had been arranged for all participants, but there were problems in the handling of the crisis. Who was the most important authority, a medical practitioner on the expedition or the person with the most knowledge of the altitude and terrain? Arguments continued whilst the sick participant deteriorated; there was an urgent need to descend from Base Camp, and then it became too late to reach a landing point to summon the helicopter that night, given that helicopters need to return to Kathmandu each night by 6 pm.

Finally, the roles of **Resource-Allocator** and **Negotiator** were used extensively on the expedition, requiring planning and organizing ability and collaborative, problem-solving skills. The latter skills were particularly in demand on the last day, on departure, as the airline claimed that the baggage allowance of 40 kg had been reduced to 20 kg whilst the expedition had been in Nepal, and after the 18 female participants had spent two days shopping in Kathmandu and were clutching a large collection of yak-bells, Gurkha knives, cheesecloth shirts, etc. And the resource-allocation of warm, clean clothes at strategic points on the return trek became a life-saver after long days and nights of dirt and discomfort.

In conclusion, participants learned new insights into each of these leadership and managerial roles as a result of this high-altitude experiential training exercise. In the Figurehead role, they learned about cross-cultural negotiating and understanding typical political issues in how to make things happen at high levels in an organization; as a leader, in gaining buy-in to executive decisions, focusing on objectives despite short-term difficulties, and applying collaborative rather than compromise solutions to problems; in liaising, achieving effective supply-chain management and the importance of everything being in the right place at the right time; in monitoring, keeping a close check on what's happening – 'health checks' can be applied to organizations as much as to people; in disseminating, relaying all information in an accurate, timely and relevant way, allowing choices to be made when appropriate; in being a spokesperson, understanding the importance of good Public Relations (PR) skills, of being upbeat and positive despite difficulties; in being entrepreneurial, of seeing opportunities all down the track and keeping focused on goals; in handling emergencies ('disturbance-handler') of the importance of calmly making decisions from the choices available, and being able to accurately judge the gravity of a situation; of allocating resources fairly and with clear knowledge of resources available; and of negotiating for maximum advantage whilst maintaining relationships with all concerned. More so than in a typical workplace, teamwork and learning as a group was significant, with such close proximity of working and living together for such an extended period.

CASE QUESTIONS
- *Do the Mintzberg roles cover all the tasks and jobs needed in an organization?*
- *Can you think of any required in your organization not included in the theory?*
- *How can a leader be competent in such a diverse variety of roles? Is this possible, or is the case scenario with many different people occupying different roles more credible?*
- *Which of these roles is currently most important in your organization?*
- *Which of these roles would you find personally the most challenging?*
- *In this particular case, which roles could be carried out only by one or two people, and which are more ubiquitous?*

NATIONAL CONTEXT AND LEADERSHIP

One of the questions increasingly asked in the more contextual emphasis on leadership favored by contemporary writers is that of **"What is the impact of national culture on leadership?"** Which has greater effects on an individual's approach to leadership, individual personality or the pressures of the local environment? This is a difficult question as many authors examining leadership neglect national cultural issues, and cross-cultural management commentators mostly do not focus on leadership.

Many widely-discussed leadership theories, popular in textbooks (Hellriegel & Slocum, 2004: 248-287) do not explore the influence of national cultural context. The Traits Model (Northouse, 2004), the Ohio State University's studies of the late 1940s, the Path-Goal model (House and Howell, 1992), Hersey and Blanchard's model (1988), and Vroom-Jago's (1988) time-driven leadership model are mainly North American-centric and see the rest of the world through this lens. The same could be said to apply to the extensive literature on Transformational and Transactional leadership (Burns, 1978 and Bass, 1985, for example, discussed in more detail in Chapter 2).

One cross-cultural insight into leadership, used as a textbook example, looks at Vietnam (Hellriegel & Slocum, 2004: 259-260) and considers the local consultative process ('xin phep') designed to show respect and build relationships. This is not relinquishing power or delegation, but ensuring that everyone feels comfortable with a decision. Cumbersome and needing time and effort, everyone discusses details exhaustively, leading to "almost too much democracy" (Barton, 2000: 20-31). Does this mean that giving attention to 'soft' issues is more obvious in Asian countries? Is this an important consideration?

As discussed in more detail in our chapters on national culture and in a companion textbook 'Managing Cultural Diversity,' Hofstede discusses *'High Power Distance'* cultures, such as many Asian countries (Philippines, India, Singapore, Hong Kong), South American countries (Mexico, Venezuela, Brazil) and many Arab and African countries, in contrast with *'Low Power Distance'* cultures such as North America, Australasia, Scandinavia and Great Britain. The former countries show the importance of rank in organizations and deference shown to bosses; the latter show lower rank-consciousness and much more familiarity (Hofstede, 1984: 65-109).

Studies of leadership have largely neglected the Asian world. Initial insights would suggest that most Asian countries exhibit *'High Power Distance'* (Hofstede, 1984: 77) and *'Ascribed status'*, as defined by Trompenaars: "acting as suits you even if nothing is achieved" (1997: 105). Trompenaars also saw Arab countries as showing the lowest percentage of respondents disagreeing with the statement "Respect depends on family background" (1997: 106).

There are obviously substantial contrasts between Eastern and Western leaders, supporting the cultural summaries of Hofstede and Trompenaars. For example, the former – characterized by *'High Power Distance'* – wanted to be leaders to have power, to take charge, to tell others what to do and avoid being a subordinate, and as a birthright. (in the Hofstede research, a distinction is made between cultures with high power distance where it is okay to show such distance - e.g. France - and such cultures where the power distance is expected to be expressed in a more subtle manner - e.g. Japan). The Westerners, by contrast saw the desire to be a leader as a personal character trait, an interest in leading, and for a more stimulating and worthwhile career. It can thus be suggested that national culture has a powerful impact on chosen leadership style, and that all studies of individual leaders and groups of contrasting leaders should take national culture into account. However, it is a field where there are still more questions than answers.

EXERCISE: How does your culture impact on your leadership style? Based on Hofstede and Trompenaars' dimensions, how do you respond to these questions:

- *Universalism and particularism: do you make decisions based on the need to preserve relationships, or to abide by the law? If your friend committed a crime, would you support him or her, or obey the law of the land as a priority? Why? What are the implications for you as a leader?*

- *Power distance: do you like people to call you by your first name, and do you also like to spend social time with your staff? Or do you think they should keep their distance, call you "Sir" or "Madam", and respect you as the boss at all times? Is this your personal preference, or the way you think you should behave in the environment where you work, which may or may not be your home country?*

- *Ascribed status: do you regard your role as leader as part of your birthright, as a task you have been brought up for all your life, which is unquestioned as an ambition for you? Or do you think you have to struggle and strive for your position, and do you think you could lose it at any moment?*

Review your answers with colleagues in the workplace and classmates on the study program. If you feel uncomfortable or uncomfortable doing this, you may also be responding in a way related to your culture! Above all, think through what this means for the way you operate as a leader in your own environment. How much of this is personality and how much is culture?

CLOSING EXERCISE: LEADERSHIP LESSONS

As discussed above, the 'Eight Questions of Leadership' help to define our leadership styles and attitudes, in an interactive way. How would you answer these questions? How about if we have still not achieved what we want to achieve? How can you achieve your desired way of being a leader? How can we define our approach to leadership, and hence our own leadership style? There are at least eight important questions we can ask to define our approach:

- *Why be a leader? What motivates you to take this challenge? Do you really want to be a leader, or are you reluctant and will do it if you have to?*
- *Do you have to be an expert in your field to be a leader in your field? Is it the most necessary feature of leadership in your context?*
- *Do you want to lead from the front and be always visible? Or do you believe in quiet leadership, behind the scenes?*
- *How do you handle your public and private life, balancing love and duty? Do you achieve your work/life balance?*
- *Why be a team player? Is it necessary and more effective to share leadership? How do you feel about leading a team? To what extent are you prepared to share ideas and plans, and devolve authority and initiative?*
- *Can leaders be managers too? Is it important to be visionary and inspirational, and be a good administrator and resource manager? Can you be both, in the context in which you work? Do you think it's necessary?*
- *Why should others follow you? Is your team following you because they have to or because you are inspirational? Are you consciously helping them achieve their potential?*
- *What will be your legacy? What will you leave behind as the mark of your leadership?*

The leadership lessons described here take one of the choices of each of the leadership questions above, and explain how this mode of leadership can be achieved. The lessons are based on being a motivated leader, an expert leader, a visible leader, a leader able to achieve a work/life balance, a team-player leader, a leader with an ability and interest in managing, a would-be inspirational leader, and one who wants to leave something specific behind him. The questions here are also relevant to those who choose another leadership route.

The way of the motivated leader – leadership lessons: do you really want to be a leader? Be honest with yourself – have you got the energy and commitment for it?

Then volunteer for tough but high-profile assignments, giving opportunities for independent action;

Be an excellent communicator – you can't be a leader without it. Get a good PR person onto it if you can't do it yourself;

Spread the word about your achievements with stories that will be repeated, to inspire others and remind them of the values they most admire. It is not enough to just sing your own praises;

If you want to be a 'real leader,' you must show genuine and robust leadership qualities – courage, passion, loyalty – not just the spin;

Choose a profession or organization where you can rise to the top and which is congruent with your own values. Start leading your peers;

Identify and represent important values which can earn you trust and respect;

You can't be the leader all the time, you need to be a good manager as well; and

Have deep and unshakeable faith in what you do and feel good about it.

The way of the expert leader – leadership lessons: if you want to be a leader where expertise is the route to respect, focus on gaining expert knowledge quickly and apply it for ideal ends. This will give you respect beyond the ordinary;

Search for patrons or mentors and build relationships to gain expert knowledge, using them to give you more opportunities to learn, and as stepping-stones to increased influence;

Keep using the expert knowledge of your specialism even if, as a leader, others can now do these expert jobs – it's a way of reducing risk in decision-making, avoiding being ripped off, and continuing to bond with all levels of the organization – you speak the same language;

If expert knowledge is respected in your organization, then use it to select good people, and to respect ability in others;

Expert knowledge has to be maintained, nothing stands still, so this has to be worked on all the time; and

Realize the limitations of an expert role that this may keep you to an operational role, and there's a long jump from here to higher ranks.

The way of the visible leader – leadership lessons: as a leader, you are always visible, even if no one can see you – they will have an image of you – and you can live up to it or not;

Some situations require more visibility than others – especially in operational roles – but there is no hiding place, even if you choose to be behind the scenes;

If you want to be a clearly visible leader, you'll never make a name for yourself without taking risks and huge responsibility;

People have to know what you stand for – you can't be visible without objectives, goals and a mission;

Being visible, you are most exposed if things go wrong, and you need to ask yourself, is this way the best use of my leadership role? and

If you are visible, show absolute confidence in a positive outcome – others are looking towards you to set an example.

The way of work/life balance – leadership lessons: as a leader you may have a lot of emotional energy – where is it going? To your job, your team members at work, or your private life? In what proportions? Is it under control? Is there a balance?

The constant exercise of leadership, and the expectations of others, can have repercussions on relationships at work and at home;

Appreciate when you might be at your most vulnerable to work/life imbalance, such as at times of stress, when passions are conflicting;

Sometimes there's a real conflict between the demands of the job and your relationships, then because balance can't be possible, you just have to make a choice; and

Take into account the views of family and friends on your leadership style – they may see things that others can't tell you.

The way of being a team player – leadership lessons: if you want to be a participative leader and a team player – you must create loyalty and trust – being autocratic is quicker and easier;

As a participative leader, be a 'primus inter pares' – first among equals, admired and respected – but promoting loyalty to the team;

Invest in getting to know your immediate subordinates and help them to know each other, so they know what each other is thinking and how they will act;

Let them know that your success depends on them, give them the clear message, you're all in it together;

Create trust and honesty, between each other and between all your team members and yourself, handling mistakes and failures in a supportive and positive way;

Start a sort of informal 'club' to which they can identify, based on achievements and abilities, and add new members to the 'club' based on the same meritocratic values;

Take team members with you to the most important and high profile events, as a reward and for their exposure and development;

But make sure they are a team and not a clique. A clique invests more in their own togetherness than in the work they must do together;

Use common interests to overcome differences in background, social status, nationality and personality;

Be a rallying-point, offer guidance and decision-making, whilst encouraging them to contribute, facilitating but not dominating discussions;

Look after their interests, their families, their promotion prospects, and all chances for improvement;

Resolve differences and falling-out between team members by listening and encouraging disputants to see the issues from the other's perspective; and

Listen to their advice, consult them on your own problems, be human and vulnerable, offer real affection and enjoy receiving it in return – it's lonely at the top.

The way of being a manager as well as a leader – leadership lessons: gain a deep understanding of how your organization works enables you to 'feel the pulse' and be engaged in managing it;

Managers who can't lead are dull and unexciting, whilst leaders who can't manage are out of control;

If you are more interested in people than things and can't do both easily, others around you will have to handle the things, and vice versa;

Identify the boundaries of your autonomy as both a leader and a manager – where do you have freedom to act, and where must you conform to guidelines?

In your areas of freedom to act, focus on maximizing the ability of your team to be successful, in terms of resources and tools to do the job, and provide them with opportunities for achievement;

Make good use of the four functions of management – firstly, planning. Be clear on what you want to achieve and keep it rooted in reality. Share your goals with your team, seek their inputs and obtain their buy-in, allocate resources as effectively and economically as you can;

Followed by organizing. Stay in touch with talented people in your own organization. Make sure they have what they need to succeed;

Then leading. Identify talent, build teams and design reporting relationships that suit your objectives. Keep communicating; and

Finally, controlling. Evaluate how well you are achieving your goals, monitor performance and take corrective action if needed. Choose key performance indicators and keep improving on the results.

The way of inspiration – leadership lessons: remind everyone (regularly) what it's all for and demonstrate that you are fully dedicated to that great purpose – actions speak louder than words but words inspire action;

Show that results can be achieved and they are for a greater purpose, appealing to people's highest aspirations;

Know your people, know their jobs, know stories about them, and show your care with symbolic acts of kindness;

Fight for the interests of your people, lobby for their cause; nothing can be achieved without them;

Be a hero to your people – and don't ask them to do anything you wouldn't do yourself – leadership is a trust earned through respect;

Represent the cause, the ideals and values of your people and be a role model, walking the talk and promoting unity through a common vision;

Offer stability and continuity in times of chaos, but also the possibility of reform and improvement;

Deal with discontent by appealing to the pride of your people in their achievements, offer to deal with genuine grievances fairly, and focus behavior on urgent current tasks;

Use the sandwich technique of giving feedback – praise, criticize (gently) and praise again; and

Even in the most extreme circumstances – always celebrate success – symbols and gestures matter.

The way of a continuing legacy – leadership lessons: do you want to be remembered, or do you want to do your job quietly and just as quietly slip away? Leaving behind a glorious legacy is not for everyone;

We are talking about what you leave for future generations. Will you leave your part of the world in a better state than you found it?

To leave something really memorable, you will probably have to make sacrifices – to give up current pleasure for future benefits. So it's worth choosing something worthwhile;

The cause you serve is important – it should be bigger than any individual, bigger than the self-interests of a minority or a corporation: it should be worthy of your best efforts, tangible and real;

Results matter and so do examples. Setting an example can have a bigger long-term impact. Live your life according to ideals that will be admired by others for generations to come;

Build your legacy into the culture of your organization, so that everyone joining this organization and becoming aware of the culture becomes aware of your legacy;

Present a clear common vision which everyone can buy into, make their own commitment to, and celebrate its achievement; and

Create memorable stories – or legends – about your achievements, with little touches that reveal your human side. To be remembered, you need to be a little larger than life, but not impossibly so.

Are you a motivated leader, and have you clearly thought through your interest in leadership? Are you an expert leader, or a generalist? Visible, or invisible? Are you able to achieve work/life balance, or not? Are you a team-player leader, or a loner? Are you a leader with an ability and interest in managing? Are you a would-be or existing inspirational leader, and do you want to leave something specific behind you, and not be forgotten? Do you take the Nelson route, or do you want to carve out a new and unique niche for yourself? The way you answer these questions should help you make your own hopes and dreams clearer and perhaps more within sight.

CONCLUSION

In this chapter we have considered a range of new leadership challenges and realities. Leadership studies have come a long way since the theories of the 1950s, and new insights are emerging every day. The task of leading is more complex than ever before – as evidenced in the case of Gerstner at IBM. Leadership competencies now involve a lot more than the decision-making and problem-solving demands of the past. We have considered a range of recent examples of new thinking on leadership, which emphasize the multifaceted nature of this job in the modern world. Above all, the role of the leader needs more reflection, and is no longer based on gut instinct. What is your choice of leadership style and approach? How do you answer the eight questions of leadership? What is the impact of your current leadership, management and business studies on the defining of your leadership role? There are many things to think about here!

REFERENCES

Barton. L. 2000. Working in a Vietnamese Voice. *Academy of Management Executive. 14* (4): 20-31.

Burns. J.M. 1978. *Leadership*. New York: Harper & Row.

De Bono. S. and Jones. S. 2007. *Managing Cultural Diversity*. Oxford: Meyer & Meyer.

Gerstner. L. 2002. *Who Says Elephants Cant Dance?* New York: Harper Collins.

Goffee. R. and Jones. R. 2000. Why Should Anyone Be Led By You? *Harvard Business Review. 62-70.*

Gosling. J. and Mintzberg. H. 2003. The Five Minds of a Manager. *Harvard Business Review. 81* (11): 54-63.

Hellriegel. D. and Slocum. J. 2004. *Organizational Behavior*. Mason, Ohio: Thomson.

Hersey. P. and Blanchard. K. 1988. *Management of Organizational Behavior*. Upper Saddle River, NJ: Prentice Hall.

Hofstede. G. 1980. Motivating. leadership and organization: Do American theories apply abroad? *Organizational Management Association. 42-63.*

Hofstede. G. 1984. *Cultures Consequences: International Differences in Work-Related Values*. Beverley Hills, CA: Sage.

Hofstede. G. 1991. *Cultures and Organizations: Software of the Mind*. London: McGraw Hill.

Hofstede. G. 1993. Cultural Constraints in management theories. *Academy of Management Executive. 7* (1): 81-94.

House. R.J. 1977. A 1976 theory of charismatic leadership. *Leadership: the Cutting Edge*. Carbondale, IL: Southern Illinois University Press.

House. R.J. and Howell. J.M. 1992. Personality and charismatic leadership. *Leadership Quarterly. 3* (2): 81-108.

Jones. S. 2003. On Top of the World: Leadership and Management Lessons from Everest. *Human Assets Middle East. 16-19.*

Jones. S. and Gosling. J. 2005. *Nelson's Way: leadership lessons from the great commander*. London: Nicholas Brealey.

Lundquist E. 2002. Gerstner's vision got IBM on course . *e-week*. September. 5. Northouse. P. 2004. Leadership: Theory and Practice. USA: Sage.

Peace. W. 2001. The Hard Work of Being a Soft Manager. *Harvard Business Review. 99-104.*

Rooke D. Torbert W 2005. Seven Transformations of Leadership. *Harvard Business Review. 54-67*

Trompenaars. F. and Hampden-Turner. C. 1997. *Riding the Waves of Culture: understanding cultural diversity in business*. London: Nicholas Brealey.

Vroom. V. H. and Jago. A. G. 1988. *The New Leadership: managing participation in organizations*. Englewood Cliffs: Prentice Hall.

Useem. M. 2001. The Leadership Lessons of Mount Everest. *Harvard Business Review. 51-58.*

Worth R 1999. What Lou Gerstner Could Teach Bill Clinton. *Washington Monthly*. 31: 9. September 1999. 8.

RECOMMENDED FURTHER READING

Bennis. W.. and Biederman. P. W. 1997. *Organizing Genius*. USA: Addison Wesley.

Bennis. W. 2001. *The Future of Leadership: Todays Top Leadership Thinkers Speak to Tomorrows Leaders*. San Fransisco: Jossey-Bass.

Campbell. D.J. Bommer. W. and Yeo. E. 1993. Perceptions of appropriate leadership style: participation versus consultation across two cultures. *Asia Pacific Journal of Management. 10* (1): 1-19.

Blanchard. Kenneth 1994. *Leadership and the One Minute Manager*. London: Harper Collins.

Boulden. Richard 2005. What is Leadership Development? Exeter: *Centre for Leadership Studies*. Research Report.

Cooper. John 2002. *Great Britons*. London: BBC

Covey. S.1992. *Principle-Centered Leadership*. New York: Simon and Schuster.

Daft. Richard 2002. *The Leadership Experience*. New York: Harcourt.

Den Hartog. D. N. House. R. J. Hanges. P. J. et al. 1999. Culture specific and cross culturally generalizable implicit leadership theories: are attributes of charismatic/ transformational leadership universally endorsed? *Leadership Quarterly. 10* (2): 219–56.

Goleman. D. 1998. What Makes a Leader? *Harvard Business Review*. November-December

Gosling. J. and Mintzberg. H. 2004. Education of Practicing Managers. *MIT Sloan Management Review*. 19-22.

Gregersen. H.B.. Morrison. A.J. & J.S. Black. 1998.. Developing leaders for the global frontier. *Sloan Management Review*. Fall. 21–32.

Grint. K. 2000. *Arts of Leadership*. Oxford: Oxford University Press.

Hamel G. 2000. Waking up IBM. *Harvard Business Review*. 137-146.

Harvey-Jones. J. 1988. *Making it Happen: Reflections on Leadership*. London: Collins.

Hiebert. M. and Klatt. B. 2001. *The Encyclopedia of Leadership; a practical guide to popular leadership theories and techniques*. Blacklick. Ohio: McGraw Hill.

House. R. J. Hanges. P. J.. Ruiz-Quintanilla. S. A.. Dorf-man. P. W.. Javidan. M.. Dickson. M. et al. 1999. Cultural influences on leadership and organizations: Project globe. *Advances in Global Leadership*. 1. 171 233. Stamford. CT. JAI Press.

Hunt. J. and Larsen. L. H. 1979. *Cross-Currents in Leadership*. Illinois: Southern Illinois. University Press.

Jones. Stephanie 1992. *Psychometric Testing for Managers*. London: Piatkus.

Keegan. John 1987. *The Mask of Command*. London: Jonathan Cape.

Kerr. S. and Jermier. J.M. 1978. Substitutes for leadership: their meaning and measurement. *Organizational Behavior and Human Performance. 22*. 374-403

Khadra. B. 1985. Leadership. ideology and development in the Middle East. In S. Hajjar Ed. *The Middle East*. pp. 109-119.

Kotter. J. 2001. What Leaders Really Do. *Harvard Business Review*. 1-12.

McFarland. L.J.. Senen. S.. and Childress.J.R. 1993. *Twenty-First Century Leadership*. New York: Leadership Press.

Mintzberg. H. 1998. Covert Leadership: Notes on Managing Professionals. *Harvard Business Review*. November-December

Pfeffer. J. 1996. Why do smart organizations occasionally do dumb things?. *Organizational Dynamics*. Summer. 33-44

Phillips. Fred 2003. *The Conscious Manager: Zen for Decision Makers*. USA: General Informatics.

Reichheld. Frederick 2001. Lead for Loyalty. *Harvard Business Review.* *79* (7): 76-84.

Rifkin. G. 1998. How Richard Branson works magic. *Strategy and Business.* *13* (4): 44-52.

Robbins. S. P. and Coulter. M. 2002. *Management.* 7th ed. Englewood Cliffs: Prentice Hall

Thomas. M. 2006. *Gurus on leadership.* UK . Thorogood Publishing Ltd.

Vries. Kets de. M.F.R. 1999.. *The New Global Leaders: Richard Branson. Percy Barnevik. and David Simon.* San Francisco: Jossey Bass.

Yukl. Gary 2002. *Leadership in Organizations.* Englewood Cliffe. N.J.: Prentice Hall.

Zaleznik. A. 2004. Managers and leaders: are they different? *Harvard Business Review.* 105-126.

CHAPTER FOUR
STRATEGY AND STRUCTURE
QUANG TRUONG

LEARNING OBJECTIVES:

- To understand the relationship between organizational strategy and organizational structure.
- To study the organization's mission for improvement to enhance overall effectiveness and efficiency (competitive advantage).
- To examine the current need for adaptation of organizations to the global arena.

Structure, together with People and Culture, forms the foundation of an organization. At the same time, the organization's competitiveness largely depends upon how well the organization manages these critical building blocs, especially the way the organization is structured and operated to achieve the highest level of efficiency and effectiveness, given the organization's business conditions.

As the world is moving toward a fully globalized economy, organizations -multi-national corporations (MNCs) and start-up companies alike- are confronting a large array of structural choices in their effort to achieve organizational goals through the best coordination of task structure and authority relationships at individual, group and organizational level. This makes structure and design considerations become even more critical for the firm's long-term strategy for survival and growth. As initially suggested by Alfred Chandler (1962), the firm's strategy decides the form of its structure, however, the strategy-structure relationship is *reciprocal*. As much as strategy drives structure, structure also drives strategy (Fredrickson, 1986). Ultimately, an appropriate fit between strategy and structure may become a source of competitive advantage for the organization.

RELATIONSHIPS BETWEEN ORGANIZATION STRATEGY AND STRUCTURE

There has been a substantial body of work dealing with the relationships between strategy and structure, but most of the studies have mainly focused either on diversification or divisionalization of the organization. Recently, Miller (1986) offers a new approach by examining the relationships between strategy and structure and proposes some functional linkages between several complex strategic and structural configurations. Most significantly, Miles and Snow (2003) focus on how organizations adapt to their environments and identify three possible reasons leading to an organization's mediocre performance by not being capable to establish a consistent link between its charted strategy (formulation capacity) and structure (delivery capacity):

- Management fails to articulate a viable organizational strategy, e.g., the death of the CEO of Daro Development Inc. left the remaining management team unable to articulate the organizations' strategy.

- Strategy is articulated, but technology, structure and process are not linked to it in an appropriate manner, e.g., Cohen Publishing Company is struggling to pursue a new strategy, but its current structure is not well suited to this task.

- Management adheres to a particular strategy-structure relationship even though it is no longer relevant to environmental conditions, e.g., Exotic Foods is being forced out of its domain but reluctant to give up its recent strategy and structure (Raymond and Snow, 2003).

As organizations are purposive and goal-oriented, it follows that the structure of an organization also is purposive and goal-oriented (Ivancevich and Matteson, 1999: 556). In other words, an organization's structure is a means to help management to achieve the objectives set by its strategy. Accordingly, Dressler (2004) suggests that organization effectiveness relies on the capacity to connect achieved performance with existing organizational patterns and to predict how these patterns will work for a company and its strategic challenges in the future. In order to fit into its evolving environments, a company should develop its strategic capabilities on the following elements:

- Purpose: the main purpose of the business and the entrepreneurial spirit are the key drivers for a company's mission, vision, and strategy;
- Structure: corporate and business structures are focusing on the task of how effectively and efficiently allocate to work;
- Processes: organizational infrastructure defines the processes of how decisions are made;
- Capabilities: team and individual capabilities subsequently challenge the skill base that is required to run the organization as its mission and goals have been outlines;
- Control: target setting and performance management dealing with the control mechanisms to ensure strategic goals are pursued as intended.

Since organizations interact with their own environments, it can be assumed that no two organizational strategies will be the same. As a practice, each organization will chose its own target market and develop its own set of products and services in support of appropriate decisions concerning the organization's technology, structure, and process. Miles and Snow (2003: 29) define four types of organizations with corresponding strategies (technology, structure and process) (see Table 4.1):

Table 4.1. Organizational Configuration and Strategy

Organizational type	Characters	Strategic focus
Defenders	Narrow product-market domain	Seldom need to make major adjustment in their technology, structure, and methods of operation; focus on improving **efficiency** of their existing operations

Organizational type	Characters	Strategic focus
Prospectors	Continually search for market opportunities. and regularly experiment with potential responses to emerging environmental trends	Are the creators of change and uncertainty to which their competitors must respond; strong concern for product and market **innovation**
Analyzers	Operate in two types of product-market domains, one relatively stable and other changing	In stable environment, they operate routinely and efficiently through use of formalized structures and processes In more turbulent environment, they watch competitors closely for new ideas, and then quickly adopt those which appear most promising
Reactors	Frequently perceive change and uncertainty occurring in their organizational and environments, but are unable to respond effectively	Due to lack of a consistent strategy-structure relationship, they seldom make adjustment of any sort until forced to do so by environmental pressures

Source: Adapted from Miles and Snow (2003: 29)

In the global context, managing a balanced strategy-structure relationship helps the firm to ensure optimal integration, coordination and control at the corporate level in terms of strategy formulation and implementation, budgeting and performance management. The chosen form of structure will essentially decide the firm's capacity of delivery (see Table 4.2).

Table 4.2. Strategy-Structure Relationship

Strategic Option	Focus	Structure	People	Culture
Price	Cost control; procedures	Mechanistic; hierarchical	Accountants; effective managers	Individual
Quality	Process management	Organic; flat	Engineers; quality circles	Individual/group
Diversification	Innovation; creativity	Boundaryless; networked	Thinkers. inventors	Team

ORGANIZATIONS AND ENVIRONMENT

In order to survive and grow, organizations must develop some kind of accommodation to the external environment in which they operate. The performance of an organization is largely dependent on how effective it responds to the forces of change.

Complexity theory (Waldrop,1992) has been used extensively in the field of strategic management and organizational studies, sometimes called 'Complexity strategy' or 'Complex Adaptive Organization' on the Internet or in popular press. Broadly speaking, complexity theory is used in these domains to understand how organizations or firms adapt to their environments. The theory treats organizations and firms as collections of strategies and structures. When the organization or firm shares the properties of other complex adaptive systems, which is often defined as consisting of a small number of relatively simple and partially connected structures, they are more likely to adapt to their environment and, thus, survive.

Taking the system view of organizations, Tosi et al. (2000: 389) define organizations as systems of related activities that import resources from their external environment which are then transformed, or changed, by these activities into products or services. These products or services may be exchanged with other organizations or groups in the organization's environment, usually for revenues that are then used to maintain the organization itself. At least eight external groups, which are called the **relevant environment** (or key external stakeholders of an organization), can be considered:

1. Markets
2. Suppliers
3. Unions
4. Competitors
5. Public pressure groups
6. Government agencies
7. Investors or fund providers
8. Technology and science

According to Thompson (1967), the relevant environment may be relatively simple or very complex. A *simple* environment contains just a few relatively homogeneous sectors (e.g., the technological environment for companies that sell long-distance service), while a *complex* environment contains many different sectors (e.g., the case of an engineering firm which specializes in the installation of manufacturing plants of different types and in different countries).

Usually, a more straightforward approach is adopted to understand how organizations are affected by focusing on two environment sectors: the market environment and the technological environment. The *market* environment is composed of individuals, groups, or institutions that use what the organization produces, giving value to that output. For business organizations, this means products such as cars, computers, steel, television sets, bread, or the ideas or services that might be provided by advertising agencies, consulting firms, or travel agencies. The market provides the organization with some sort of exchange in return for its output. The *technological* environment consists of the techniques and the processes that the organization uses to produce the product or service, and the ideas or knowledge underlying the processing or the distribution of the product or service (Tosi et al., 2003: 390). That is where technology and science are translated into useful applications.

The degree of uncertainty or environmental change can have major implications for the internal structure of the organization (Burns and Stalker, 1961; Lawrence and Lorsch, 1969). In the *stable* environment, the degree of changes is relatively small, occurring in small increments, with small impacts on the structure, processes, and output of the organization. On the contrary, the *volatile* environment is often more turbulent, with more intense and rapid changes. The Ansoff (1990) 4-dimension matrix (market penetration, market development, product development, and diversification) provides a meaningful way to establish the relationship between the market and the products, on which a company can design its market or product strategy per market scenario.

For simplicity, there are four basic organizational types corresponding to the environmental conditions of which they are a part:
1. The mechanistic organization
2. The organic organization
3. The technology-dominated mixed
4. The market-dominated organization

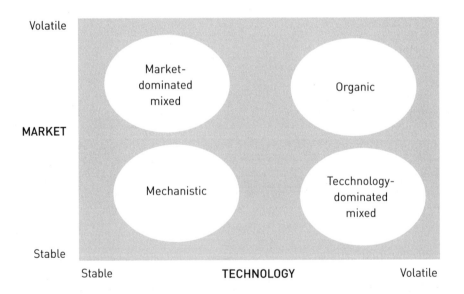

Figure 4.1. Environment-Structure Relationship

Source: Tosi et al. (2000 : 392)

Mechanistic *versus* Organic Organizations

As illustrated in Figure 4.1, when it is stable and predictable in both market and technology environments, there will be a **mechanistic** organization, in which its structure is characterized by extensive departmentalization, high formalization, a limited information network, and centralization (Robbins, 2003: 440). The reason for being mechanistic is that when the market and the technology are stable, the mechanistic form is most efficient and efficiency (small, simple, repetitive and standardized activities) is required for survival (Blauner, 1964). Typical examples of this structural type are automobile manufacturers, steel producers, and fast food restaurants. In contrast, an *organic* organization is more suitable for volatile markets and technology conditions, in which structure is flat and relationships and jobs are more loosely defined to allow an easier process of adapting to the changing environment (Tosi et al., 2000: 393). Examples of organic organizations are specialized consulting firms, advertising agencies, research units, or software development teams. The following tables (see Tables 4.3 and 4.4) show the differences between the two organization types and their relationships with the organization strategy.

Table 4.3. Mechanistic versus Organic Organizations

Mechanistic	Organic
• High specialization • Rigid departmentalization • Clear chain of command • Narrow spans of controls • Centralization • High formalization e.g.: McDonalds, Wendy's, Burger King	• Cross-functional teams • Cross-hierarchical teams • Free flow of information • Wide spans of control • Decentralization • Low formalization e.g.: Lucent, Unilever

Source: Robbins (2003: 440)

Table 4.4. Strategy and Structural Options

Strategic Option	Structural Option
Price	**Mechanistic**: hierarchical structure; tight control; extensive work specialization; high formalization; high centralization
Quality	**Mechanistic/organic**: mix or loose structure; high division of labor; process management; (group) participation
Innovation	**Organic**: flexible structure; low specialization; low formalization; decentralized

Box 4.1. Organic Structure

International Creative Management (ICM) is a talent agency firm that represents famous and important artists of the likes of Richard Gere, Goldie Hawn, Faye Dunaway, and William Baldwin, just to name a few. The job of Ed Limato, ICM's vice chairman, is to facilitate and to manage the careers of these stars. His market is the entertainment business, firms, theater and television producers.

You can imagine how unpredictable that market is. So, how does Ed Limato develop a strategy and plan for the careers of his clients? He doesn't and "There's no plan in this business." He says.

> Anybody who tells you he has a strategy –it's all [a lie]. That's what they tell a client to sign him up: "We have a plan....There is no plan...we go to work. We get our hands on every script. we try to get offers on everything. Then we discard what isn't good enough. We say 'no' nicely. Any agent who says he has a plan is snow balling you. There is no plan. It's hard work."

ICM is an organic organization. It has to respond to the different needs of its customers, the producers of films, plays and music. You can, from just what you know about these businesses, imagine the uncertainty and volatility of the demands in that market. To deal with it, ICM and Ed Limato have to be flexible.

Source: Adapted from Reginato (1998); quoted in Tosi et al. (2000: 393).

ORGANIZATION'S MISSION FOR IMPROVEMENT

Every organization has a mission and desire for improvement in its continuous drive toward achieving an excellent level of efficiency and effectiveness. An organization can achieve this level of performance by developing and maintaining an 'appropriate' structure, a 'motivated' workforce and a 'winning' culture. The organization's delivery capacity (through its excellent management system) of these three components will give an organization the necessary competitive advantages to survive and grow in a highly competitive environment (see Figure 4.2.).

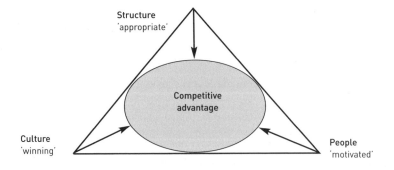

Figure 4.2. Components of an Organization and its Competitive Advantage

In this context, a wide range of studies has led to the identification of critical factors to organizational excellence. The most significant works are:

- Peters and Waterman (1982) identified 43 U.S. companies from a variety of American industries that had a fine track record over 1961-1980 on several financial criteria and that were also known to be innovative and responsive to changing internal conditions.
- Likert (1961) focused on the efficacy of good human relations in organizational settings and provided considerable data to prove that employee-oriented supervision, cohesive groups, and good communication at work are associated with high group productivity.
- Bowers and Seahore (1966) studied 40 agencies of an American life insurance company on how the style of the organization influences the performance of the organization.
- Bennis and Nanus (1985) interviewed 90 American leaders, of whom 60 'successful' corporate chief executives and 30 'outstanding' leaders from the public sector.
- Thune and House (1970) attempted to determine whether formal long-range planning, an important component of professional management, contributes to corporate performance or not.
- Lawrence and Lorsch (1967) studied 10 U.S. business units in the plastics, container, and packaged food industries to find out whether the fit between the nature of the task environment of the organization and the structure of the organization is a significant influencer of organization performance.
- Child (1974; 1975) sought to understand the relationship between the nature of a company's business environment and the kind of organizational structure the company needed to have.
- Miller and Friesen (1984) enquired whether changes in organizational structure lead to changes in organizational performance and if so, what sort of organizational changes.

KEYS TO ORGANIZATIONAL EXCELLENCE

The above mentioned studies indicate a large range of factors that contribute to organizational excellence, including (Khandwalla, 1992: 68-69):

1. *Mission, vision of excellence, and core values:* Organizations acquire a distinctive identity when they are charged by some mission, when certain goals that constitute a vision of excellence are widely shared, accepted and practiced not just by the top management but by every level across the organization, and when certain core values such as quality, service delivery, or innovation are held in high esteem by the employees of the organization. Mission, vision, and core values can bind individuals and groups together, and give them a collective inspiration, and elicit a dedication few other mechanisms can. Organizational leadership plays a critical role in institutional building.

2. *Style of management:* The distinctive way of goal setting, control, coordination, organizing, leading, managing external stakeholders, and other management functions are performed by top management comprises the style of management. A number of studies suggest that the style of management is a significant determinant of organizational performance.

3. **Strategic management:** Operating goals, policies, and strategies for achieving goals, and management focus are also known to critically contribute to organizational excellence. Goals and strategies never work in isolation. They have to be worked out into policy frameworks in the context in which the organization is operating, and they often include elements of environment or contingency management.

4. **Structure and systems:** It is proven that faulty structures or management systems can impede excellence or make it difficult to obtain. Management systems include systems for functional management, such as personnel management, management of financial and performance control, marketing management, operations management, coordination of inter-functional activities, etc. Management systems are designed to take care of the relatively repetitive or routine activities of the organization.

5. **Organizational renewal processes:** These include organizational learning, creativity, innovation, leadership and mobilization for fresh tasks. These understudied processes seem to grow in importance as organizations operate in increasingly complex, turbulent environments or take on bigger more complicated tasks.

ORGANIZATION ADAPTATION TO THE GLOBAL ARENA

Today business environment is becoming increasingly global, competitive and dynamic. New technologies are becoming more advanced, in short cycle, more user-friendly and network-driven. In order to sustain their competitive advantage, companies should demonstrate better innovation and learning ability than their competition. Given the on-going speed and the scope of the globalization process, it is expected that there will be mainly two types of organizations which will be able to succeed in this global competitive environment (Hilb, 2006: 14):

1. Innovative small local companies which form a virtual network of worldwide business partners to develop niche markets on a global basis.

2. Global group firms which form a confederation of small innovative subsidiaries and employ associates who do well for the customers, the colleagues, the shareholders and the environment in which they operate.

THE 'GLO-CAL' COMPANY

A 'glo-cal' company emerges from the above-mentioned concept which has the following organizational goals to achieve (Hilb, 2006: 95-96):

1. Development of the **social structure** which by creating necessary freedom to act for employees, satisfies their individual and group psychological needs, and in doing so acts as a mediator in a personal and social sense;

2. Realization of a high level of self-organization by involving participants at all levels of the company;

3. Introduction of a **network structure** comprising the least possible number of management levels, the largest possible span of trust (opposed to control), as well as delegation of decisions and subsequent action to the lowest possible position;

4. Introduction of a **'tent approach.'** which is effectively oriented towards output and involves an organizational culture which is flexible enough to adapt to changing environmental conditions.

As such, glo-cal companies can be coordinated, integrated and controlled according to three different approaches (see Table 4.5).

Table 4.5. Coordination Dimensions in International Companies

Coordination Dimension/Approach	Ethnocentric *(colonial)*	Polycentric *(federalistic)*	Geocentric *('glo-cal')*
Cultural Coordination	Home Country	Subsidiary Country	Mix of the best of transferable strengths of the Home. Third Country and Subsidiary Country
	Culture is dominant worldwide	Culture is dominant in each country	Cultures are created in each country
Market Coordination	Home Country Marketing exported worldwide	Country-specific marketing activities	Global Marketing approach
HRM Coordination	Subsidiary General Managers are Home Country expatriates	Subsidiary General Managers are all locals	The best people are at the top of each subsidiary (irrespective of nationality)
Structural Coordination	Centralistic organization	Decentralized organization	Integrated 'Glo-cal network'
e.g.:	Gillette	Toyota	ABB, Nestle, 3-M, Unilever

Source: Adapted from Hilb (2006:96)

IMPLICATIONS TO DEVELOPING AND EMERGING COUNTRIES

The globalization has deeply affected all organizations on a large scale and scope, both in a positive and in a negative sense. Multinational corporations (MNCs) and start-up companies alike have been actively adjusting their structures (internal capacity) to meet the demands of the changing business environment (external opportunity). The need for restructuring and self-adjustment is even more critical and urgent for organizations of all kinds (public and private, profit and non-profit) in the drive toward full integration into the world mainstream. One of the positive benefits of globalization is that developing and emerging countries (especially the ex-socialist countries and the mixed ('market economy with socialist characters') economies like China and Vietnam, can adapt the 'best practices' from well established and well managed enterprises from the West to turn their suboptimal organizations (processes. systems and mechanisms) into high performance organizations (see Box 4.2.). The dilemmas that these organizations are commonly facing can be summarized as follows (see Table 4.6.):

Table 4.6. Current Issues Facing Organizations in Developing and Emerging Economies

Areas for improvement	Dilemmas
• Competition	• Centralization *versus* decentralization
• Organization design	• Efficiency *versus* effectiveness
• Human resources	• Staff *versus* line
• Speed	• Control *versus* commitment
• Quality	• Short-term *versus* long-term
• ICT technology	• Change *versus* stability
• Business strategy	• Transparency *versus* discretion

Box 4.2. Internal Problem Areas of Indian Organizations

Third World organizations often run into a host of internal problems because of limited capacity to manage complexity, socio-cultural conservatism, social stratification in the larger society impeding cooperation in the workplace, government control, political interference, etc. In an on-going study among 80 Indian public and private sector organizations performed by the Indian Institute of Management, Ahmedabad, of fifteen internal problem areas that were hindering even progressive organizations, the following are found to be most widespread:

• Delay in solving problem
• Lack of commitment to goals
• Lack of opportunities to staff for personal growth
• Unproductive meetings and discussions
• Poor communication, inadequate information from colleagues

The correlations of the fifteen internal problem areas with ten indicators of organization performance revealed the following problem areas as those with the most widespread negative impact on organizational performance:

- Lack of clear goals
- Lack of skilled manpower
- No teamwork
- High turnover among professional staff
- Lack of opportunities to staff for personal growth
- Delay in solving problems

Source: P.N. Khandwalla, Organizational Designs for Excellence. New Delhi, Tata McGraw-Hill Publishing Co.
Ltd., 1992: 217.

QUESTIONS FOR DISCUSSION
- *Why should an organization's structure be linked to its strategy?*
- *Choose one organization which is familiar to your knowledge and experience and describe the issues that it is facing at the moment.*
- *What are related structural issues organizations are facing as a result of globalization?*

Box 4.3. Strategy before Structure
by Jeffrey A. Krames*

Why Peter Drucker got it right 50 years ago, and the lessons IT managers still need to learn today:
Organizational structure is one of those amorphous topics that many managers would prefer to ignore. That explains why the majority of the best-selling business books of the last decades, contains little on how an organization *should* be structured. Most authors and consultants have touted flat structures regardless of a company's size or strategy, and the boldest have taken it further by prematurely declaring the 'death of hierarchy.'

Peter Drucker was among the first to write about the importance of fewer layers and the importance of designing an organization to fit the objectives of the enterprise. He also warned of the perils of a bad structure:

"Organization is not an end to itself but a means to the end of business performance and business results. Organization structure is an indispensable means; and the wrong structure will seriously impair business performance and may even destroy it" (1988: 45).

As organizations grow larger and markets become more complex, creating a crystal-clear strategy and a structure that enables the organization to achieve its goals becomes mission critical. In developing both, top management must be sure that key functions like IT are properly aligned so that it is of maximum value to the firm.

The Knowledge Revolution and The Future of IT
In the last decade countless experts have spoken fervently of the new Information Age that arrived with new technology breakthroughs such as faster computers, smarter software and the Internet. However, Drucker saw the information boom almost two decades earlier. In a 1988 piece for the *Harvard Business Review*, Drucker described the organization of the future:

"We are entering a third period of change: the shift from the command-and-control organization...to the information, the organization of knowledge specialists" (1988: 53).

Drucker saw this paradigm shift as so fundamental to a corporation that achieving it would require a new structure to ensure that information moves freely throughout the company. The old ways would clog the works: rigidly structured departments and divisions, silos, walls, bureaucracy -all were enemies to what Drucker later called the 'Knowledge Revolution.'

Regardless of what we call it, the proliferation of information today is rapidly changing the DNA of our organizations. The role of IT is likely to undergo seismic shifts as organizations grapple with the realities of a truly global marketplace. The 'old' ways will not work for two essential reasons:

- Organizations that are not structured for 'boundaryless' communication and information flows will fall behind as faster, more nimble competitors eat their lunch.

- The kinds of information that managers require as the world within - and more important the world outside - will undergo massive shifts in the years to come.

This transformation will be sparked, not by better microchips or faster computers, but by increasingly demanding customers, the ever-changing dynamics of the industry, and global competition. Managers will have to work smarter than ever before: *"The key is not electronics; it is cognitive science"* (Drucker,1988: 45-53).

Information then - more specifically, the utilization of information - is likely to be far more important to a corporation than its selection of hardware and software. Technology alone seldom provides competitive advantage. It is how a manager uses that information that can give one company an edge over another. *"What has made it possible to routinize processes is not machinery; the computer is only the trigger. Software is the reorganization of work, based on centuries of experience, through the application of knowledge and especially of systematic logical analysis"* (Drucker, 1988: 45-53).

The winners of the future will be organizations that recognize the ever-increasing value of information - and create an organization designed to use information to make better decisions, create better products, and abandon the obsolete. Companies need to have an information strategy that is not only consistent with the strategy of the firm, but one that helps the company to speed its learning curve across a great number of areas.

As a result, tomorrow's knowledge-based corporation must be structured in such a way that literally puts senior IT professionals at the table with other senior managers. They cannot be expected to learn these things 'through channels' [or layers] of an organization. This will require not only a new structure, but also a new mindset. Top management must recognize that information and the people who deliver it are as important to the company as primary functions like marketing and sales. Information professionals must also change.

It is incumbent upon IT to better understand the intricacies of the organization, the customers and markets it serves, its products and services and more. The inertia to maintain the status quo is a force of itself: *"...a substantial majority of executives in all organizations spend most of their time worrying whether we need a fourth [carbon] copy and very little on what we use the report for. Organizations have a gravity, the weight is constantly being pushed into being problem focused and mediocrity-focused, and one has to fight it all the time"* (Drucker, 1988: 45-53).

IT cannot be viewed like some minor service function that is treated like a second class citizen. That is a prescription for failure: *"Increasingly,"* proclaimed Drucker: *"performance in these new knowledge-based industries will come to depend on running the institution so as to attract, hold, and motivate knowledge workers. The key to maintaining leadership in the economy and the technology that are about to emerge is likely to be the social position of knowledge professionals and social acceptance of their values"* (1988: 45-53).

What makes these issues - the role of IT professionals, how they fit into the structure, their 'social' position, etc. -so critical now? In a knowledge-based economy, how an organization collects and disseminates information is as important as the information itself. Hording information, a practice that was commonplace for most of the last century, must be banished once and for all. In this century, the success of a corporation will depend. at least in part. on getting the right information to those closest to the customers and to the market.

Lastly, the entire management team must quickly develop an 'outside-in' perspective. That is, they must understand and view their firm from the perspective of their customers, non-customers, and suppliers. Absent that fundamental shift, it is more likely than not that the information that is collected and compiled will be of diminishing value to the senior management team. Management must never forget that *"results exist on the outside,"* (Drucker, 1988: 45-53) in the marketplace, not within the four walls of a corporation. Those organizations that embrace and act on this essential Druckerism will likely gain a competitive advantage over those firms that are still structured 'inside-out.' Of course, the final test will be how quickly an organization acts on the information they collect, for, in the end, *„the ultimate test of management is business performance"* (Drucker, 1988: 45-53).

* Jeffrey A. Krames is a noted leadership authority and best-selling author.
His most recent book is Jack Welch and the 4E's of Leadership (McGraw-Hill. 2005).
Source: http://www.microsoft.com/business/executivecircle/content/article.aspx?cid=2001andsubcatid=301

CONCLUSION

In this chapter, the relationships between strategy and structure within organizations were discussed. Appropriate structure is essential to achieving the goals formulated in the organization's strategy. Thus, both structure and strategy are the result of specific choices that are made by the organization, and they can also be changed in response to the new conditions of the environment. The impact of the environment on the organization is believed to greatly influence the choices in the design of the structure, either in a mechanistic, organic, technological or market style, which ultimately lead to achieving organizational excellence. There have been several approaches toward this end, which have been suggested in recent years and have been practiced by organizations in their pursuit for better competitiveness in an increasingly globalized environment. An answer to that reality is often thought to be a mixture of both global and local: the 'glo-cal' structure.

REFERENCES

Ansoff, I. 1990. *Corporate Strategy*. New Jersey: Prentice Hall.

Bennis, W. and Nanus, B. 1985. *Leaders: The Strategies for Taking Charge*. New York: Harper and Row.

Blauner, R. 1964. *Alienation and Freedom*. Chicago: University of Chicago Press.

Bowers, D.G. and Seahore, S.E. 1966. "Predicting organizational effectiveness with a four-factor theory of leadership". *Administrative Science Quarterly, 11*(2): 238-263.

Chandler, A. 1962. *Strategy and Structure*. MIT Press.

Child, J. 1974 and 1975. Managerial and organizational factors associated with company performance, Part I and II. *Journal of Management Studies. 11*(3): 175-189 and *12* (1): 12-27.

Drucker, P. 1988. The coming of the new organization. *Harvard Business Review. January-February. 66*(1): 45-53.

Hilb, M. 2006. *Glocal Management of Human Resources*. University of St. Gallen. IFPM Series.

Ivancevich, J.M. and Matteson, M. T. 1999. *Organizational Behavior and Management* (5th Ed.). McGraw-Hill International Editions.

Khandwalla, P.N. 1992. *Organizational Designs for Excellence*. New Delhi: Tata McGraw-Hill Publishing Co. Ltd.

Lawrence, P.R. and Lorsch, J.W. 1967. *Organization and Environment*. Boston: Harvard University Graduate School of Business Administration.

Likert, R. 1961. *New Patterns of Management*. New York: McGraw-Hill.

Miles, R.E. and Snow, C. 2003. *Organizational Strategy. Structure and Process*. Stanford University Press.

Miller, D. 1986. Configurations of strategy and structure: towards a synthesis. *Strategic Management Journal. 7*(3): 233-249.

Peters, T. and Waterman, R.H. 1982. *In Search of Excellence: Lesson from America's Best Run Companies*. New York: Harper and Row.

Robbins, S.P. 2003. *Organizational Behavior* (10th Ed., International edition). Upper Saddle River: Pearson Education/Prentice Hall.

Thompson, J.D. 1967. *Organizations in Action*. New York: McGraw-Hill.

Thune, S. and House, R. 1970. Where long-range planning pays off. *Business Horizon*. August, pp. 81-87.

Tosi, H.L.. Neal, P.M. and Rizzo, J.R. 2000. *Managing Organizational Behavior* (4th Ed.). Blackwell Publishers Inc.

Waldrop, M.M. 1992. *Complexity: The Emerging Science at the Edge of Order and Chaos*. New York: Touchstone.

RECOMMENDED FURTHER READINGS

Autry, R.H.. 1996. What is Organization Design. http://inovus.com/organiza.htm

Daft, Richard L. 2004. *Organization Theory and Design* (8th Ed.). Thomson Learning/South-Western.

Dessler, S. 2004. *Organization and Performance Management: from Basics to Best Practices.* London: Universal Publishers.

Fredrickson, J. 1986. The strategic decision process and organizational structure. *Academy of Management Journal. 11*: 280-297.

Grandori, A.and Soda, G. 2006. A relational approach to organization design. *Industry and Innovation.13* (2): 151-172.

Hellriegel, D. and Slocum Jr., J.W. 2004. *Organizational Behavior* (10th Ed.). Thomson Learning/South-Western.

McNamara, C. 1997. Basic overview of organizational life cycles. http://www.managementhelp.org/org_thry/org_cycl.htm, accessed on January 19th. 2007.

Robbins, S.P. and Coulter, M. 2002. *Management* (7th Ed.). Upper Saddle River: Pearson Education/Prentice-Hall.

Roper, K. S. and. Jackson III, I.J. 2001. Building organizational structure on a foundation of strategy. *The Contractors Management Journal,* 12: 6-11.

Zott, C. and Amit, R. 2004. Business strategy and business model: extending the strategy-structure-performance paradigm. *Working Paper Series* 2004/84/ENT/SM/AGGRD 8. Wharton/INSEAD Alliance Center for Global Research and Development, 31 pages.

CHAPTER FIVE
ORGANIZATIONAL DESIGN – PRINCIPLES
QUANG TRUONG

LEARNING OBJECTIVES:

- To define what is organizational structure.
- To examine the key elements of organizational structure.
- To explain how environmental, strategic, and technological factors affect the design of organizations.
- To describe the traditional organizational design alternatives.
- To explain the need for continuous structural adjustment to cope with environmental change conditions.
- To examine the contemporary organizational designs for global competition.

Organizational structure (also known as Organizational design or Organizational architecture) refers to a firm's formal reporting relationships, procedures, and controls (Galbraith, 1995; Harris and Raviv, 2002). It is considered by many to be "the anatomy of an organization, providing a foundation within which the organization functions" (Dalton et al., 1980: 49). In concrete terms, an organizational structure defines how job tasks are formally divided, grouped, and coordinated (Robbins, 2003: 425). It is also seen as a framework, which "focuses on the differentiation of positions, formulation of rules and procedures, and prescriptions of authority" (Ranson et al., 1980: 2).

DEFINING ORGANIZATIONAL STRUCTURE

Basically, an organization is a collection of individuals, groups or departments that work together to perform the common tasks of the organization. Thus, in order to understand the actual situation and the delivery capacity of an organization, the analysis should focus on the three levels (individual, team/group, and department) to examine their specific characteristics, and the nature of relationships among groups and departments that make up the organization in interacting with its environment.

FORMAL ORGANIZATIONS

The divisions and departments in an organization are created through two processes, namely structural differentiation and structural integration (Tosi et al., 2000: 396). **Structural differentiation** is the process of unbundling all of the work activities in an organization, separating specific sets of activities from others. **Structural integration** is necessary when differentiation has occurred for the need of coordinating the activities of different subunits. The set of decisions about how differentiation and integration is achieved in an organization is called **organizational design**.

To decide on the form of the organizational structure, it is essential to answer the following three questions:

1. How the work will be differentiated? (division of labor)
2. How the work is then grouped into organizational subunits? (departmentalization)
3. How the relationships between the subunits are defined? (distribution of authority)

There are six key elements that managers need to address when they design their organization's structure: work specialization, departmentalization, chain of command, span of control, centralization and decentralization, and formalization (e.g., Daft, 2001) (see Table 5.1).

Table 5.1. Key Design Questions and Design Options for Organizational Structure

Key Questions	Design Options
1. To what degree are tasks subdivided into separated jobs?	Work specialization
2. On what basis will jobs be grouped together?	Departmentalization
3. To whom do individuals and groups report?	Chain of command
4. How many individuals can a manager efficiently and effectively direct?	Span of control
5. Where does decision-making authority lie?	Centralization and decentralization
6. To what degree will there be rules and regulations to direct employees and managers?	Formalization

A mechanistic organization is essentially a **bureaucracy** which is often associated with Max Weber, a German sociologist and economist in the early 1890s. The word bureaucracy often brings to mind rigidity, incompetence, red tape, inefficiency, and ridiculous rules. In principle, though, the basic characteristics of a mechanistic system may make a bureaucratic organizational design feasible or even desirable in some situations (e.g.,Hellriegel and Slocum, 2004: 355-356) (see Box 5.1).

Box 5.1. "Bureaucracy is Dead"

This statement is false. Some bureaucratic characteristics are in decline. And bureaucracy is undoubtedly going through changes. But it's far from dead.

Bureaucracy is characterized by specialization, formalization, departmentalization, centralization, narrow spans of control, and adherence to a chain of command. Have these characteristics disappeared from today's modern organizations? No. In spite of the increased use of empowered teams and flattered structures, certain facts remain: (1)

Large size prevails. Organizations that succeed and survive tend to grow to large size, and bureaucracy is efficient with large size. Small organizations and their non-bureaucratic structures are more likely to fail, so over time, small organizations may come and go but large bureaucracies stay. Moreover, while the average business today has considerably fewer employees than those 30 years ago, these smaller firms are increasingly part of a large, multi-location organization with the financial and technological resources to compete in the global marketplace; (2) Environmental turbulence can be largely managed. The impacts of environmental uncertainties are substantially reduced by management strategies such as environmental scanning, strategic alliances, advertising, and lobbying. This allows organizations facing dynamic environments to maintain bureaucratic structures and still be efficient; (3) Bureaucracy's goal of standardization can be increasingly achieved through hiring people who have undergone extensive educational training. Rational discipline, rather than that imposed by rules and regulations, is internalized by hiring professionals with college and university training. They become pre-programmed. In addition, strong cultures help achieve standardization by substituting for high formalization; (4) Finally, technology maintains control. Networked computers allow management to closely monitor the actions of employees without centralization or narrow spans of control. Technology has merely replaced some previously bureaucratic characteristics, but without any loss of management control.

In spite of some changes, bureaucracy is alive and well in many venues. It continues to be the dominant structural form in manufacturing, service firms, hospitals, schools and colleges, in the military and in voluntary associations. Why? Because it's still the most efficient way to organize large-scale activities.

Source: S.P. Robbins. Organizational Behavior. New Jersey: Pearson Education. Inc., 2003, p. 444.

KEY ELEMENTS OF ORGANIZATIONAL STRUCTURE

An organizational structure is the formal framework by which job tasks are divided, grouped, and coordinated. When managers develop or change an organization's structure, they are engaged in organizational design -a process that involves the six key elements as described below (Robbins and Coulter, 2002: 256).

1. **Work specialization** is the degree to which tasks in an organization are divided into separate jobs; also known as **division of labor**. In the late eighteenth century. Adam Smith was the first to prove that division of labor contributed to increased employee productivity. Early in the twentieth century. Henry Ford used this concept in an assembly line, where every worker was assigned a specific, repetitive task. By doing so. Ford was able to produce one car in every ten seconds with relatively low-skilled workers. By the late 1940s, most manufacturing jobs in industrialized countries were being done with high work specialization (Robbins, 2003: 426).

    A mechanistic organization typically has a high division of labor, e.g., in manufacturing, banking, insurance, the fast-food industry, etc. In theory, the fewer the tasks a person performs, the better he or she may be expected to perform them.

However, a continued increase in the division of labor may eventually become counter-productive, as workers who perform only very routine and simple jobs that require relatively limited skills may become bored and frustrated. The results may be low quality and productivity, high turnover and absenteeism (Hellriegel and Slocum, 2004: 357). In contrast, the organic organization tends to reduce the cost of high turnover by delegating decision-making to lower levels *(ibid)*. Most managers today see work specialization as an important organizing mechanism, but not as a source of ever-increasing productivity (Robbins and Coulter, 2002: 257).

2. **Departmentalization** is the basis by which jobs are grouped together. Every organization has its own specific way of classifying and grouping work activities along the five common forms of departmentalization, namely: functional, geographical, product, process and customer departmentalization (Robbins and Coulter, 2002: 258) (see Table 5.2).

Table 5.2. The Five Common Forms of Departmentalization

Type of departmentalization	Advantages/disadvantages
Functional	• Efficiencies from putting together similar specialties and people with common skills. Knowledge, and orientations • Coordination within functional area • In-depth specialization • Poor communication across functional areas • Limited view of organizational goals
Geographical	• More effective and efficient handling of specific regional issues that arise • Serve needs of unique geographic markets better • Duplication of functions • Can feel isolated from other organizational areas
Product	• Allows specialization in particular products and services • Managers can become experts in their industry • Closer to customers • Duplication of functions • Limited view of organizational goals
Process	• More efficient flow work activities • Can only be used with certain types of products
Customer	• Customers' needs and problems can be met by specialists • Duplication of functions • Limited view of organizational goals

Source: Adapted from Robbins and Coulter (2002: 258)

Large organizations may use all of the forms of departmentalization as described above to optimally cover geographically or divisionally dispersed markets and integrate related planning and support activities. In the same fashion, cross-function teams are complemented traditional departmental lines to create maximum synergy and coordination effect.

3. **Chain of command** refers to the hierarchical arrangement of authority and responsibility, which used to be the cornerstone in the design of organizations in the 1970s (Robbins, 2003: 429). It is an unbroken line of authority that extends from the top of the organization to the lowest echelon and clarifies who reports to whom. Its complementary concept, the **unity of command** principle, holds that no subordinate should receive direction from more than one superior. For this purpose, the **organization chart** is essential to prevent confusion of authority line and duplication of responsibility in an organization.
   The concepts of chain of command and unity of command have become less relevant in recent years due to the far-reaching advancements of information and telecoms technology (ICT) and the growing trend toward employee empowerment. For instance, with the modern technologies (networked computer and mobile devices), a low-level employee can access information or reach his or her subordinate in seconds for a quick decision or approval without going through lengthy and cumbersome formal channels as before. Self-managed and cross-functional teams are also being used, which have significantly changed the landscape of organizations in the globalization era.

4. **Span of control** answers the question how many employees can a manager efficiently and effectively direct. It reflects the number of employees reporting directly to one manager and thus, determines the number of levels and managers an organization has. Following is an example of two organizations, both of which have 4.096 employees; one organization has a span of four and the other a span of eight. The wider span would have two fewer levels and approximately 800 fewer managers, which would save $40 million a year on an average of $50.000 per manager per year (see Table 5.3).

Table 5.3. A Comparison of Contrasting Spans of Control

Organizational level	Organization I (assuming span of 4 members)	Organization II (assuming span of 8 members)
1	1	1
2	4	8
3	16	64
4	64	512
5	256	**4.096**
6	1.024	
7	**4.096**	
Comparison	Span of 4 Operatives: 4.096 Managers (levels 1-6): 1.365	Span of 8 Operatives: 4.096 Managers (levels 1-4): 585

Source: Adapted from Robbins (2003: 430).

As illustrated from Table 5.3, by keeping the span of control to the minimum (5-6 employees) a manager can, in principle, maintain close control. However, he or she has to deal with three drawbacks: (1) additional management levels imply more costs; (2) it makes vertical communication more complex as many layers tend, to slow down decision-making processes and isolate upper management; and (3) it encourages tight supervision and at the same time discourages employee autonomy and empowerment.

In today's global environment, the trend has been toward higher spans of control in consistency with the company's efforts to reduce costs, cut overhead, expedite decision-making, increase flexibility, get close to customers, and empower employees (with high investment in employee's training) (See Box 5.2).

Box 5.2. Few Entrepreneurs Understand Span of Control

Pat Harpell learns a lesson that many entrepreneurs fail to learn: Having too many people report to you can undermine your effectiveness.

Harpell runs Harpell Inc., a trans-active marketing services company she founded in 1982 in Maynard. Massachusetts. USA. As her firm grew, she added managers. Eventually she had 18 people reporting directly to her. It took her a few years but she finally recognized that she had to reduce the number of people over whom she had direct control. "I realized I was the bottleneck." Harpell says. "By limiting the number of people reporting to me, I was able to look beyond day to day and focus upon building a unique brand and position for the company." Today, Harpell has only six people reporting directly to her and she has the time to focus on important issues.

Harpell's experience is not unusual among entrepreneurs. As a group they tend to want to do everything, supervise everyone, and have all decisions come through them. A study of entrepreneurs found that among two dozen popular management principles, span of control was the least appreciated. Only 23 percent of the respondents agreed that "span of control shouldn't be too large." and just 16 percent believed "top managers cannot deal with all problems personally."

Source: Stephen P. Robbins. Organizational Behavior. New Jersey: Pearson Education. Inc./Prentice Hall, 2003, p. 431.

---

5. **Centralization and decentralization** define where the locus of power lies in the organization. The hierarchy of authority is closely related to **centralization** which refers to a situation in which decision-making is concentrated at a single point or level in the organization. A mechanistic organization has as many levels in its hierarchy as necessary to achieve tight control; whereas an organic organization has few levels, which makes communication and coordination easier and fosters innovation (Hellriegel and Slocum, 2004: 357) (see Table 5.4.).

Table 5.4. Factors Influencing the Level of Centralization and Decentralization

More centralization	More decentralization
• Environment is stable	• Environment is complex. uncertain
• Lower level managers are not as capable or experienced at making decisions as upper level managers	• Lower level managers are capable and experienced in making decisions
• Lower level managers do not want to have a say in decisions	• Lower level managers want a voice in decisions
• Decisions are significant	• Decisions are relatively minor
• Organization is facing a crisis or the risk of company failure	• Corporate culture is open to allowing managers to have a say in what happens
• Company is large	• Company is geographically dispersed
• Effective implementation of company strategies depends on managers retaining say over what happens	• Effective implementation of company strategies depends on managers having involvement and flexibility to make decisions

Source: Robbins and Coulter (2002, p. 262).

As organizations have consistently tried to make their structures more flexible and Responsive, there is a growing trend toward more decentralization and delegation. For Example, multinational corporations like Unilever have given their 'managers in the field' more discretion to quickly respond to the specific demands of the local markets.

6. **Formalization** refers to the degree to which jobs within the organization are standardized. The degree of formalization can vary widely between organizations and even within organizations. Where formalization is low, job behaviors are relatively non-programmed and employees have a great deal of freedom to exercise discretion in their work (Robbins, 2003: 432).

ORGANIZATIONAL PARADIGM SHIFT

In coping with rapidly changing business environments, traditional approaches to organizing work (especially 'scientific management' pioneered by Frederick Taylor and 'principles of management' proposed by Henry Fayol) which seem to work well into the 1950s and 1960s, are being questioned and re-evaluated. A paradigm shift (see Table 5.5) occurred in organizations as managers search out structural designs that will best support and facilitate employees doing the organization's work - one that can achieve efficiency but also have the flexibility that is necessary for today's complex, diverse and dynamic environment (Robbins, 2003: 256).

Table 5.5. Paradigm Shift in Organizations

Characteristics	Old Paradigm	New Paradigm
Scope	Domestic	International
Work force	Homogeneous	Culturally diverse
Employee wants	Economic security	Personal growth
Resource management	Exploitative	Ecologically sensitive
Values	Masculine	Feminine

Source: Daft (1995: 22).

ORGANIZATIONAL LIFE CYCLES

Organizations progress through different life cycles just like human beings do. For example, people go through infancy, childhood, teenage, mature and aging phases. Start-up organizations grow in the same fashion. Features of new organizations are usually markedly different from older (often much larger) organizations (Table 5.6).

Table 5.6. Organizations Life Cycles and Corresponding Typical Features

Features/Phase	Birth	Youth	Midlife	Maturity
Size	Small	Medium	Large	Very large
Bureaucratic	Non-bureaucratic	Pre-bureaucratic	bureaucratic	Very bureaucratic
Division of labor	Overlapping tasks	Some departments	Many departments	Extensive. with small jobs and many descriptions
Centralization	One-person rule	Two-leader rule	Two department heads	Top management heavy
Formalization	No written rules	Few rules	Policy and procedure manuals	Extensive
Administrative intensity	Secretary. no professional staff	Increasing clerical and maintenance	Increasing professional and staff support	Large. multiple departments
Internal systems	Non-existent	Crude budget and information system	Control systems in place; budget. performance reports. etc.	Extensive planning. financial and personnel added

Lateral teams. task forces for coordination	None	Top leaders only	Some use of integrators and task forces	Frequent at lower levels to break down bureaucracy

Sources: Compiled by Carter McNamara. http://www.managementhelp.org/org_thry/org_cycl.htm. 2-2007; Richard L. Daft, *Organization Theory and Design* (5th Ed.). San Francisco etc.: West Publishing Co., 1995, p. 178; Robert E. Quinn and Kim Cameron, "Organizational life cycles and some shifting criteria of effectiveness." *Management Science, 29*, 1983, pp. 31-51.

KEY FACTORS AFFECTING ORGANIZATIONAL DESIGN

There is no such 'one-fits-all' model which perfectly matches the requirements for structural design of an organization. More often than not, an organizational design decision may help solve one set of problems, but may create others at the same time. Organizational design aims at minimizing the reasons of organizational ineffectiveness, which are commonly faced by all types of organizations:

- Lack of goal clarity: strategic goals are not clear or linked to particular aspects of the organizational design.
- Ineffective links to customers: the design does not effectively integrate the demands of customers.
- Lack of external fit: the design does not fit the requirements of the environment.
- Lack of internal alignment: the design of the organization is internally inconsistent.

An effective organizational design should take into account the three primary elements: environmental, strategic and technological factors (see Figure 5.1.).

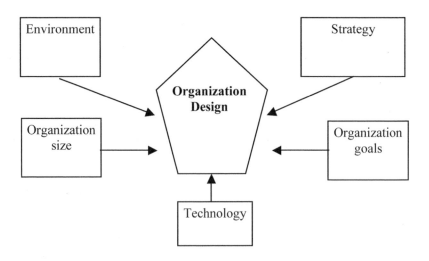

Figure 5.1. Structural Design Factors

Source: Adapted from Hellriegel and Slocum (2004: 348)

ENVIRONMENTAL FACTORS

An organization's **environment** is composed of institutions or forces outside the organization that potentially affect the organization's performance. They can be considered as 'external stakeholders' of the organization, like suppliers, distributors, customers, competitors, government regulatory agencies, unions, pressure groups, and the like. In business, the (external) environment represents the opportunities and threats that are supposed to match with the (internal) capacity of delivery of the organization.

For an effective design decision, the environmental factors that an organization needs to be aware of are: (1) the characteristics of the present and possible future environment, and (2) how they affect the organization's ability to function effectively (Hellriegel and Slocum, 2004: 348).

As illustrated in Figure 5.2, there is evidence that relates the degrees of environmental uncertainty to different structural arrangements. For instance, the more scarce, dynamic, and complex the environment, the more organic a structure should be. On the reverse, the more abundant, stable, and simple the environment, the more the mechanistic structure will be preferred (Robbins, 2003: 444).

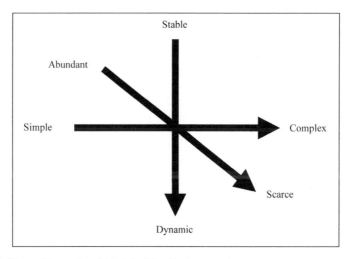

Figure 5.2. Three-Dimensional Model of the Environment

Source: Robbins (2003: 444).

STRATEGIC FACTORS

An organization's structure is the essential vehicle to help managers achieve its objectives. It is therefore logical that organizational structure should follow the organization's overall strategy. Establishing an effective organizational structure requires that managers understand and formulate the organization's strategic direction (mission. vision) first, and then modify the structure of the organization to effectively pursue that direction. In other words, the primary goal of the designed structure is to support the execution of the organization's chosen strategy, and thereby enhancing the organization's competitive advantage. In case management makes a significant change in its organization's strategy, the structure will need to be modified to accommodate and support this change (Amburgey and Dacin, 1994; Chandler, 1962).

Fundamentally, strategy formulation involves answering the three critical questions:

1. Who are the organization's customers? (target customer. segment. market)
2. What are their needs and wants? (the products and services the organization provides)
3. How will the organization satisfy these needs and wants of the customers? (organization's capacity of delivery)

As a logical process, an organization should first strategically target 'external' customers, then develop an organizational structure that best meets their needs and wants. Organizational structure design should equally take into account the needs of the organization's 'internal' customers. Most companies fail to recognize the paramount importance of serving their internal stakeholders, who in the era of knowledge economy, actually form the core assets of the company.

The emphasis on the internal customers is essential in structural design due to the fact that if the organizational structure does not provide internal customers with effective communication, processes for ease of execution, and appropriate support systems, external customers cannot be served effectively (Roper and Jackson, 2001: 6). Also, information should flow in every direction and throughout all levels within the organization, and back to the customers in the form of execution. The two-way information flow ensures that the designed organizational structure will support all of the activities that the organization performs for customers in the delivery of products and services. Furthermore, value chain analysis adds another dimension to structural design in addressing the external interests, from the initial contact with the business alliances (suppliers and distributors) and customer, to ending with the completion of the project.

As already described in the previous chapter, an innovation strategy needs the flexibility of an organic structure; while cost minimizers and quality-focused strategies seek the efficiency and stability in process management of the mechanic structure.

TECHNOLOGICAL FACTORS

Technology is a process by which an organization transfers its inputs into outputs. Every organization utilizes at least one (mostly state-of-the-art) technology for converting financial, human, and physical resources into products or services to serve the target customers. For instance, automobile manufacturers such as Ford, GM, Toyota, Nissan, Renault, Volvo, Mercedes, etc. predominantly used an assembly line to make their products. On the other hand, universities may use a number of instruction technologies, e.g. lectures, case study, group discussion, business game, simulation method, and so forth to effectively deliver their curriculum.

There have been numerous studies on the technology-structure relationship (e.g. Glick et al., 1991; Roberts and Grabowski, 1999; Thompson, 1967), which suggest that in general technology influences the design of an organization. The common theme that differentiates technologies is their degree of routine. *Routine* activities are characterized by automated and standardized operations, whereas *non-routine* activities are customized (Robbins, 2003: 442), such as in furniture restoring, custom shoes-making, and genetic research. As such, routine tasks are associated with taller and more departmentalized structures. It is also found that degree of routine is strongly associated with formalization through the presence of rule manuals, job description, and other formalized documentation, which is typical in mechanistic organizations, such as bank and insurance companies (see Table 5.7).

Table 5.7. Technology, Structure and Effectiveness

	Unit Production	Mass Production	Process Production
Structural characteristics	Low vertical differentiation	Moderate vertical differentiation	High vertical differentiation
	Low horizontal differentiation	High horizontal differentiation	Low horizontal differentiation
Most effective structure	Low formalization Organic	High formalization Mechanistic	Low formalization Organic

Source: Robbins and Coulter (2002: 266).

Task interdependence, such as *pooled* (when departments and teams are relatively autonomous), *sequential* (when one department or team must complete certain tasks before others can perform their tasks), and *reciprocal* (when the outputs from one team or department become the inputs for others, and *vice versa*) can also be used in designing the appropriate structure (see Figures 5.3. and 5.4).

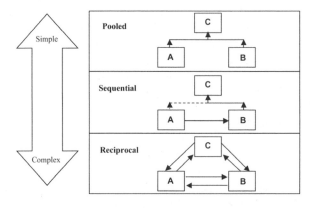

Figure 5.3. Types of Task Interdependence in Organizational Design

Source: Hellriegel and Slocum (2004: 353).

As illustrated in Figure 5.3., the Pooled form, characterized by pooled interdependence, which requires mediating technology (low complexity and high formalization), can be seen in such organizations as banks, retail stores and post office. The Sequential interdependence option, which relies on long-linked technology (moderate complexity and formalization), is often chosen to organize mass production, assembly line and school cafeteria. British Petroleum (BP) uses sequential interdependence to deliver gasoline and other products to a variety of customers (Hellriegel & Slocum, 2004: 353-354). On the contrary, the Reciprocal interdependence is most appropriate for hospitals, research labs and universities, and often uses intensive technology (high complexity and low formalization) to design the logical flow of works.

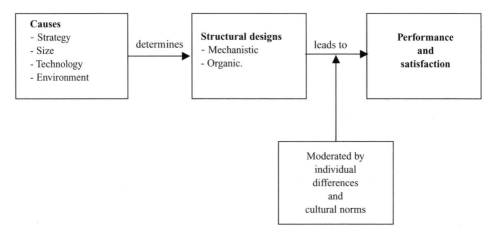

Figure 5.4. Organizational Structure: Determinants and Outcomes

Source: Robbins (2003: 446).

Box 5.3. Technology is Reshaping Organizations

In today's chaotic, uncertain, and high-tech world, there is essentially only one type of design that is going to survive. This is the electronically configured organic organization.

We are undergoing a second Industrial Revolution and it will change every aspect of people's lives. The changes that large corporations used to take a decade to implement now occur in one or two years. Companies that are successful will be designed to thrive on change. And the structure of those organizations will have common characteristics.

Ten years from now there will be nothing but electronic organizations. Brick-and-mortar organizations won't go away, but click-and-mortar will become the only means to survive. In addition, every organization will need to keep its fingers on the pulse of its customers. Customer priorities will change rapidly. What customers will pay a premium for will become a commodity so rapidly that those who lose touch with their customers will be candidates for extinction. Consumers are gaining the ability to compare the prices of hundreds of competitors rather than just two or three. This is going to dramatically drive down prices. Consumer products in Britain, for instance, will come down 10 to 15 percent between 2000 and 2003. If firms don't improve their productivity to match these drops in prices, they'll be out of business.

Technology allows firms to stay closer to customers, to move jobs to where costs are lowest, and to make decisions much more rapidly. For instance, executives at Cisco Systems can monitor expenses, gross margins, the supply chain, and profitability in real time. There no longer need to be surprises. Every employee can make decisions that might have had to come from the top management ranks a few years ago. At the end of a quarter, individual product managers at Cisco can see exactly what the gross margins are on his or her products, whether they are below expectations, and determine the cause of any discrepancy. Quicker decision-making at lower levels will translate into higher profit margins. So instead of the CEO or chief financial officer making 50 to 100 different decisions in a quarter, managers throughout the organization can make millions of decisions. Companies that don't adjust to create this capability will be non-competitive.

Source: This argument was presented by J. Chambers. "Nothing except e-companies." *Business Week*, August 28, 2000, pp. 210-12; see also A. Gore. "I'm a little skeptical...Brain don't speed up." *Business Week*, August 28, 2000, pp. 212-14; both were reprinted in Robbins (2003:448).

Questions for discussion
- *Can you answer the questions which were raised at the start of this chapter:*
  - *How the work will be differentiated? (division of labor)*
  - *How the work is then grouped into organizational subunits? (departmentalization)*
  - *How the relationships between the subunits are defined? (distribution of authority)*
- *Why is bureaucracy not dead, but still alive even in the global context?*
- *In order to remain competitive in a fast changing environment as today. which principles managers should observe and apply in designing their organization's structure?*
- *Describe the factors that influence greater centralization and those factors that influence greater decentralization.*
- *Discuss on the radical impacts brought about by the emergence of e-organizations as suggested in Box 5.3. ("Technology is reshaping organizations").*

CASE STUDY

Using a Combination Structure

Chris Smith and Steve Kinney, the owner of Aspen Earthmoving, wanted to improve their organization. The existing organizational structure was a functional design. Project managers at the company operated very autonomously. Each manager approached their segment of the business as their own with responsibility for selling, growing the revenue, and cost management. Their performance was evaluated primarily on their gross profit contribution to the company, although customer satisfaction was also a factor. According to Smith and Kinney, the accounting department was properly focused on the total operations and on providing support to the owners in running the company, but it was not providing the level of support and training that the project managers needed. Smith and Kinney believed that the interface between the accounting personnel and project managers at the project delivery level could significantly improve gross profits from each project.

Smith and Kenny concluded that the right answer was to blend the accounting and administrative functions. This solution combines elements of functional, divisional, and matrix designs.

An administrative director was hired and assigned responsibility over the administrative aspects of the company. The accounting department staff was used to provide support to the project manager at the direction of the administrative director. The administrative director is a member of the management team and provides reports to the team. The administrative director does not report to the functional manager of the accounting department but is responsible for many of the administrative support aspects of project management, including tracking job costs, handling contract billings, and enhancing gross profits on projects.

To further strengthen project performance, project supervisors were identified and given responsibility for all aspects of project construction. This addition to the project staffing structure provided additional training opportunities for project personnel and freed up the project managers to maintain project control and customer service.

The administrative director and project supervisors have made contributions to further enhancement on each project that have more than offset their costs and also improved the level of customer satisfaction. Additionally, the structure has improved teamwork and morale in the company. Smith and Kenny believe that these changes have created a true spirit of supporting co-workers and maintaining internal customer satisfaction while increasing productivity and profitability.

Source: Kenneth S. Roper and I.J. Jackson III, "Building organizational structure on a foundation of strategy." *The Contractors Management Journal,* December 2001, p. 9.

CONCLUSION

After having discussed the relationships between strategy and structure, this chapter looked further into the key factors affecting organizational design, such as environmental, strategic and technological factors. An appropriate organizational structure should be built on its own characteristics, which reflect its business scope, strategic orientation, composition of workforce, culture and value chain. Given the globalized business environment of today, the new forms of organization are typically more dynamic and organic.

REFERENCES

Amburgey. T.L. and Dacin. T. 1994. As the left foot follows the right? The dynamics of strategic and structural change. *Academy of Management Journal.* December. pp. 1427-1452.

Chandler Jr.. A.D. 1962. *Strategy and Structure.* Cambridge. MA: MIT Press.

Daft. R.L. 1995. *Organization Theory and Design* (5th Ed.). San Francisco. etc.: West Publishing Co.

Daft. R. L. 2001. *Organization Theory and Design* (7th Ed.). Cincinnati: OH: South-Western.

Dalton. D.R. Todor. W.D.. Spendolini. M.J.. Fielding. G.J. and Porter. L.W. 1980. Organization structure and performance: a critical review. *Academy of Management Review*. January. p. 49.

Galbraith. J. 1995. *Designing Organizations*. Jossey-Bass.

Glick. W.H. Wang. Y. and Huber. G.P. 1991. Understanding technology-structure relationships: theory development and meta-analytic theory testing. *Academy of Management Journal.* June. pp. 370-399.

Harris. M. and Raviv. A. 2002. Organization design. *Management Science*. 48: 852-865.

Hellriegel. D.and Slocum. Jr.. J.W. 2004. *Organizational Behavior* (10th Ed.). Mason. Ohio: South-Western.

McNamara. C. 2007. http://www.managementhelp.org/org_thry/org_cycl.htm. accessed on 20-04-2007.

Ranson. S. Hinings. B. and Greenword. R. 1980. The structuring of organizational structures. *Administrative and Science Quartely.* March. p. 2.

Robbins. S.P. 2003. *Organizational Behavior* (10th Ed.). New Jersey: Pearson Education International/Prentice Hall.

Robbins. S.P. and Coulter. M. 2002. *Management* (7th Ed.). New Jersey: Pearson Education. Inc./Prentice Hall.

Roberts. W.R. and Grabowski. M. 1999. Organizations. technology. and structuring. in S.R. Clegg. C. Hardy. and W.R. Nord (Eds.). *Managing Organizations: Current Issues.* Thousand Oaks. CA: Sage. pp. 159-171.

Roper. K.S. and Jackson III. I.J. 2001. Building organizational structure on a foundation of strategy. *The Contractors Management Journal.* December. p. 6.

Thompson. J.D. 1967. *Organizations in Action*. New York: McGraw-Hill.

Tosi. H.L.. Neal. P. M. and Rizzo. J.R. 2000. *Managing Organizational Behavior* (4th Ed.). Blackwell Publishers Inc.

RECOMMENDED FURTHER READINGS

Athey. S. and Roberts. J. 2001. Organizational Design: Decision Rights and Incentive Contracts. *The American Economic Review.* 91 (2): 200-205.

Buchanan. D. and Badham. R. 2000. *Power. Politics. and Organizational Change: Winning the Turf Game.* London. etc.: Sage Publications.

Greenwood. R. and Hinings. C.R. 1988. Organizational Design Types. Tracks and the Dynamics of Strategic Change. *Organization Studies. 9* (3): 293-316.

Nadler. D.. Tushman. M. and Nadler. M.B. 1997. *Competing by Design: The Power of Organizational Architecture*. New York: Oxford University Press.

Mintzberg. H. 1992. *Structure in Fives: Designing Effective Organizations*. Upper Saddle River: Prentice Hall.

Morgan. G. 1997. *Images of the Organization*. Thousand Oaks: Sage Publications.

Groth. L. 1999. *Future Organizational Design.* New York: Wiley & Sons.

Roberts. J. 2004. *The Modern Firm: Organizational Design for Performance and Growth*. New York: Oxford University Press.

CHAPTER SIX
ORGANIZATIONAL DESIGN – STRUCTURES
QUANG TRUONG

LEARNING OBJECTIVES:

- To understand the pressures and forces for change typical felt by organizations, including financial, from employees, from competitors and from customers.

- To appreciate other related pressures: from globalization and technology.

- To understand the need for change as part of the philosophy of the learning organization, and to create a learning organization.

In the previous chapters, we have addressed the question: Why do organizations differ? Some organizations are structured along more mechanistic lines, while others follow the organic model. We have also reviewed all the major forces that influence a particular choice of design. These findings are useful to a manager for deciding the critical question of how to design the appropriate organizational structure which would best fit both external and internal requirements.

What organizational designs do Ford. Toshiba, Gillette, Toyota, Unilever, Procter and Gamble, and e-Bay have? It is believed that some organizational designs are better suited to certain basic organizational types with different set of characteristics. For example, the mechanistic organization is likely to be more effective if the product or functional organizational design is used, and the mixed-type organization seems better suited to the matrix structure, whereas the organic type is likely to use the project organizational structure to optimize its interaction with the environments.

ORGANIZATIONAL DESIGN ALTERNATIVES

Activity grouping and output grouping are the two most common approaches to structural design, as described in Figure 6.1.

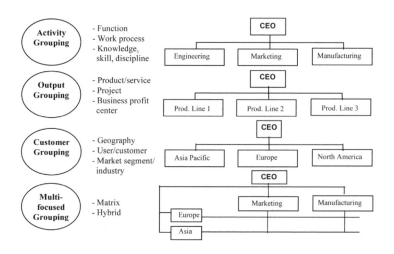

Figure 6.1. Structural Design Options for Activity and Output Grouping

Source: Daft (1995: 203)

SIMPLE STRUCTURE

Most organizations start as entrepreneurial ventures with a simple structure with low departmentalization, wide spans of control, authority centralized in a single person, and little formalization. The simple structure is commonly used by small businesses in which the owner and the manager are one and the same (see Table 6.1).

Table 6.1. Characteristics of the Simple Structure

Strengths	Weaknesses
Fast; flexible; inexpensive to maintain; clear accountability	Not appropriate as organization grows; reliance on one person is risky

Source: Robbins and Coulter (2002: 267)

FUNCTIONAL STRUCTURE

In a functional structure, activities are grouped together by common function from the bottom to the top of the organization. For example, all accountants are located in the Finance department, and the vice president or director of finance is responsible for all financial activities. The same applies for marketing, research and development (R & D), manufacturing, and so forth.

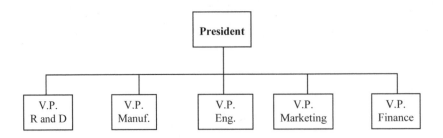

Figure 6.2. Functional Structure

Table 6.2. Summary of Functional Structure Characteristics

Context	Structure: Functional Environment: low uncertainty, stable Technology: routine, low interdependence Size: small to medium Goals: internal efficiency, technical quality
Internal systems	Operative goals: functional goal emphasis Planning and budgeting: cost based-budget, statistical reports Formal authority: functional managers
Strengths	1. Allows economies of scale within functional departments 2. Enables in-depth skill development 3. Enables organization to accomplish functional goals 4. Is best in small to medium-sized organizations 5. Is best with only one or a few products
Weaknesses	1. Slow response time to environmental changes 2. May cause decisions to pile on top, hierarchy overload 3. Leads to poor horizontal coordination among departments 4. Results in less innovation 5. Involves restricted view of organizational goals

Source: Daft (1995: 204); adapted from Duncan (1979: 429).

PRODUCT STRUCTURE

In the product organization, major units are formed around different products or services. It is also used as the generic term for what is sometimes called a *divisional structure or self-contained* units. With this structure, division can be organized according to individual products, services, product groups, major projects or programs, divisions, businesses or profit centers. The distinctive feature of a product structure is that grouping is based on organizational outputs. The product organization simplifies some managerial problems, but creates others as shown in Table 6.3.

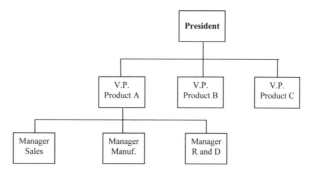

Figure 6.3. Product Structure

Table 6.3. Summary of Product Structure Characteristics

Context	Structure: Product Environment: moderate to high uncertainty, changing Technology: non-routine, high interdependence among departments Size: large Goals: external effectiveness, adaptation, client satisfaction
Internal systems	Operative goals: product line emphasis Planning and budgeting: profit center basis -cost and income Formal authority: product managers
Strengths	1. Suited to fast change in unstable environment 2. Leads to client satisfaction because product responsibility and contact points are clear 3. Involves high coordination across functions 4. Allows units to adapt to differences in products, regions, clients 5. Best in large organizations with several products 6. Decentralizes decision-making
Weaknesses	1. Eliminates economies of scale in functional departments 2. Leads to poor coordination across product lines 3. Eliminates in-depth competence and technical specialization 4. Makes integration and standardization across product lines difficult

Source: Daft (1995: 208); adapted from Duncan (1979: 431).

GEOGRAPHICAL STRUCTURE

Geographic structure is another structural grouping on the basis of users or customers. Each region of the country may have distinct tastes and needs to be addressed. In this structure, each geographic unit includes all functions required to manufacture and market products in the region, in the same fashion as the product organization. For multinationals (MNCs), self-contained units are created for different countries and parts of the work for optimal coordination. For instance, in the late 1980's Apple Computer reorganized from a functional to a geographical structure to facilitate manufacture and delivery of Apple computers to customers around the world (see Figure 6.4.).

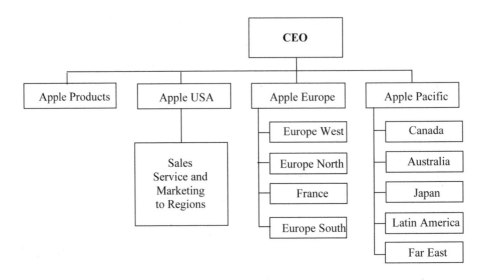

Figure 6.4. Geographical Structure for Apple Computer (1990's)

Source: Based on Markoff (1989); quoted in Daft (1995: 210).

Box 6.1. San Diego Zoo

Once upon a time, a groundskeeper at the San Diego Zoo might have swept cigarette butts under a bush if he was tired or rushed - that made it the gardener's problem, not his. And the gardener would have tended to the plants, but as far as she was concerned, it was someone else's job to deal with the visitors. Such attitudes are gone now, replaced by a desire to make sure visitors enjoy their visits from beginning to end. Zoo attendance has increased, despite a decline in southern California tourism and competition from Sea World and Disneyland. The zoo director credits the employees' new sense ownership for that success.

Traditionally, the San Diego Zoo was managed through its fifty functional departments -animal keeping, horticulture, maintenance, education, and so on. Today, cross-functional teams are jointly responsible for the success of specific parts of the zoo. Team members like the groundskeeper and the gardeners now work together to get the job done and a horticulturalist may double as groundskeeper or construction worker if that's what it takes. Teams manage their own budgets and schedule their own vacations. And cross-training makes all team members knowledgeable enough to answer visitor's questions.

Source: Thomas A. Stewart, "The search for the organization of tomorrow." *Fortune*, 18 May 1992. pp. 22-98; and Rabul Jacob, "Absence of management", *American Way*, 15 February 1993, pp. 38-41; quoted in Daft (1995: 206).

HYBRID STRUCTURE

An organization's structure may be multi-focused in that both product and function. or product and geography, are emphasized at the same time. The structure that combines characteristics of both is called **hybrid structure**. By doing so, firms can take advantage of the strengths of each form and avoid some of the weaknesses experienced in practice. For example, Xerox Corporation recently reorganized itself into a hybrid structure, with nine nearly independent product divisions and three geographical sales divisions. It was intended that the new hybrid structure will provide the coordination and flexibility needed to help Xerox get products to market faster than its competitors (Driscoll, 1992) (see Table 6.4.).

Table 6.4. Summary of Hybrid Structure Characteristics

Context	Structure: Hybrid Environment: moderate to high uncertainty. changing customer demands Technology: routine and non-routine. with some interdependencies between functions Size: large Goals: external effectiveness and adaptation. plus efficiency within some functions
Internal systems	Operative goals: product line emphasis. some functional emphasis Planning and budgeting: profit center basis for divisions; cost basis for central functions Formal authority: product managers; coordination responsibility resting with functional managers
Strengths	1. Allows organization to achieve adaptability and coordination in product divisions and efficiency in centralized functional departments 2. Results in better alignment between corporate and division-level goals 3. Achieve coordination both within and between product lines
Weaknesses	1. Has potential for excessive administrative overhead 2. Leads to conflict between division and corporate departments

Source: Daft (1995: 213)

MATRIX STRUCTURE

The matrix structure often is the answer when organizations find that neither the functional, product, geographical, nor hybrid structures combined with horizontal linkage will work. For example, the matrix form can be used when one sector of the environment requires technological and another sector seeks rapid change within each product line. Matrix structure is often used to manage complex projects.

Although the matrix is a strong form of horizontal linkage, this form of structure will only be appropriate when the following conditions are met:

1. Pressure exists to share scarce resources across product lines and the organization is typically medium-sized and has a moderate number of product lines.
2. Environmental pressure exists for two or more critical outputs, such as for technical quality (functional structure) and frequent new products (product structure).
3. The environmental domain of the organization is both complex and uncertain, which require a high degree of coordination and information interchange (communication) in both vertical and horizontal directions (see Figure 6.5. and Table 6.5.).

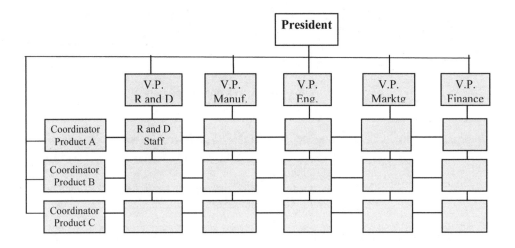

Figure 6.5. The Dual-Authority in a Matrix Structure

Table 6.5. Summary of Matrix Structure Characteristics

Context	Structure: Matrix Environment: high uncertainty Technology: non-routine. many interdependencies Size: moderate. a few product lines Goals: Dual - product innovation and technical specialization
Internal systems	Operative goals: Equal product and functional emphasis Planning and budgeting: Dual system - by function and by product line Formal authority: joint between functional and product heads

Strengths	1. Achieve coordination necessary to meet dual demands from environment
	2. Flexible sharing of resources across products
	3. Suited to complex decisions and frequent changes in unstable environment
	4. Provide opportunity for functional and product skill development
	5. Best in medium-sized organizations with multiple products

Weaknesses	1. Causes participants to experience dual authority, which can be frustrating and confusing
	2. Means participants need good interpersonal skills and extensive training
	3. Is time-consuming ; involves frequent meetings and conflict resolution sessions
	4. Will not work unless participants understand it and adopt collegial rather than vertical-type relationships
	5. Requires dual pressure from environment to maintain power balance

Source: Daft (1995: 218); adapted from Duncan (1979: 429)

NEED FOR CONTINUOUS STRUCTURAL ADJUSTMENT

In principle, either form of structure as described above -functional, product, geographical, hybrid or matrix- provide managers the necessary tool to operate the organization more effectively and efficiently in response to its environmental conditions. As the business situation is changing rapidly and drastically, senior managers need to evaluate periodically the organization's structure to determine whether it is still appropriate to the new requirements. Usually, many organizations first start with one structure, then reorganize to another form to renew its capacity to respond to the new external challenges. For example, Compaq Computer Corporation switched from a functional structure to a product structure for about a year to develop new products and then switched back to a functional structure to reduce internal competition among its product lines (Davis,1987).

It is, therefore, essential that organizational structure should always remain in alignment with organization actual needs. in order to prevent the following symptoms of structural deficiencies (Daft, 1995: 221),

1. Decision-making is delayed or lacking quality;

2. The organization does not respond innovatively to a changing environment;

3. Too much conflict is evident.

Box 6.2. Ciba-Geigy Canada, Ltd.

By getting rid of the bosses, Ciba-Geigy's agricultural chemicals plant in Ontario has boosted up productivity by 30 percent. Plant workers set schedules, manage jobs, create job descriptions, interview new job applicants, and handle numerous decisions and tasks once handled by their supervisors. For Director of Production Gerry Rich and his team of workers, the 'post-boss paradigm' is a dream come true.

When Rich first came to Ciba-Geigy, he found twelve managers and supervisors watching over ninety employees who 'seemed to be leaving their ability to think at the factory gate.' Productivity was low, and standards of quality were slipping. Rich decided to throw out the management rulebook in a daring effort to turn the plant around. Production workers served on the design team along with representatives from management, the warehouse, the administrative office, and the chemical lab. Ultimately, the plant was redesigned for participative management, with production, warehouse, and maintenance at the center of the new organization. The structure looks something like the rings on a dartboard, with administration and support services, such as the lab, forming layers surrounding the center. On the very outside are the managers -now called advisers- whose primary jobs are to facilitate teamwork and act as liaison between teams. Many of the old-style managers couldn't adapt; by the end of the reorganization, two of the plant's three foremen and half of the management staff had left the company. As Rich outed it, "People who can't change, you have to ask to work in an authoritarian environment -somewhere else."

Clearly, the loss of the bosses hasn't hurt at Ciba-Geigy.

Source: John Southerst, "First, we dump the bosses",
Canada Business, April 1992, pp. 46-51; quoted in Daft (1995: 233).

Box 6.3. Reengineering the Corporation

Hammer and Champy define reengineering as "fundamental rethinking and radical redesign of processes to achieve dramatic improvements in critical contemporary measures of performance, such as cost, service, or speed." Meeting customer demands for ever more customized goods and services requires a process focus: "It is not product but the processes that create products that bring companies long-term success. Good products don't make winners, winners make good products."

Reengineering the corporation involves several steps. First, top management adopts 'discontinuous thinking', by which managers find and drop 'outdated rules and fundamental assumptions that underline current business operations.' Second, top executives make an unwavering commitment to radical change, set ambitious goals, and initiate the reengineering process. Third, they must enlist the support of their organization by presenting a factual, lengthy 'case for action.'

   Hammer and Champy identify several recurring characteristics of successful reengineering projects, including:

- The combination of several jobs into one
- Workers empowered to make decisions
- Process steps performed in 'natural order'
- Process teams replace functional teams
- Focus of performance measures and compensation shifts from activity to results
- Managers become coaches, not supervisors
- Executives become leaders

Conclusion

Reengineering the Corporation argues for a new approach to organize a business. It outlines the way to implement the new approach, using many examples, including Ford, IBM Credit, Taco Bell, and Bell Atlantic. It presents a strong case for a recommitment by business to 'swing for the home run.'

Source: Micheal Hammer and James Champy, Reengineering the Corporation. New York: Harper Business, 1993.

CONTEMPORARY ORGANIZATIONAL DESIGNS FOR GLOBAL COMPETITION

The on-going globalization process has not only changed the worldwide business landscape, but has also greatly affected the way of doing business and the form of organizational structures in almost all sectors and industries. As a general rule, for all organizations to function effectively, their organizational designs must not be static, but have to change to reflect new threats and opportunities in the external environment. In this regard, several new forms of organizational designs have been introduced and tried by organizations during the past decades. In particular, the following new types of organizational structures have emerged in response to certain deficiencies in traditional organization designs and to rapid changes in the environment.

Box 6.4. General Electric

General Electric is a leader among global technology organizations. but like all businesses today it feels increasing competition in the world marketplace. GE remains competitive by staying in touch with the rapidly changing global scene and reorganizing to meet new challenges.

Several years ago, the company's $3 billion lighting division scrapped its traditional vertical hierarchy for an organization design in which a team of only nine to twelve senior executives oversees about one hundred processes or programs worldwide. Cross-functional teams work together on virtually all division processes, from designing new products to improving the yield on production machinery. Day-to-day activities are managed by the teams themselves. The role of senior executives is to allocate resources and ensure coordination among the numerous programs and processes, not to supervise the work teams.

The shift to a horizontal organization has led to significant gains for GE. It has reduced costs and shortened product development time, enabling the company to get products to markets faster. It has also allowed the giant company to be as responsive to its worldwide customers as if it were a small, local organization. GE knows that staying in tune with customers will be increasingly important in a world of heightened global competition.

And changes in GE's training and evaluation processes keep the company innovative and responsive. GE's team workers are evaluated -and compensated- based not just on the individual work they do but, more important, on the new cross-functional skills they learn. By encouraging and nurturing the desire and ability of the workers to improve and innovate. GE's systems keep the company competitive domestically and able to face increasing global competition.

Source: from John A. Bryne, "The horizontal corporation", *Business Week*, 20 December 1993, pp. 76-81; and Noel M. Tichy and Stratford Sherman, *Control Your Destiny or Someone Else Will*. New York: Currency Doubleday, 1993.

General Electric (see Box 6.4.) is not the only large corporation looking for new ways to cope with the ever-increasing competitive environment, in both domestic and global markets. For instance, prominent American manufacturers such as Gillette, Xerox, Hewlett-Packard, Dow Chemical, 3M, Coca-Cola, General Motors and Dupont sell more of their products outside the U.S. than they do at home. Likewise, companies such as Nestle (Switzerland), Philips (Netherlands), Michelin (France), Sony and Honda (Japan), Samsung (South Korea), Bayer (Germany), Northern Telecom (Canada), and Unilever (UK/Netherlands) all receive almost half of their annual sales from foreign countries. As their businesses are gradually grown in scope and scale (size), and complexity, the issues of integrating, coordinating and controlling their activities on the corporate level become more urgent than ever.

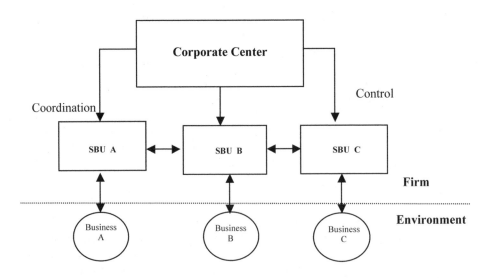

Figure 6.6. Global Integrating Structure

Source: De Wit and Meyer (2005: 14)
SBU is Strategic Business Unit

MULTINATIONAL DESIGN

Large multi-business firms like General Motors, Toyota, Unilever, Hyundai, and British Petroleum, which operate in various countries, each of which has its own set of customers and legal framework, and the like to deal with. They are called multinational organizations because they produce and sell products or services in many countries and continents. In so doing, they attempt to maintain coordination among products, functions, and geographic areas (three dimensions). In practice, managing the 3-dimension cooperation is not always an easy task, especially when operating divisions are separated by distance and time and most often have to deal with cross-cultural problems (diverse languages and cultures).

The model in Figure 6.7 illustrates how organizational design and global strategy fit.

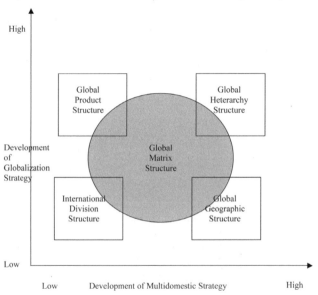

Figure 6.7. Matching Organizational Structure and International Strategy

Source: Adapted from Roderick and Poynter (1995); quoted in Daft (1995: 245).

Many companies are developing overseas operations to take advantages of the globalization of markets. They typically evolve through four phases, starting with a domestic, shifting to an international, then moving to a multinational structure, and finally transforming into a global structure to fully exploit the full potential market. Generally, a global product structure is typically best suitable when a company has many opportunities for globalization, i.e. its products can be standardized and sold worldwide (e.g., Gillette). A global geographic structure is typically used when a company's products or services have local country advantages, i.e. they do best when tailored to local needs and cultures (Daft, 1995: 253).

When large companies have to succeed on two dimensions -global and local- simultaneously, a matrix or a heterarchy form of structure can be appropriate.

NETWORK DESIGN

A network design, sometimes called a *modular organization*, focuses on sharing authority, responsibility, and resources among people, departments, and/or other organizations that must cooperate and communicate frequently to achieve common goals (Hellriegel and Slocum. 2004: 368). For example, Nike and Reebok have virtually no production facilities of their own. Both organizations currently contract their manufacturing to companies in Indonesia and Vietnam, where labor is cheap and plentiful. Similarly, Dell and Gateway buy computer components made by other companies and perform the final assembly themselves to put together customized PCs. Doing so saves these companies from having to make major investments in plants and equipment and permits them to do what they do best to satisfy customer needs.

A network organization exists only when most of the following factors operate in support of one another (Hellriegel and Slocum, 2004: 368).

- Distinctive competence
- Responsibility
- Goal setting
- Communication
- Information technology
- Organization design. and
- Balanced view

VIRTUAL ORGANIZATION

The fast and far-reaching developments in information and communication technologies (ICT) in recent years have both pushed and enabled organizations to move toward a more advanced networked form, called a virtual organization.

A virtual organization seeks to coordinate and link people from many different locations to communicate and make decisions on a real-time basis (Markus et al., 2000; Maznevski and Chudoba, 2000). In such an organization, users of sophisticated personal computers can easily access company databases and work together as if they were in the same room. The optimal use of videoconferencing, electronic blackboards, scanners, faxes, and groupware help organizations, especially those operating on a global basis, to share costs, skills, access to markets and expertise.

Box 6.1. British Petroleum's (BP) Virtual Organization

When John Brown. BP's CEO, took over for David Simon in 1995, he knew that for BP to be successful, he had to develop an organization that learns and gets all employees involved in solving problems. He believed that the people closest to BP's assets and customers should make decisions.

To implement his strategy, he created virtual teams. These teams enable people separated by time, distance, and geography to share their knowledge. If it is easy for people to communicate, connect, and share knowledge, Browne believes that they will. To make doing so easier, BP produces videos that can be viewed on its Intranet, has created electronic yellow pages that can be searched in a variety of ways, and encourages people to list interests, expertise, and experiences that they are willing to share with anyone who wants to contact them. BP's virtual organization relies on a growing system of sophisticated PCs that permit users to tap into the company's databases. All of its PCs are connected to BP's Intranet, which contains more than 40.000 home pages. These home pages are sites on which functional experts offer guidance based on the experience they have gained in dealing with a multitude of issues and problems. There are sites for sharing technical data on the mud used as drilling lubricants and for sharing information about processes that are available to reduce the amount of pipe that gets stuck in wells. There is a site where people can raise questions and exchange information. Brown's idea was to create an organization that would enable the best minds to solve a problem, even if it meant scouring the world for these people.

British Petroleum used the virtual team design to learn and pass on lessons from its exploration and development of the Andrew oil field in the North Sea to contractors and suppliers. People who had encountered similar exploration problems in the Gulf of Mexico shared information quickly with those in the Andrew field. Using virtual teams, BP and its contractors and suppliers were able to figure out radical ways to cut developmental costs and time. By fully utilizing the expertise of its own people and working closely with contractors and suppliers. BP saved an estimated $30 million or more in the Andrew field's first year of operation. But this estimate, according to Browne, does not take into account benefits that are harder to measure, such as the ability to see the expression in someone's eyes during a videoconference when that person makes a commitment. Each member of Browne's staff and each general manager of a business unit is a member of at least one virtual team. These teams allow people to share information with each other continuously. Browne recently participated in a management conference that connected people in Johannesburg with others in Singapore.

Source: Quoted in Don Hellriegel and John W. Slocum, *Organizational Behavior* (10th Ed.). Mason, Ohio: South-Western, 2004, p. 371

GUIDES TO ACTION I

As an Organization Designer, keep these guides in mind:

1. Decide whether your organization should act like a large or small company. To the extent that economies of scale, global reach, and complexity are important, introduce greater bureaucratization as the organization increases in size. As it becomes necessary, add rules and regulations, written documentation, job specialization, technical competence in hiring and promotion, and decentralization.

2. If responsiveness, flexibility, simplicity, and niche finding are important, subdivide the organization into simple, autonomous divisions that have freedom and a small company approach.

3. Grow when possible. With growth, you can provide opportunities for employee advancement and greater profitability and effectiveness. Apply new management systems and structural configurations at each stage of an organization's development. Interpret the needs of the growing organization and respond with the management and internal systems that will carry the organization through to the next stage of development.

4. Don't cut support personnel to reduce overhead without first examining inefficient processes throughout the organization. Unless tasks assigned to support personnel can be handled in other ways, cutting support staff can seriously damage the health of the organization.

5. When layoffs are necessary, handle them with care. Treat departing employees humanely. Give them plenty of notice, allow them to leave with dignity, and offer assistance, such as severance pay and job leads.

Source: Richard L. Daft, *Organization Theory and Design* (5th Ed.).
San Francisco etc.: West Publishing Co., 1995, p. 184.

GUIDES TO ACTION II

As an Organizational Designer, keep these guidelines in mind:

1. Develop organization charts that describe task responsibilities, vertical reporting relationships, and the grouping of individuals into departments. Provide sufficient documentation so that all people within the organization know to whom they report and how they fit into the total organization picture.
2. Provide vertical and horizontal information linkages to integrate diverse departments into one coherent whole. Achieve vertical linkage through hierarchy referral, rules and plans, new positions, and vertical information systems. Achieve horizontal linkage through paper work, direct contact, liaison roles, task forces, full-time integrators, and teams.
3. Choose between functional or product structures when designing overall organization structure. Use a *functional* structure in a small or medium-sized organization that has a stable environment. Use a *product* structure in a large organization that has multiple product lines and when you wish to give priority to product goals and to coordination across functions.
4. Implement *hybrid* structures, when needed, in large corporations by dividing the organization into self-contained product divisions and assigning to the product division each function needed for the product line. If a function serves the entire organization rather than a specific product line-structure that function as a central function department. Use a hybrid structure to gain the advantage of both functional and product design while eliminating some of the advantages.
5. Consider a *matrix* structure in certain organization settings if neither the product nor the functional structure meets coordination needs. For best results with a matrix structure, use it in a medium-sized organization with a small number of products that

has a changing environment and needs to give equal priority to both products and functions because of dual pressures from the environment. Do not use the matrix structure unless there is truly a need for a dual hierarchy and employees are well trained in its purpose and operation.

6. Consider a *structural reorganization* whenever the symptoms of structural deficiency are observed. Use organization structure to solve the problems of poor-quality decision making, slow response to the external environment, and too much conflict between departments.

Source: Richard L. Daft, *Organization Theory and Design* (5th Ed.).
San Francisco etc.: West Publishing Co., 1995, p. 224.

GUIDES TO ACTION III

As an Organizational Designer, keep these guidelines in mind:

Analyze the global forces at work that influence your company, and respond by designing new domestic or international structures that enable international competitive advantage.

Move the organization through the four stages of international evolution, including domestic, international, multinational, and global. Maintain congruence between stages of development, strategic orientations, resource flows, structure, market potential, and facilities location.

Shift to a horizontal structure with self-managed teams or a dynamic network structure to maintain domestic competitiveness in the face of global competitive forces. Use self-managed teams to gain motivation and commitment of employees and a dynamic network structure to maintain a fluid responsiveness to the changing international environment.

Choose a global product structure when the organization can gain advantages with a globalization strategy. Choose a global geographic structure when the company has advantages with multi-domestic strategy. Choose an international division when the company is primarily domestic and has only a few international opportunities.

Develop international strategic alliances, such as licensing, joint ventures, and consortia, as fast and less expensive ways to become involved in international sales and operations. Implement a matrix structure when the opportunities for globalization and multi-domestic opportunities are about equal. Implement a heterarchy* when the organization is truly global and is responding to many global forces simultaneously.

Keep these guides in mind when analyzing the following case.

* The *global heterarchy structure* occurs for huge multinational firms with subsidiaries in many countries that try to exploit both global and local advantages, and perhaps technological superiority, rapid innovation, and functional control.

CASE STUDY

Company Y

Company Y is a USA-based company that sells more than $2 billion annually in products and services for a variety of industrial applications. It has facilities and offices in dozens of locations throughout the world. The organization has a strong domestic product structure that has been in place for ten years. An international division exists that has responsibility for the company's international operations.

A consulting study of the international division suggested that the division develops country specialists who are well-regarded and helpful to product division managers; the study further suggested that the specialists be given some authority to influence international decisions made by product managers.

The international division vice president reports directly to the CEO and has veto power over international acquisitions and international capital appropriations. Product line managers often work with international managers to gain acceptance of their proposed international actions.

The international vice president has set up a new structure with four regional managers reporting to him. The regional managers are stationed in the United States of America and travel about 50 percent of the time to provide regional and country information to product line managers. Field managers eventually will be stationed in every country with multiple operations; they will support marketing and business development efforts of the global business units. Current field managers report to one of the four regional managers.

The international vice president believes the success of the international division comes from maintaining quality working relationships with the product divisions. The company is considering three possibilities for the future direction of the international division. The first is to continue to grow in influence and to continue adding regional and country managers. The second is to help each product group develop its own in-house capacity to conduct effective international operations; this could eventually mean the demise of the international division as now defined. The third idea is to develop in-house expertise within each division and to maintain strong international expertise at the corporate level. This would enable the corporate international division to act as an independent international agent and provide advice to divisions on such matters as finance, counter-trade, and marketing.

Questions for discussion

1. At what stage of international evolution (domestic. international. multinational or global) is Company Y? Explain.
2. What problems do you think Company Y is experiencing with its present structure?
3. Which of the three alternatives you think should be adopted for the future international structure at Company Y? Consider advantages and disadvantages of each alternative.

Source: Daft (1995: 256); based on *New Directions in Multinational Corporate Organization*. New York: Business International Corporation, 1981.

CONCLUSION

In this chapter, the practice of structural design in several settings in the forms of functional, product, geographical, hybrid and matrix structures are discussed. Given the fast changing and globalized environment of today, these structural designs are not ever-lasting, but often have to be adjusted to the new requirements. The appropriate forms of organizational design for the globalization era can be a combination of the matrix structure, the network structure, and the virtual structure.

REFERENCES

Daft, R.L. 1995. *Organization Theory and Design* (5th Ed.). San Francisco etc.: West Publishing, Co.

Davis, J. E. 1987. Who's afraid of IBM? *Business Week*. 29 June, pp. 68-74.

De Wit, R. and Meyer, R. 2005. *Strategy Synthesis: Resolving Strategy Paradoxes to Create Competitive Advantage*. London: Thomson Learning.

Driscoll, L. 1992. The new thinking at Xerox. *Business Week*. 22 June. pp. 120-21.

Duncan, R. 1979. What is the right organization structure? Decision tree analysis provides the answer. *Organizational Dynamics*. Winter. p. 429.

Hammer, M. and Champy, J. 1993. *Reengineering the Corporation*. New York: Harper Business.

Hellriegel, D. and Slocum Jr., J.W. 2004. *Organizational Behavior* (10th Ed.). Mason. Ohio: South-Western.

Markoff, J. 1989. John Sculley's Biggest Test. *New York Times*. 26 February. pp. 1-26; quoted in Daft (1995:210).

Markus, M., Manville, L.B. and Agres, C.E. 2000. What make a virtual organization work? *Sloan Management Review*. 42(1):13-7.

Maznevski, M.L. and Chudoba, K.M. 2000. Bridging space over time: global virtual team dynamics and effectiveness for virtual organizations. *Organization Science*. 11: 473-492.

Robbins, S.P. and Coulter, M. 2002. *Management* (7th Ed.). New Jersey: Pearson Education. Inc./Prentice Hall.

Roderick, E. W. and Poynter, T.A. 1989. Organizing for Worldwide Advantage. *Business Quarterly*. Summer. pp. 84-89.

RECOMMENDED FURTHER READINGS

Dawson, P. 1994. *Organizational Change: a Processual Approach*. London: Paul Chapman Publishing, Ltd.

French, W.L., Bell Jr., C.H, and Zawacki, R.A. 1994. *Organization Development and Transformation: Managing Effective Change*. Sydney, etc: Irwin.

French, W.L. and Bell Jr., C.H. 1995. *Organization Development* (5th ed.). New Jersey: Prentice Hall, Inc.

Novarro, T. 2000. *Restructuring your Organization: a Reorganization Guide*. Colorado: TGN&Associates.

Paton, R.A. and McCalman, J. 2000. *Change Management: a Guide to Effective Implementation* (2nd ed.). New Delhi: Response Books.

Thornhill, A. Lewis, P., Millmore, M. and Saunders, M. 2000. *Managing Change: a Human Resource Strategy Approach*. London, etc.: Prentice Hall/Pearson Education.

CHAPTER SEVEN
ORGANIZATIONAL DEVELOPMENT AND CHANGE
SILVIO DE BONO AND STEPHANIE JONES

OPENING CASE: GENERAL ELECTRIC (GE) (PART ONE)

A widely quoted example of organizational development and change, regarded as the fastest growing company on the planet from 1981 to 2001, General Electric achieved the status of being the company with the largest market value in the world in 2001. Constantly ranked among the top six Fortune 500 companies, General Electric made 600 acquisitions in these two decades. In the process, the company revenue of General Electric exceeded the combined Gross Domestic Product (GDP) of UAE, Kuwait, Oman, Qatar & Bahrain.

General Electric was historically a significant corporation. When the Standard & Poor Index (S&P Index) of top 500 companies was formed in 1957 with 500 companies, General Electric was already one of the most prominent. In 1997 only 74 of these 500 remained, such was the level of corporate attrition over time. Survival is not a given, nor is it a norm. Survival is an exception, and hence the need for continuous organizational development and change. In recent times, only twelve companies have regularly outperformed the S&P Index. Only two companies have outperformed the S&P Index despite their industries underperforming – and one was General Electric.

Founded in 1878, General Electric now has operations in over 100 countries, and employs over 300,000 people worldwide. Revenues of US$ 131.7 billion were achieved as a result of its two-decade process of organizational development and change, representing earnings of US$ 15.1 billion and assets of US$ 575.0 billion. This represents a nearly 300% increase in most measures. The company remains a diversified conglomerate.

One of the main factors in the company's transformation was the CEO of the 1980s and 1990s, the legendary Jack Welch. Tough and uncompromising, sometimes innovative and sometimes conservative, Welch dominated the American corporate scene with unique prominence in this era. Now on the international lecture circuit and with several "how I did it" books to his credit, Welch may be seen as a one-off rather than as a blueprint for organizational development and change. But his story is epoch-making and successful enough to have attracted wide attention among practitioners and academics.

Amongst America's corporate leaders, Welch maintained an envied leadership position for many years:

Table 1: Leaders' rank order by perceived success

Rank 1998	Rank 1999	Rank 2000	Rank 2001	Name	Company
1	1	1	1	Jack Welch	GE
2	2	2	2	Bill Gates	Microsoft
8	6	6	3	Warren Buffett	Berkshire Hathaway
4	3	3	4	Lou Gerstner	IBM
7	8	11	5	Nobuyuki Idei	Sony
5	13	7	6	Andy Grove	Intel
15	7	15	7	Hiroshi Okuda	Toyota
	5	10	8	Michael Dell	Dell

Source: Financial Times, 2001

Welch was born as an only child to a hard working father Irish immigrant father and a loving mother. "If I have any leadership style", he reflected, "or a way of getting the best out of people, I owe it to her." In his book *Straight from the Gut*, Welch writes that he saw his mother as the most influential person in his life. A self-confident, bright and popular student, he was a life-long sports fanatic, able to keep up a scratch handicap in golf despite leading one of the USA's top organizations. Growing up with a speech impediment – a stutter that wouldn't go away – Welch had to be trained to face the press and analysts, especially as CEO.

Welch joined GE in 1960 after gaining his PhD in Chemical Engineering, but decided to leave GE after only one year. He didn't like all the rules and levels of authority, but he quickly moved up the GE bureaucracy to become the general manager (GM) of a new factory. Eight years after joining GE he was in charge of the $26million per year GE plastics business unit, and by 1973, he became the head of Strategic Planning for a portfolio of businesses. In 1977, he was chosen by the CEO to become the sector executive of the consumer products division. He won the seven-man race to become the GE CEO in 1981.

Welch inherited a complex and diverse organization. It was divided into 150 business units, and nine levels of management existed between the CEO and the shop floor workers. This proliferation of bureaucracy, and its extinction, became Welch's main goal in the early years of his leadership. Additionally, he focused on the few laggards in the company – more than a few – and the minimal synergy between the GE companies.

This case is continued in the next two chapters.

CASE QUESTIONS:
- *What were the pressures for change at GE at the beginning?*
- *Do you consider two decades a long, short or expected amount of time to achieve such improvements in the company's revenue situation?*
- *Is the background to Welch relevant to the story?*
- *Do you think the historic background and long-term existence of GE as a company was an advantage or a burden to its efforts to change?*
- *Do you think that the fact that Welch was a lifelong GE employee made it easier or more difficult for him to undertake a major change at the heart of the organization?*
- *Why was Welch voted top of the CEO poll for so long?*

See further discussion questions in the next two chapters.

LEARNING OBJECTIVES:

In this chapter, 'Organizational Development and Change', our purpose is to help you:
- Understand the pressures and forces for change typically felt by organizations, including financial pressures, those from employees, and those from competitors and from customers
- Appreciate other related pressures: from trends towards globalization to changes in technology
- Understand the existence of the need for change as a regular part of the philosophy of the learning organization, and to create a learning organization

In terms of content, this chapter includes:
- An introduction to organizational diagnosis to understand problems and challenges – is there a need for incremental or rapid response to change?
- The issue of assessing employee readiness for change and ability to cope with stress
- Analyzing resistance to change - individual and organizational
- Overcoming resistance to change through empathy, communication and participation

This chapter begins with attempts to define change (and four different perspectives), and then considers approaches to change, taking two radically different viewpoints.

DEFINING CHANGE

In diagnosing the need for change, we need to define change itself. Hayes (2002), in arguing that most organizations strive to maintain or improve their competitiveness, suggests this is achieved through 'Change Management,' defined as a decision-making procedure which modifies or transforms organizations to be both effective and efficient. Carnall (1999) defines efficiency as achieving stated goals within given resource constraints; and effectiveness as the efficient use of resources to reach immediate goals, but including the need to adapt to changing circumstances in the long-term. Organizational effectiveness, another key concept in the issue of change, may be assessed through different perspectives:

The goals perspective measures effectiveness by how far the organization satisfies pre-set identifiable goals. Attaining these goals is interpreted as organizational effectiveness (Goodman & Pennings. 1980).

The systems perspective is founded on the basic survival instinct. Effectiveness is measured by how far parts of the organization function well together and by the relationship of the whole organization with the environment.

The organizational development perspective measures effectiveness through the process of organizational learning aimed at promoting renewal and long-term survival. Beer (1980) defines Organizational Development as a systems-wide process of:

a   data collection
b   diagnosis
c   action planning
d   intervention and evaluation

The process is aimed at enhancing congruence between organizational structure, process, strategy, people and culture while developing creative organizational solutions for self-renewal.

The political arena perspective regards organizations as a set of internal and external constituencies pursuing their own objectives where organizational effectiveness is measured by the values of the most powerful constituency. A constituency's power is determined by the importance of its contribution to the input-transformation-output process: the more central and indispensable the contribution to the survival of the organization, the greater the power of the constituency.

TWO APPROACHES TO THE STUDY OF CHANGE

There are two approaches to the study of change: a passive approach and an active approach. The former, called '**Determinism Approach**' (Wilson. 1992), presents the premise that organizations are affected to a large extent by external forces, namely the economic situation, the environment and the context in which they operate. Thus, managers, or change agents, are limited in their ability to effect change as the main determining forces lie outside their realm of control. Wilson stresses that the interplay between the organization and the environment is the key determinant of strategic change.

Burns (2000) regards this approach as 'over-fatalistic' and argues that if managers, when acting as change agents, do not believe in their ability to change course, they will not be proactive but will react to external forces after events have taken place. He concludes that "Scope for choice ... is likely to be more pronounced when change, particularly major change, is on the managerial agenda" and not overly subject to deterministic forces.

The alternative route is the '**Voluntarism Approach**' which bases its premise on the ability of managers or change agents to affect outcomes through a choice of strategy. This view stresses that the quality of strategic choices made can promote or undermine organizational effectiveness. Effective change management will depend on the conceptual model and tools selected, on change management skills and on the confidence on the part of the manager in his ability to change course. This perspective hinges on the process of change (see figure below).

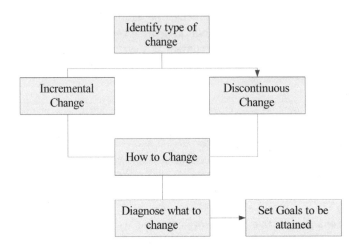

Figure 1: The Process of the Voluntarism Approach as developed by Nadler and Tushman (1995)

To understand the process, we must first identify the type of change in question. Once this is identified, it will pave the way as to how the organization can change and to decide on the elements to change. The final step is to set the goals to be attained in order to visualize a directional path towards which to strive. Nadler and Tushman (1995) suggest that organizations go through periods of minor, or incremental, change which consist of small, continuous adjustments across units. Taken as a whole, such adjustments create substantial change.

However, in cases of a big disturbance, these times are punctuated by major upheaval. These considerable spurts of change usually affect many companies which go through periods of 'punctuated equilibrium', termed as discontinuous change or Burke (2002) 'transformational change'.

DIFFERENT CLASSICAL MODELS OF CHANGE

Lewin's model of change: The intentional management of change can be approached from two perspectives: one may effect change by actively pushing for it, while another may achieve change by decreasing resistance to the process. According to Lewin (1951), when change is achieved by intensifying the forces for it, the situation is characterized by tension and aggression. On the other hand, when change is brought about by diminishing the resistance against it, the atmosphere is comparably less tense. Thus, the end result may be of a more permanent nature than a situation filled with aggression. Lewin advocated a three-step approach in the intentional management of change in order to achieve a sustainable state:

1   unfreeze or unlock from the existing level of behavior;
2   change or move to a new level; and
3   refreeze behavior at the new level.

Lewin's three-step model has been considered a cornerstone in the management of change. Most models have been built on this basic premise and follow the process of unfreezing, change and refreeze if one delves deep enough into their construction.

Lewin's model helps us to see in perspective the needs of employees and how they fit into the picture. In terms of drivers for change, employee readiness can be a very important factor. But more frequently they become a restraining force or barrier against the achievement of change. The achievement of sustained change is impossible without the process of overcoming individual and organizational resistance. These can be pinpointed using Lewin's force field analysis:

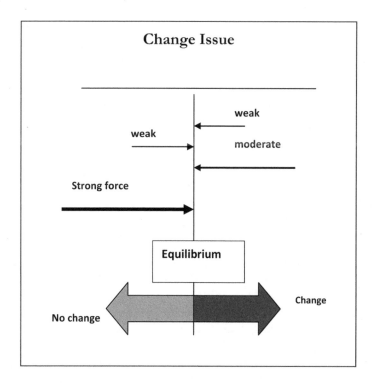

Figure 2: Force Field Diagram (Source: Lewin, 1951)

The Force Field Analysis is carried out in this specific order:

a   An investigation of the current situation and a projection of the desired state;
b   The identification of what will happen if no action is taken;
c   A listing of the forces driving and resisting change;
d   The examination of the validity of all the forces;
e   The allocation of a score for each force according to its strength or weakness;
f   The positioning of the forces according to their allocated score to determine whether the situation can be unblocked to effect change;
g   An attempt to reach a new equilibrium either by increasing the forces or by decreasing the restraints; and
h   Keeping in mind that increasing or decreasing the current forces may unleash new forces, whether for or against.

Weisbord's six box model: A second model which focuses on internal alignment is Weisbord's Six Box model, which approaches change through an open-systems model targeting what needs to be done internally. This model is termed 'descriptive' by Burke (2002) with the leadership role coordinating the remaining five elements. The effectiveness of the organization is measured by the content and interplay of the six boxes (Hayes. 2002).

Weisbord (1976) suggested that there were six key areas in which 'things must go right' if an organization is to be successful (Stahl. 1997). The model proposes a diagnostic tool for identifying the key areas by addressing the questions in each of the boxes.

Weisbord argues that an effective organization diagnosis can trigger improvement if carried out correctly. He advises that the 'diagnosis,' defined as identifying a problem by determining the gap between the ideal and the reality, must be carried out by the same persons solving the problem so that they learn from the present and try to improve the future. The boxes (shown in Figure 3) describe Purpose, Structure, Relationships, Rewards, Helpful Mechanisms, and Leadership. The Purpose refers to what the business is actually doing and whether the reasons for being in the particular sphere are still congruent with the existing environment and a future direction. The answers can identify whether the core business is still in line with the environment's demands or whether there is a misalignment which may signal a need for change.

The Structure diagnosis refers to clarifying "functional responsibilities and staff accountabilities." Weisbord's model talks of a matrix structure where persons may have a dual role or be answerable to two different persons. Thus, this investigation should clarify who does what and where the responsibility lies in preparation for the possibility of change. Weisbord focuses the diagnosis for Relationships to look for dysfunctions in the quality of the relationships. When people do not work well together, they are not able to "buy into" a new direction. This also helps us to understand the positioning of employee and organizational resistance.

The rewards diagnosis is directed at the empowerment of people to participate in the decision-making process; their contributions are also recognized in a psychological manner. Helpful mechanisms refer to adequate tools for working, namely systems and required information technology. Is there a gap between the existing and the required systems to produce a good-level product? The Six Box Model can only be effective if the diagnosis is understood and activated. If a gap or variance is diagnosed, the need for change should be translated into a strategic plan with definite time frames involving leadership and employees. Organization transformation can only be effected if employees 'buy in' to the new direction.

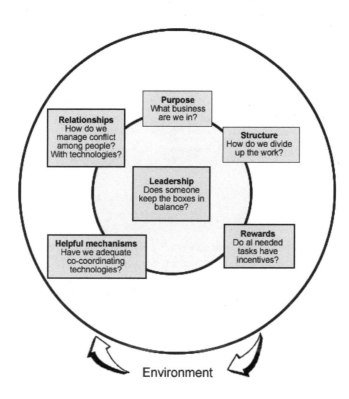

Figure 3: Weisbord Six Box Organizational Model.

Source: Weisbord (1976).

KOTTER'S INTEGRATIVE MODEL TOWARDS CHANGE (1980)

This model comprises one set of organizational processes and six structural elements which interplay and impact each other while potentially driving or constraining behavior. In the short-run, organizational effectiveness can be measured by the cause and effect relationships that relate all the elements of the system to each other (Hayes. 2002). The structural elements are always responsive to external information in order to influence the key organizational processes to maintain alignment with the environment.

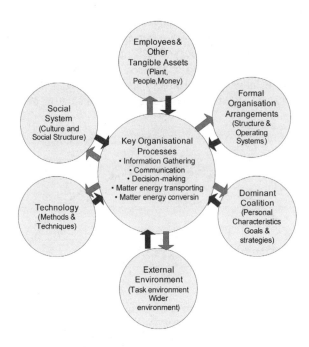

Figure 4: Kotter's integrative model towards change (1980)

The lighter-colored arrows signify a source of potential behavior and constraints.The darker-colored arrows show sources of impact.

According to Kotter (1980) in the medium term, the role is inverted and it is the onus of the organizational processes to ensure the alignment of the six structural elements with each other.

This may be done through ensuring that the key processes are kept in 'efficient and effective state' to enable 'fit' between the six elements. Failure to do this will bring about a misalignment or 'poor fit' between the elements which will trigger waste of resources and misinformation.

In the long term, the onus is once more on the six structural elements which must adapt themselves as required to maintain organizational effectiveness. Kotter predicts that one or two structural elements will exert dominance on the key processes and emerge as the driving force. This will nudge the other elements to follow to maintain alignment, not without possible conflict. But it is imperative that sustained misalignment is not allowed to operate for a long time as this will endanger the survival of the organization.

Kotter (1980) developed this model after extensive research carried out in 1975 and 1976 of twenty-six organizations. At the time, the model was regarded as quite unique and revolutionary. The model is effective in its simplicity yet complex enough to include all the necessary variables impacting organization development and change.

The **Nadler and Tushman** Congruence Model for Organizational Behavior (1980) is also based on an open system with an emphasis on transformation and way that the component parts Relate to each other. The model delineates four types of input which influence the transformation process, namely the environment, external resources, history and strategy. The authors include the issue of history as they feel that there is evidence to suggest that the way organizations function today can be influenced by past events.

Strategy, as a final input, is different from the other inputs as it represents a series of decisions the organization has to make to maximize the value of its resources within the demands, constraints, and opportunities of the environment and the historical framework. Strategy is presented as an aligning factor between the organization and the environment which determines the organization's outputs. Organizational outputs are assessed at different levels, namely, at the product level and at the organizational performance level represented by group functioning and by individual level functioning. Nadler and Tushman (1980) submit that organizational performance may be evaluated by goal attainment, resource utilization and adaptability to a changing environment. Nadler and Tushman view organizations as made up of four major components, "the task, individuals, the formal organizational arrangements and the informal organization." An analysis of the task includes basic work flows, the knowledge required for the work, the rewards, the degree of uncertainty and constraints inherent in the work (see figure below), 'A Congruence Model for Organization Analysis'.

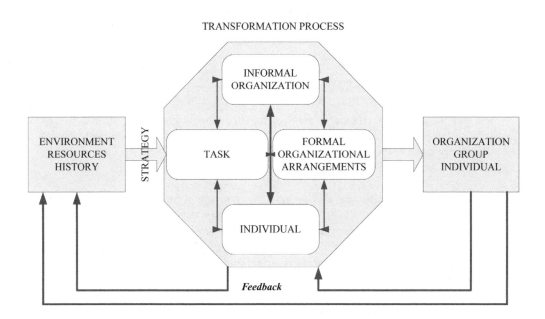

Figure 5: Nadler & Tushman transformation process (1980 : 47)

The factors to consider with reference to individuals are the nature of the individual knowledge and skills, their preferences, expectations and perceptions. The formal organizational arrangements include the structures, processes, methods and procedures required to get individuals to perform the tasks. One facet is organizational design which focuses on how jobs are grouped together into units and the coordinating and control mechanism used to link the units. Another facet is how jobs are designed within the organization while a third perspective is the physical work environment. The last facet is the system used to attract, develop and evaluate human resources.

The informal organization centers on those processes and arrangements which, although not written and formalized, influence behavior a great deal. Once the components have been established, the critical issue is how they interact and fit together. The degree of congruence between each set of components will render organizational performance more effective. Effectiveness is reached when there is congruence between strategy and the environment and 'fit' between the internal components (Nadler & Tushman. 1989).

However, Nadler and Tushman (1989) submit that although congruence may provide effectiveness in the short-term, it may hamper performance in the long-term. An organization with high congruence, according to the authors, "can be resistant to change" and may insulate it from environmental changes and render it inflexible to respond in a timely manner.

The key issue is how to maintain congruence during a change process in a large-scale organizational change. Nadler and Tushman (1989) approach change from two dimensions: (1) the scope and (2) the positioning of change. The scope refers to the range targeted by change: incremental change focuses on a subsystem of the organization and is made within the context of the organizational strategies. It does not address fundamental changes in the direction of the business; nor does it deal with changes in power or culture. Strategic change, however, addresses the whole organization and focuses on the organizational frame, bending it, reshaping it and sometimes breaking it.

The positioning of the change in relation to key external events can be reactive or anticipatory. Reactive changes respond to an event or series of events while anticipatory change precedes events perceived to happen in the near future. Four classes of change result as follows (see figure below) 'Organization Frame Bending'.

The incremental changes are less in intensity than the strategic changes. Thus, the former, which are less difficult, are usually managed through normal management processes. Strategic changes, on the other hand, are more difficult and intense, especially in highly complex settings. Re-creations are extremely difficult, traumatic and risky, and managers prefer to resort to re-orientations, or frame-bending, rather than to frame–breaking change.

The Learning Organization is also a relevant concept as indicating an organization with the continuous capacity to change (Robbins, 2003). Resistance to change is less here, as a true Learning Organization has been intentionally designed to keep improving and re-

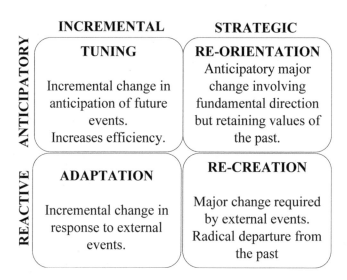

Figure 6: Nadler & Tushman scope and positioning of change (1989 : 196)

inventing itself. In this kind of environment, employees are more willing to put aside old ways of thinking, learn openness and transparency, understand how their organization really functions, and set and achieve their own vision for the business. A commitment to change must be part of the management's plan, and the corporate structure must be flexible and 'boundary-less.' Cross-functional teams are common in Learning Organizations. The culture must be geared towards supporting and resolving functional conflict. Learning Organizations must have people with a shared vision; who are prepared to abandon old ways; who operate as a system of interrelationships; who believe in open communication; and who sublimate their personal self-interest and fragmented departmental interests for the good of the organization's shared vision.

A STRATEGIC ANALYSIS OF CHANGE USING A SWOT ANALYSIS

A SWOT (Strengths, Weaknesses, Opportunities and Threats) analysis provides an internal and external environmental scan of the organization to project a position as a foundation for strategic formulation. The so-called 'home' or internal scan studies the internal sectors of the organization, giving each sector a subjective strength or weakness score in order to mentally visualize the state of the company as a whole. The external scan attempts an analysis of the 'outside' environment in order to spot positive and negative competitive openings of interest to the organization.

A SWOT Analysis is a subjective exercise but it is helpful in developing a 'fit' between the organization's internal strengths and external opportunities. It is also useful to delineate the organization's weaknesses and to work to overcome them if they hamper it from pursing an opportunity. Such an analysis follows a 'voluntarism' approach in so far as change would be planned following an analytical exercise to promote competitiveness.

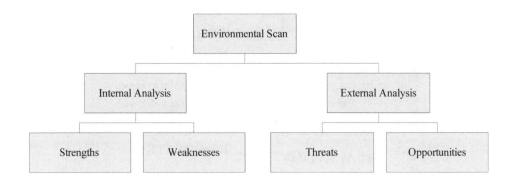

Figure7: SWOT Analysis flow diagram

A STRATEGIC ANALYSIS OF CHANGE USING A PEST ANALYSIS

PEST Analysis is concerned with the pure environmental, external influences of an organization. It is undertaken to promote a reaction to such influencing factors and stands for:

P - Political, legal influences comprising environmental regulations and protection, consumer protection, employment laws

E - Economic influences including growth or stagnation, taxation, international trade, competition, inflation

S - Social factors comprising demographics, income distribution, labor/social mobility, lifestyles, attitude to work, education, health and welfare

T - Technological factors including investment on research and development, innovation and Information Technology

CLOSING CASE: PATAGONIA

This is an example of a company involved in constant organizational development which doesn't need to change. Here we explore the emergence and development of a radical, innovative company based in the USA named Patagonia. Its profile in a recent issue of *Fortune* represents a considerable departure for a magazine typically hailing supreme capitalists, Wall Street wiz kids and other financially over-achieving organizations and captains of industry. The interesting point about Patagonia is that it deliberately doesn't want to change – and the organization is finding it just as difficult to resist pressure towards what it sees as negative changes, as many companies find it challenging to keep up with change.

Founder Yvon Chouinard "took his passion for the outdoors and turned it into an amazing business" – but the passion came first and the business came later. With Al Gore's scary movie 'An Inconvenient Truth' making almost everyone feel uncomfortable, Chouinard cashed in on a hot topic, but he doggedly doesn't see it that way. "There is no business to be done on a dead planet" is one of his favorite slogans, exhibited at Patagonia at the headquarters operation at Ventura, California. He maintains a strong level of personal control of the organization and it is dominated by his personality, but there is a strong dose of transformational leadership behind this.

For example, in the 'factory' of Patagonia, life is dominated by the surfing report. If the waves are good, staff members are encouraged to be out there out there surfing. The statistic that 350 employees produce $270 million in revenues shows a high level of individual productivity, of around $770,000 (compared with $380,000 sales per employee in 2001 at General Electric), not bad for a 35 year old outdoor clothing and equipment company, with a radical and non-corporate way of operating, described by Chouinard as 'highly experimental.'

It is certainly entrepreneurial, and Chouinard – now 68 – with his 'outdoorsy' and 'no suits' rule, also has a vision, of opposing the "endless consumption and discarding" nature of contemporary society. Cutting down forests, polluting oceans, and bulldozing wetlands are anathema to him. Putting his 'save the planet' obsession first, he doesn't play by the normal rules of business. His book – Let My People Go Surfing – was described by Fortune as a mix of "memoir and green business primer."

Chouinard does not care that most of his competitors are bigger than he is, and he has no intention to grow his business much larger than it is. Without necessarily setting out to do so, Patagonia has gained a more powerful influence on its customers' lifestyles than some of its largest competitors, such as Billabong, for example. Although the latter espouses a laid-back, sun-drenched beach-bound lifestyle, it lacks the underlying philosophy of Patagonia. The accent on recycling, day care, paternity leave, and a catalogue which makes social statements shows Patagonia as a company with a conscience – which is genuinely entrepreneurial, and uniquely visionary, especially in the conscience-struck early 21st century.

The role of the leader in presenting an attractive message for employees and in transforming people – there are 900 applications for every job opening at Patagonia – is clear in Chouinard's case. He provides idyllic working conditions and facilities and appears easygoing, but he demands excellence, gets it, and is always a perfectionist (a more task-oriented than relationship-oriented trait, but for Chouinard it works with his relationships too). He stretches people in terms of their commitment to product improvement and by making the company's output more and more environmentally-friendly. Staff members are self-selecting in terms of those joining the firm – they have already bought into the concepts and vision of the organization. Chouinard wants people to "think in unique and independent ways," seen as highly self-actualizing – definitely transformational.

The management structure at Patagonia tends to be flat, with Chouinard at the helm and everyone else (including his son) playing their part in a more or less equal way. He makes good use of cross-hierarchical and cross-functional teams in creating new products, especially in the endless pursuit of recycling and anti-pollution, such as making fleece jackets out of discarded soda bottles. He is never satisfied with existing solutions: teams of Patagonia staff members have developed a revolutionary new wetsuit material. As Chouinard argued, if we think about the future of the planet – we may have no more snow, but the waves are getting bigger – so this makes business sense too. And he may be making these decisions in a more timely way than most (except Al Gore) appreciate.

There is typically a low level of formalization at Patagonia, and the organization possesses a comprehensive information network, especially to develop its "focus on doing things right, and then profits come." Chouinard relies on participative decision-making, because he wants to access the drive and brains of everyone in the organization. He keeps the company privately held, to avoid compromising his values and those of his people. If there was a clear pursuit of endless growth, as in many organizations (more typical of *Fortune's* choices for profiles), there would be a clash with the Patagonia view of producing "nothing polluting" and "developing endless recycling" and deciding on the best sources of fabrics for the environment. The level of involvement of staff in the daily operation of Patagonia is impressive, as team members subscribe to the image of the "highly influential anti-business experimental company". The company records only 3 to 8% of growth per year, as huge chunks of revenues are given away to worthy causes, often at employee suggestion and nomination.

Despite the espoused aims of "putting the Earth first, ignoring fashion, and making clothes that do not wear out", the wide variety of customers in Patagonia's 23 stores call them "Patagucci or Pradagonia". For all Chouinard's rejection of big business, he knows how important it can be in spreading the word of his vision. Believing that the most powerful pressure to improve the environment will come from the consumer, he made a strong impact on Wal-Mart, and gained their commitment to sustainability, convincing Wal-Mart to make important green initiatives. Patagonia led the growth of the preference for organic cotton, creating a new industry. He realized the real difference would come when the 'big boys' adopted his ideas, not just a small niche of customers. Thus, his visionary entrepreneurship could have a stronger foundation. Other initiatives for spreading the word include his 'One Per Cent for the Planet' fund – which he created in 2001 – of which now 500 companies have joined. With French-Canadian parents, a social misfit who liked climbing and surfing as typically loner activities, living close to the wild and off the land and once arrested for "wandering around aimlessly without means of support", Chouinard now speaks at the universities of Harvard, Stanford and Yale about his pet theme of business and the environment.

Thus, this radical climbing equipment business that started in 1972 can be seen as a genuinely visionary and entrepreneurial company. Chouinard, transformational and relationship-oriented, lives and breathes a flat structure, the use of teams, and empowerment. Yet Chouinard is in control: "I don't want a Wall Street grease ball running my company" he argues. If he did, he may not get 900 applicants for every job, and 25 year old classics of his fleece jackets selling on EBay for $4,000. So he doesn't want to change the carefully-constructed and unique business he has developed.

CASE QUESTIONS:
- *What are the pressures for change facing Patagonia which Chouinard regards as negative?*
- *How could a business become more like Patagonia? Or would it seem insincere or fake to try to change to become like them?*
- *Do you think the Patagonia model can be sustained?*
- *Could it be appropriate for larger companies?*
- *Would you like to work for a company like this?*
- *Do you see Patagonia as a "Learning Organization"?*

CONCLUSION

This chapter has reviewed definitions and the theoretical foundation to the change process, especially in an organizational developmental context. Here, we have considered different perspectives on change, the Determinism and Voluntarism approaches to change, and frameworks such as those by Lewin, Weisbord, Kotter and Nadler and Tushman's concepts of change methodologies. The Learning Organization concept, and the use of SWOT and PEST analyses also help organizations to decide on the way forward. Assessing employee readiness for change and overcoming the inevitable resistance are also crucial considerations within a change initiative. How to manage the change itself and preserve the company's knowledge base with Knowledge Management are also major developmental issues. Our cases on GE and Patagonia contrast organizations which are dissatisfied with their status quo and also want to transform themselves into a company which has built a model culture and is fighting hard to preserve it.

REFERENCES

Beer. M.. Eisenstat. R.A.. Spector. B. 1990.. Why change programs don't produce change. *Harvard Business Review. 68* (6): 158-66.

Burke. W. 2002. *Organisational Change. Theory and Practice*. Thousand Oaks CA: Sage.

Burns, J.M. 2000. *Transformational Leadership: democratic or despotic?* Thousand Oaks CA: Sage

Campbell. J.P 1977. New perspectives on organizational effectiveness. in Goodman, P.S., Pennings. J.M. and Associates Eds. *On the Nature of Organizational Effectiveness*. San Francisco: Jossey-Bass.

Carnall. C.A. 1982. *The Evaluation of Work Organization Change*. Farnborough: Gower.

Carnall. C.A. 2003. *Managing Change in Organizations*. London: Prentice Hall.

Casey. S. 2007. The Coolest Company of the planet. *Fortune* 12th April. 2007. 155: 6

Emery. M. and Purser. R.E. 1996. *The Search Conference: A Powerful Method for Planning Organizational Change and Community Action*. San Francisco: Jossey Bass Public Administration.

Hayes. J. 2002. *The Theory and Practice of Change Management. London: Palgrave.*

Kotter J.P. 1980. *An Integrative Model of Organizational Dynamics*. In E. Porter, D. Nadler and C. Cammann (eds), Organizational Assessment. New York: Wiley.

Kotter. John P. 1995. Why Transformation Efforts Fail. *Harvard Business Review March*.

Kotter. John P. 1996. *Leading Change*. Boston: Harvard Business School Press.

Lewin. K. 1951. *Field Theory of Social Science.* New York: Harper & Row.

Nadler. D.A. and Tushman. M.L.. 1980. A Model for Diagnosing Organizational Behavior. *Organizational Dynamics.* 47

Nadler. D.A. and Tushman. M.L. 1989. *Organizational Frame Bending: Principles for Managing Reorientation.* San Francisco: Jossey-Bass.

Senge. P. 1990. *The Fifth Discipline. The Art and Practice of The Learning Organization.* Kent: Mackays of Chatham.

Stahl. Steve A. and David A. Hayes ed. 1997. *Instructional models in reading.* Marwah. NH: Lawrence Erlbaum Associates.

Welch. J. 2001. *Straight from the Gut.* New York: Warner.

Welch. J. 2005. Speaker Series September 18. 2002. Available from: http://mba.tuck.dartmouth.edu/cgl/downloads/JackWelch.pdf [Accessed 13 November 2006]

Welch. J. 2005. *Winning.* New York: HarperCollins.

Welch. J. 2006. Press release. book tour stop February 09. 2006. Available from: http://www.24-7pressrelease.com/pdf/2006/02/09/press_release_10871.pl

Weisbord, J. 1976. *Group and Organization Management.* Thousands Oaks CA: Sage

Wilson, D.C. 1992. *A Strategy of Change: concepts and controversies in the management of change.* London: Routledge

RECOMMENDATIONS FOR FURTHER READING

Ansoff. I.H. 1990. *Implanting Strategic Management.* London: Prentice Hall.

Barr. P.S. Stimpert. J.L. Huff. A.S. 1992. Cognitive change. strategic action. and organizational renewal. *Strategic Management Journal. 13.*15-36.

Child. J. Smith. C. 1987. The context and process of organizational transformation – Cadbury Limited in its sector. *Journal of Management Studies. 24* (6): 565-93

Goldstein. J. 1988. A far-from-equilibrium systems approach to resistance to change. *Organizational Dynamics.* 16-26

Hannan. M.T. Freeman. J. 1984. Structural inertia and organizational change. *American Sociological Review. 49.* 149-64

Kanter. R.M. 1989. The new managerial work. *Harvard Business Review. 67* (6): 85-92.

Klein. K.J. Sorra. J.S. 1996. The challenge of innovation implementation. *Academy of Management Review. 21* (4) 22-42.

Leana. C.R. Barry. B. 2000. Stability and change as simultaneous experiences in organizational life. *Academy of Management Review. 25* (4): 753-9

Marshak. R.J. 1993. Managing the metaphors of change. *Organizational Dynamics. 22* (1): 44-56.

Nadler. D.A. Tushman. M.L. 1990. Beyond the charismatic leader: leadership and organizational change. *California Management Review. 32* (2): 77-97.

Nemeth. C.J. 1997. Managing innovation: when less is more. *California Management Review. 40*:1. 59-74

Zaltman. G. Duncan. R. 1977. *Strategies for Planned Change.* Toronto: Wiley.

Zeffane. R. 1996. Dynamics of strategic change: critical issues in fostering positive organizational change. *Leadership & Organization Development Journal.* 17:7

CHAPTER EIGHT
THE PROCESS OF ORGANIZATIONAL CHANGE
SILVIO DE BONO AND STEPHANIE JONES

OPENING CASE: GENERAL ELECTRIC (GE) (PART TWO)

What was the process employed by Jack Welch to effect the changes at General Electric? One of his first transformational initiatives was the remodeling of the General Electric portfolio of businesses, into three broad areas: short cycle, long cycle, and capital, or financial services. What was the thinking behind this ? It was a convenient division of types of businesses by the needs for investment, the customer base, and the kind of people who worked there. The Consumer Products division included Industrial System products, NBC (the media business acquired by GE during Jack Welch's leadership, mostly as a contrast to the existing businesses and 'to inject new blood' and new thinking through its radically different people) and plastics businesses. This division also included Specialty Materials. But all these businesses had one thing in common – there was a relatively short period of time between the inception of new policies and their fruition in terms of new products and services.

By contrast, the Long Cycle Division included businesses which were subject to a long development period, and needed investment, and people with mindsets to match. Typical long cycle businesses within the General Electric portfolio included Aircraft Engines – highly successful and trusted in the aircraft manufacturing industry – but it could take three to five years to produce a new aircraft engine, including all the testing and modifications. This division also included Medical Systems, Power Systems and Transportation Systems. All these businesses provided products and services which took months and usually years to deliver and implement for clients. They were more risky but enjoyed higher margins than the short cycle businesses. The trusted brand name of General Electric played a key part here. People in charge of purchasing aircraft engines and medical equipment – on the efficiency and reliability of which people's lives depend – did not want to take chances on an unknown brand. Here, the experience of GE and its reputation paid off.

Third, Welch created the Capital Division, in which he set up a whole new business for GE in financial services. This was a new but highly profitable area, and again GE could leverage the value of having a long-established brand name, even if this was a new business for the company. Capital included Commercial Finance, Consumer Finance, Equipment Management, and Insurance. They were not exactly general or electric, but the way Jack Welch saw it, they were an important part of the new GE.

Financial reports show that during Welch's leadership, there had been exponential growth. Market value rose dramatically, as did net income and revenues, reflecting around 300% growth in each case. This achievement represented a number of factors at work: Jack Welch's vision of the future, based on a 'Manufacturing – Service based economy' and his leadership drive and focus; the 1980s economic recession in the USA and the need to be competitive in tough times; globalization, increased competition, and the rise of high tech industries; the well-known financial strength of GE as a firm, in terms of its ability to invest and take risks, and its creditability, in terms of borrowing ability.

However, there were many obstacles to be overcome on the way. The impact of history and tradition were too strong for rapid change. Employees felt that the company was in fine shape. "If it ain't broke, don't fix it" was a favorite motto, so they created a good deal of resistance to Jack Welch's thinking. The bureaucracy of GE, disliked so much by Welch, was an on-going stumbling block, and took years to be freed up. The GE Management Style was traditionally cautious and slow-moving, inflexible and time-honored. In particular, the organization structure revealed bloated ranks at the top of the business, not adding much value but protecting their territories. Some had come up through the ranks out in the field, and felt it was their entitlement to move up to the comfortable and prestigious environment of the head office.

In the process of the changes Welch introduced, he liquidated 1/5th of the USA $ 21 billion asset base; cut the workforce by more than 18%, and the overstuffed ranks of head office were reduced from 2,100 to 900. He sold 71 and acquired 118 businesses in this 20 year period, and changed a toaster and oven firm to a high growth services firm. In four years of shutting down businesses, laying off staff, and making asset sales, there was not a single labor slowdown or strike at GE – Welch was careful to square things with the unions. This case is continued in the next chapter.

CASE QUESTIONS:
- *Explain the rationale of dividing GE into three sections – can you think of any way in which Jack Welch could have done this differently?*
- *What was the thinking behind letting go such large numbers of employees? Could the change process have been successfully executed whilst keeping these people?*
- *What were the strengths of GE in creating and sustaining such a huge corporate change process for two decades?*
- *What were some of the most important barriers Welch had to overcome during this transformation?*
- *See the next chapter for further discussion questions.*

LEARNING OBJECTIVES:

In this chapter, 'The Process of Organizational Change', we will be focusing on the following objectives, and how you can:
- Develop awareness of change processes and how these are managed in different companies
- Appreciate the difference between interpersonal methods, team methods and organizational methods in the change process
- Be able to create a simple road map for change, with milestones and goals

In the process of helping you with these learning objectives, we will be looking at:

- An introduction to initiatives contributing to an effective change process
- The process of promoting change in organizations - through interpersonal, team and organizational methods
- Goal-setting and documenting the change process
- Essential stages in the change process

First of all, we will examine employee readiness for change, and why resistance to change occurs and is quite a normal reaction and state of affairs for many employees; we will then consider factors contributing to change management and reactions to change, especially mistakes made in the change process; and we will think about how the whole process of change can be managed effectively. A final case based in China explains how change can be implemented in a challenging cultural setting.

ASSESSING EMPLOYEE READINESS FOR CHANGE

The short series of questions are intended to help students diagnose the situation in their respective companies. In answering 'yes' to these questions, 'then the change process can begin. Otherwise there will be a need to back-track and sort out these issues first:

EXERCISE:
- *Do people throughout the organization share values or visions?*
- *Does the organization have a good track record in implementing change smoothly?*
- *Is there a high degree of co-operation and trust throughout the organization (as opposed to animosity and conflict)?*
- *Does the organization's culture support risk-taking (as opposed to being highly bureaucratic and rule-bound)?*
- *Are people able to handle change (as opposed to being worn out and disturbed by recent, unsettling changes)?*
- *Does the organization reward people who take part in change and improvement efforts (as opposed to punishing those who try but fail)?*
- *Will people be able to maintain respect and status when the change is implemented (as opposed to losing them as a result of the change)?*
- *Will the change be gradual and slight (not causing a disruption of status quo)?*

RESISTANCE TO CHANGE

If you are not answering 'yes' to the questions above, you may be encountering resistance to change. Eales-White (1996) considers that the reasons for resistance to change are many and vary with the circumstances, but whenever there is a perceived possibility of loss of position or status, of inequitable treatment, or the loss of the use of present competencies, there is the strong likelihood that resistance to change will emerge. An obvious organizational implication is that those initiating change should reassure all concerned as clearly as possible about those areas in which there is no need for concern and in those areas in which there will likely be benefits, along with establishing realistic expectations about the pains and challenges that will occur.

When considering organizational change, one is also bound to consider the organization's human resource policies and practices that are inevitably interdependent with change. Essentially, resistance to change can occur simply because the organization does not have, or has not envisaged the implementation of reward schemes, training and development, industrial relations and other broad human resource processes that can reinforce the change process and assist individuals in accepting it as their own. From this perspective, organizational change can never be successful unless it is 'owned' by the senior management of the organization. See Goldstein (1988) and Maurer (1996) for a further discussion here.

The leadership style adopted by change agents, or other members of the organization that are in a position to influence the direction the change process will take, is also another crucial factor towards minimizing resistance to change by the members of the organization. This point holds true in that, despite the fact that the senior management of the organization must own the change process, middle and junior management have been identified as the single major cause of collapse of such processes (see Lawrence. 1954). For the change process to be successful, it requires a leadership style that is usually incongruent with the traditional leadership styles adopted by middle and junior management within organizations.

It is clear that the dominant leadership style in organizations undergoing large scale change must probably feature or move towards extensive use of employee involvement at all levels. Furthermore, leadership must be a team and team process variety. That is, leadership must be conceptualized as a highly interactive, shared process, with members of all teams developing skills in this process. However, middle management in traditional organizations tends to think that the contribution that low level employees can make to improvements is slight. Moreover, the presence of change agents and senior managers drawn from elsewhere in the organization tends to expose this tier of management to unusual outside scrutiny, leaving few middle managers committed to the principle of change and participative management with regard to their own subordinates.

When considering change processes within organizations, the lack of training is another potential detractor towards the success of the process. Organization members need to develop competencies for the new assignments that will be precipitated by change. This means that change agents must anticipate and be on top of the emerging training needs.

Both theory and practice suggest that change processes in organizations are liable to fail unless the reward system of the organization is changed in a timely fashion. It can prevent the institutionalization of the change process in several ways. It may not reward the behavior that is needed to make the changed system work. Worse yet, it may even reward behavior that is the antithesis of what is needed to make the changes work. (See a further discussion in Piderit,2000).

Lack of feedback from organization members on the process of change may lead to a situation whereby change agents and the owners of the change process think that the process is succeeding, whilst the situation will reveal otherwise once it's too late.

Accurate feedback must be sought on two levels. First, feedback must be sought at the interpersonal level. Such feedback should be solicited, fairly immediately after the event concerned and specific. There is a strong possibility of cynicism creeping in (Reichers, Wanous & Austin. 1997). Above all, feedback should be reported in terms of the impact on the person who is providing the feedback. In fact the rationale for such feedback is to improve the relationship between the person and the change process itself. Secondly, feedback must be sought at an organization unit basis. Such feedback is most effective if it is reported directly to the manager or team who can take remedial action, in contrast with senior management. Beer, Eisenstat, and Spector (1990) also provide a useful summary of why many change programs fail to achieve the extent of change required.

FACTORS CONTRIBUTING TO CHANGE MANAGEMENT

While internal or external change agents or a combination may be needed for major or complex organizational changes or major organizational systems changes, most changes are more likely to succeed by following several basics of change management:

Clarify reality and the need for change. Changes are sometimes driven by unsubstantiated opinions, assumptions, and biased information. It is thus very important to conduct a diagnosis that accurately portrays reality and to establish the need for change. Changes for the sake of change, change for the wrong reasons, or unneeded change are all counterproductive. A reality check could be made by evaluating internal information, conducting surveys and interviews, or perhaps benchmarking best practices.

Develop a results-oriented strategy for change. Results-centered changes seek specific and, as much as possible, measurable improvements accomplished during a reasonable time frame.

Involve key stakeholders in planning and managing changes. The key stakeholders could include top management, if they can influence the outcome of the changes made. It could also include a cross-section of managers and employees as well as union officials. Involvement improves the quality of decisions and increases commitment. Expedient changes that bypass the key stakeholders will usually increase resistance to change. When the key stakeholders have some level of involvement in the planning and execution of change, the change will have a high probability of success.

Build in reliable feedback mechanisms to monitor and manage the change process. Timely and accurate feedback helps the change agent assess the impact of the change process and determine whether the process is having the desired effects on the organization. The process itself may be further fine-tuned or changed to evade potential pitfalls or stalling of the process due to resistance.

Ensure that enabling structures are aligned to facilitate and reinforce the desired changes. Enabling structures could include mission statements, goals, resources, organization designs, reward and valuing systems, policies, and training. An organization may launch a team building program only to discover that there is nothing in the reward system to value teamwork. Innovation, risk-taking and collaboration may be encouraged in an organizational culture that historically has not valued such behaviors. People may be asked to perform tasks or to utilize skills without the training to do what they are expected to do. It is imperative that enabling structures be aligned to support desired changes if the changes are expected to be maintained. This area of change management is often overlooked.

A useful summary in looking at the change process is given below. The first six columns present different variables required for effective change while the last column (in bold) shows the result.

Table 1: Elements of change

VISION	COMMUNICATION	DECISION	TOOLS	INCENTIVES	ACTION PLAN	REAL CHANGE
-	COMMUNICATION	DECISION	TOOLS	INCENTIVES	ACTION PLAN	CONFUSION
VISION	-	DECISION	TOOLS	INCENTIVES	ACTION PLAN	RESISTANCE
VISION	COMMUNICATION	-	TOOLS	INCENTIVES	ACTION PLAN	FEAR
VISION	COMMUNICATION	DECISION	-	INCENTIVES	ACTION PLAN	FRUSTRATION
VISION	COMMUNICATION	DECISION	TOOLS	-	ACTION PLAN	DISAPPOINTMENT
VISION	COMMUNICATION	DECISION	TOOLS	INCENTIVES	-	CHAOS

Thus, there is a need to have all the elements in place to achieve real change, and if there is something missing, the change efforts can fail – producing confusion, resistance, fear, frustration, disappointment and/or chaos – or a combination of these. Therefore any change initiative needs careful preparation, and clearly identified elements.

REACTING TO CHANGE

According to Kotter (1996: 3), the incidence of change in organizations has grown tremendously over the past two decades: "Although some people predict that most of the reengineering, re-strategizing, mergers, downsizing, quality efforts, and cultural renewal projects will soon disappear, I think that is highly unlikely." Kotter feels that the macro-economic forces propelling change may grow even stronger over the next few decades. Then more organizations will be pushed to reduce costs, improve the quality of products and services, locate new opportunities for growth, and increase productivity. But in too many situations, attempted improvements have been disappointing, "and the carnage has been appalling, with wasted resources and burned-out, scared, or frustrated employees" Kotter (1996: 4) argues.

It also depends on the thinking behind change:

Change as needed: the extent of factually necessary alterations within the company and its periphery

Change as wanted: attitudes of those people/organizational units involved in the change towards goals and measures of the change process

Change as possible: opportunity of the individual/organizational unit to execute the change process, based on knowledge and ability (Kruger, 1996).

Kotter (1996: 4-15) has identified eight major mistakes which help explain the failure of many change initiatives:

Error # 1: Allowing too much complacency: Kotter suggests that one of the greatest mistakes made when trying to change organizations is to rush on without establishing a high enough sense of urgency in managers and employees. This error is fatal because transformations always fail to achieve their objectives when complacency levels are high. Change interventions without the necessary communications will not be effective (see chart above).

When there is a failure to create sufficient urgency at the beginning of a business transformation, it is often due to overestimating how much change can be forced on an organization, and underestimating how hard it is to drive people out of their comfort zones. Kotter (1996: 5) argues that this can be caused by a lack of patience: "Enough with the preliminaries, let's get on with it." People become defensive, and morale and short-term results fall. By creating anxiety rather than urgency, they create even more resistance to change.

Kotter (1996: 5) considers that complacency is too high in most organizations today: "Too much past success, a lack of visible crises, low performance standards, insufficient feedback from external constituencies," and more are characterized by comments such as: "Yes, we have our problems, but they aren't that terrible and I'm doing my job just fine," or "sure we have big problems, and they are all over there." Without a sense of urgency, people won't give that extra effort and will resist change initiatives from above.

Error # 2: Failing to create a sufficiently powerful guiding coalition: Kotter insists that in successful transformations, "the president, division general manager, or department head plus another five, fifteen, or fifty people with a commitment to improved performance pull together as a team." (1996: 6). This must form a powerful coalition, as individuals alone cannot have all the assets needed to overcome tradition and inertia except in very small organizations. Efforts that lack a sufficiently powerful guiding coalition can make apparent progress for a while, but then get undermined.

Failure in this case is usually associated with underestimating the difficulties in producing change and thus the importance of a strong guiding coalition. Kotter argues that even when complacency is relatively low, firms with little history of transformation or teamwork often undervalue the need for such a team or assume that it can be led by a staff executive from human resources, quality, or strategic planning instead of a key line manager. No matter how capable or dedicated the staff head, guiding coalitions without strong line leadership never seem to achieve the power that is required to overcome inertia. Thus support from the highest levels in these guiding coalitions is imperative.

Error # 3: Underestimating the power of vision: Urgency and a strong guiding team are necessary but insufficient conditions for major change on their own. Of the remaining elements that are always found in successful transformations, none is more important than a powerful vision. Vision plays a key role in producing change, according to Kotter, by helping to direct, align, and inspire actions on the part of large numbers of people. Without an appropriate vision, a transformation effort can easily dissolve into a list of confusing, incompatible, and time-consuming projects that go in the wrong direction or nowhere at all. Without a sound vision, the reengineering project in the accounting department, the new 360 degree performance appraisal from human resources, the plant's quality program, and the cultural change effort in the sales force either won't add up in a meaningful way or won't stir up the kind of energy needed to properly implement any of these initiatives.

Knowing the difficulty in producing change, some people try to manipulate events behind the scenes and avoid any public discussion of future direction, Kotter observes. But visions are needed to guide decision making, otherwise the smallest of decisions can generate heated conflict that reduces energy and morale. Kotter (1996: 9) suggests a useful rule of thumb: "whenever you cannot describe the vision driving a change initiative in five minutes or less and get a reaction that signifies both understanding and interest, you are in for trouble."

Error # 4: Under-communicating the vision by a factor of 10 (or 100 or even 1,000) Major change is usually impossible unless most employees are willing to help, often to the point of making short-term sacrifices. But people will not make sacrifices, even if they are unhappy with things as they are, unless they think the potential benefits of change are attractive and unless they really believe that a transformation is possible. Without strong communication, it is impossible to capture employees' hearts and minds. Interventions at this point can include communications programs with newsletters and videos, personal meetings with members of the leadership, and giveaways bearing the vision message.

Kotter has identified three patterns of ineffective communication, all driven by habits developed in times of stability: Firstly, a group develops a transformational vision and then proceeds to sell it by holding just a few meetings or sending out only a few memos, but are surprised when people don't seem to understand the new approach. Secondly, the head of the organization spends a considerable amount of time making speeches to employee groups, but most of the managers are silent. Thirdly, much more effort goes into newsletters and speeches, but some highly visible individuals still behave in ways that are against the vision, and the result is that cynicism goes up while belief in the new message goes down.

Communication, Kotter suggests, comes in both words and deeds. The latter is generally the most powerful form. Nothing undermines change more than behavior by important individuals that is inconsistent with the verbal communication. And yet this happens frequently, even in well-known companies.

Error # 5: Permitting obstacles to block the new vision The implementation of any kind of major change requires action from a large number of people. New initiatives fail, Kotter argues, when employees feel disempowered by barriers in their way. Sometimes these are imaginary and no external barriers exist. Sometimes the obstacle is the organizational structure. Narrow job categories can undermine efforts to increase productivity or improve customer service. Compensation or performance-appraisal systems can force people to choose between the new vision and their self-interests. Perhaps worst of all are supervisors who refuse to adapt to new circumstances and who make demands that are inconsistent with the transformation.

Many employees act as barriers because they do not believe that the organization needs major change. Or it might be because they are concerned that they cannot produce both change and the expected operating results. Some companies are inexperienced in handling such personnel problems among executives, others are afraid of confrontation. Sometimes there is worry about losing a talented contributor. Kotter sums it up by saying "whenever smart and well-intentioned people avoid confronting obstacles, they dis-empower employees and undermine change (1996: 11)."

Error # 6: Failing to create short-term wins: Kotter emphasizes that real transformation takes time. Complex efforts to change strategies or restructure businesses risk losing momentum if there are no short-term goals to meet and celebrate. Most people need to see compelling evidence within six to eighteen months that the change initiative is producing the expected results; otherwise they may give up or start resisting the efforts.

To achieve a successful transformation, managers must actively look for ways to obtain clear performance improvements, such as by establishing goals in the yearly planning system. They must achieve these objectives, and reward the people involved with recognition, promotions, or bonuses (in general, with whatever counts for those people within their organizations as 'rewards'). In change initiatives that fail, Kotter argues that managers either assume that things will happen or become so caught up with their vision that they don't worry much about the short term.

Kotter points out that although employees often complain about being forced to produce short-term wins, under the right circumstances that kind of pressure can be a useful element in a change process. When it becomes clear that quality programs or cultural change efforts will take a long time, urgency levels usually drop. "Commitments to produce short-term wins can help keep complacency down and encourage the detailed analytical thinking that can usefully clarify or revise transformational visions," Kotter (1996: 12) maintains.

Error # 7: Declaring victory too soon: After a few years of hard work, a major change effort can be argued as successful with the first major performance improvement, but the suggestion that the job is mostly done at this stage can be a great mistake. Change often means culture change, which for an entire company can take three to ten years (or even longer) and new adjustments can be fragile and subject to regression.

Kotter has studied several change efforts operating under the re-engineering theme, and in most cases victory was declared and the expensive consultants were paid and thanked when the first major project was completed. This was despite little, if any, evidence that the original goals were accomplished or that the new approaches were being accepted by employees. Within a few years, the positive changes that had been introduced began to disappear, and some have disappeared without trace. Declaring victory too soon, Kotter feels, is like stumbling into a hole on the road to meaningful change: "and for a variety of reasons, even smart people don't just stumble into that hole. Sometimes they jump in with both feet (1996: 14)."

Error # 8: Neglecting to anchor changes firmly in the corporate culture: In the final analysis, Kotter argues, change takes root only when it is planted into the corporate culture. Until new behaviors become social norms and shared values, they disappear when the pressures associated with a change effort are removed. The new culture must be adopted wholesale by the organization as a whole. This complex process, suggests Kotter, can be the result of a conscious attempt to show people how specific behaviors and attitudes have helped improve performance. Anchoring change also requires that sufficient time be taken to ensure that the next generation of management really does personify the new approach. The culture change must be exemplified from the top. If promotion criteria are not reshaped, transformations rarely last. Smart people miss the mark here when they are insensitive to cultural issues, considers Kotter: "economically-oriented finance people and analytically-oriented engineers can find the topic of social norms and values too soft for their tastes. So they ignore culture – at their peril."

THE 'EIGHT MISTAKES'

None of these change errors would matter so much in a slower moving and less competitive world, Kotter believes (1996: 15). Handling new initiatives quickly is not an essential component of success in relatively stable or monopolistic environments. "The problem for us today is that stability is not longer the norm. And most experts agree that over the next few decades the business environment will become only more volatile," Kotter reflects. Making any of the eight errors common to transformation efforts can have serious consequences (as explained in our table below, showing the results of leaving out important change elements). In slowing down the new initiatives, creating unnecessary resistance, frustrating employees endlessly, and sometimes completely stifling needed change, any of these errors could cause an organization to fail to achieve the change they hope for.

Table 2: Eight errors common to organizational change efforts and their consequences

Common Errors
• Allowing too much contentment and gratification • Failing to create the right team to guide the change process • Not giving vision its due importance – hence little direction • Not communicating with team members the change process • Allow obstacles to interfere the change program • Failing to develop short term wins to indentify with immediate results • Communicating an early victory • Failing to place change in the corporate culture

Consequences
• New strategies are not implemented according to expected design and level • Acquisition doesn't achieve expected synergies • Re-engineering process is not guided by time frame and cost • Rightsizing (downsizing) does not bring along expected savings • Quality programs fail to deliver expected results

Source: Kotter (1996: 16)

"These errors are not inevitable. With awareness and skill, they can be avoided or at least greatly mitigated. The key lies in understanding why organizations resist needed change, what can overcome destructive inertia, and, most of all, how the leadership that is required to drive that process in a socially healthy way means more than good management", as Kotter points out.

SUCCESSFUL CHANGE AND THE FORCES THAT DRIVE IT

Kotter reflects that people who have been through difficult, painful, and not very successful change efforts often end up drawing both pessimistic and angry conclusions. Suspicious of the motives of those pushing for transformation, they worry that major change is not possible without also creating huge upheaval. During change processes, bosses become monsters and many of the management appear to be incompetent. "After watching dozens of efforts to enhance organizational performance via restructuring reengineering, quality programs, mergers and acquisitions, cultural renewal, downsizing and strategic redirection, I draw a different conclusion," Kotter (1996: 17) surmises hopefully. Evidence suggests that most public and private organizations can be significantly improved, at an acceptable cost, "but often we make terrible mistakes when we try because history has simply not prepared us for transformational challenges," he considers.

THE GLOBALIZATION OF MARKETS AND COMPETITION

People of Kotter's generation (in their 50s and 60s) did not grow up in an era when transformation was common. With less global competition and a slower moving business environment, the norm back then was stability and the ruling motto was, as in the GE case: "If it ain't broke, don't fix it." As Kotter observed, change occurred incrementally and infrequently. If a typical group of managers in 1960 were told that business people today, over the course of eighteen to thirty-six months, would be trying to increase productivity by 20 to 50 per cent, improve quality by 30 to 100 percent, and reduce new-product development times by 30 to 80 percent, they would have laughed at you. "That magnitude of change in that short a period of time would have been too far removed from their personal experience to be credible," Kotter (1996: 18) suggests.

The challenges we now face in the early 21st century are different. A globalized economy is creating both more challenges, problems and more opportunities for everyone, forcing organizations to make dramatic improvements not only to compete and prosper but just to survive. The process of globalization is being driven by a broad and powerful set of forces associated with technological change, international economic integration, domestic market maturation within developed countries, and political developments such as self-determination, democratization, the diminution of communist type of societies and rise of free market forces.

No organization is immune to these forces, Kotter argues. Even companies that sell only in small geographic regions can feel the impact of globalization. The influence route is sometimes indirect, Kotter describes. Toyota beats GM, GM lays off employees, belt-tightening employees demand cheaper services from the corner dry cleaner and grocery store.

In a similar way, school systems, hospitals, charities and government agencies are being forced to try to improve. The problem is that most managers lack preparation and previous experience to guide them through all this. They need to learn how to implement positive change, using a multi-step process that creates power and motivation sufficient to overwhelm inertia. Secondly, they need strong leadership, not just excellent management. Kotter sees this as an important distinction.

THE EIGHT-STAGE CHANGE PROCESS

Kotter considers that the methods used in successful transformations are all based on the insight that major change will not happen easily. Even if an objective observer can clearly see that costs are too high, products are poor, customer requirements are not being met, the change process can still fail. This may be because of inward-looking cultures, bureaucracy, office politics, a lack of trust, no teamwork, arrogance and complacency, a lack of leadership in middle management, and the common human fear of the unknown.

Table 3: Eight step stage change process:

Establishing a sense of urgency
-> Examining the external market competitive reality
-> Identifying and discussing real as well as potential crisis in the market that will have an adverse effect on the organization.

Creating the guiding coalition
-> Ensuring that an effective team is developed in order to effect the necessary changes
-> Ensuring that there is enough team synergy within the appointed group – where all members are moving in the same direction, at the same speed and at the same time.

Developing a vision and strategy
-> Developing a correct vision which is understood by the respective members
-> Developing the correct and workable strategies to achieve the vision

Communicating the change vision
-> Actively communicatin at all times in order to ensure change
-> Having the guiding coalition role model the behavior expected of employees

Empowering broad based action
-> Ensuring the correct organizational changes to achieve the desired goals
-> Moving away from traditional 'conservatisim' to a more risk-taking approach

Generating short term wins
-> Planning and creating immediate wins to show commitment and results
-> Visibly recognizing and rewarding people who made the wins possible

Consolidating gains and producing more change
-> Using increased credibility to change all existing systems and procedures towards more effective management
-> Recruiting the right people who can actively support change
-> Re-invigorating the process with new projects, themes, and change agents

Anchoring new approaches in the culture
-> Anchoring the new results as part of the corporate culture (over time)
-> Achoring changes as part of the norms of success
-> Developing means to ensure leadership development succession

To be effective, a method designed to alter strategies, re-engineer processes or improve quality must tackle these barriers. The diagram lists and categorizes the strategy Kotter recommends, and illustrates the stages of the change process. The first four steps in the transformation process help to loosen up the system in an organization and prepare it for change. Phase five to seven then introduce many new practices. The last stage consolidates the changes in the corporate culture and helps to make them stick. Kotter observes that people under pressure to show results will often try to skip phases in a major change effort. They often try to transform organizations by undertaking only steps 5, 6, and 7, especially if it appears that a single decision – to reorganize, make an acquisition, or lay people off – will produce most of the needed changes. Alternatively, they race through each step without ever finishing the job. Or they fail to reinforce earlier stages as they move on, and as a result the sense of urgency dissipates or the guiding coalition breaks up. When any of the early stages are neglected, the organization cannot establish a solid enough base on which to proceed. And without the follow-through that takes place in the final step, it is difficult to make the changes last.

Kotter (1996: 23) argues that successful change of any magnitude goes through all eight stages. Although one normally operates in multiple phases at once, skipping even a single step or getting too far ahead without a solid base almost always creates problems. Normally, people skip steps because they are feeling pressures to produce. They may invent a new sequence or order of change (or they may take some steps as less important). Most major change initiatives are made up of a number of smaller projects that also tend to go through the multi-step process. So at any one time, you might be halfway through the overall effort, finished with a few of the smaller pieces, and just beginning other projects.

INITIATING AND MANAGING CHANGE

In terms of getting started on a change initiative, Eales-White (1996) differentiates between initiating change for ourselves, in ourselves, in others and through others:

- Initiating change for ourselves: This could be any change in our business or personal circumstances, where we are acting in a proactive way. Here, we try to find what we think will help us. In business terms, it could vary from deciding we want to change the nature of our work with our existing employer to deciding to change employers and look for a new job in a new organization.

- Initiating change in ourselves: We have identified a strength we want to develop or a weakness we want to overcome – we have climbed the learning ladder out of unconscious incompetence in some areas and want to progress.

- Initiating change in others: We want to persuade someone to change – to become different or do something different, as that will benefit us or that person, or both parties.

- Initiating change through others: This can occur when we are in reaction or initiation mode.

In terms of being in reaction mode in a change process, some business examples would include:

- The Managing Director of a subsidiary is given demanding profitability targets by the board of the parent company. Reaching the target will be up to others as well as to the MD, so the MD's reaction could be one of powerlessness and frustration.
- A new performance appraisal is being introduced, where there has been little or no consultation with section heads. Section heads will not only need to use the new instrument on subordinate managers, but also ensure that they carry it out throughout the company. They will have to perform effectively in carrying out appraisals of their subordinates.

THE FOUR PERSUASION APPROACHES

Eales-White suggests four approaches to persuasion as can be seen from the following:

Table 4 : The four persuasion approaches

I= incentives	L= logic	E= Empathy	G= Group
Incitement to action through the use of one or more of • Financial rewards • Non-financial rewards • Praise • Flattery • Threats (open and veiled) • Criticism	Correct or incorrect use of the intellectual faculty whereby conclusions are drawn through connecting facts (or opinions serving as facts) in a structured way	The power of entering into the feeling and spirit of another person and so appreciating her or him fully	The creation or use of a common understanding of a shared vision

Source: Eales-White (1996)

The use of **incentives** means we use the 'stick' and the 'carrot' to encourage desired behavior, to motivate people to perform. Sometimes, when we are supported by positional power, we try to persuade them to do what we think is best for them. When we praise or blame, we are in the incentive persuasion mode. If we are feeling insecure we shall often use the negative side to try to control others. If we are at a higher level of development, we shall use the positive side to encourage and support others. As is often the case, the way we say things will determine whether we are seen as using negative 'incentives' or rational 'logic.'

Logic is used to develop knowledge, decide rationally and, sometimes, to win arguments using the 'incorrect use of reasoning' or prejudicial approach.

With **Empathy**, we display good questioning and listening skills, and supporting body language. It is very powerful as we effectively communicate to other people the message that we care for them, we understand them and we know and appreciate their point of view. We are explicitly acknowledging their value and importance as human beings and individuals. Most people respond to such an approach. Sometimes, when using the empathy persuasion mode, we may be seen as manipulative (exposing others and not ourselves) or non-assertive falling over to please.

A **Group** persuasion mode uses vision and ideas, trying to generate or develop a group or team spirit. The approach can be used at any level – international, national, company and team – and can be very powerful as we all have our dreams and can be inspired by the visionary.

ASSESSING YOUR OWN PERSUASION MODE

In the following table, you are asked to consider the points out of 20 which you would allocate to each persuasion approach. This numbered system helps you to differentiate between strong, moderate or weak use of a particular approach when making your decision about yourself. If you ask your colleague to complete the questionnaire about you, he or she may be able to produce an accurate profile of his or her perception. When interpreting the results, a gap of a few points between you and your colleague is not significant, and so your approximation does not matter.

Table 5 : Assessing your persuasion mode

Development level	Classification	Approach	Result	Duration
Security and self-esteem	'Strong leader'	'Inspire and control'	Do with commitment but without understanding	Until retirement or removal of leader
Growth	'Questioning coach'	'Involve and explore'	Do with commitment and understanding	Permanent

Source: Eales-White (1996)

Thus, the ways of persuading vary according to the developmental stage of the company, and the behavior of the leader and their approach. The results vary, and so does the duration of this leader. The way we persuade people to make the change we want them to make can differ according to the level of the relationship, the nature of the relationship, and the specific situation.

Think of a specific individual you know. Think of your relationship with that person, and cast your mind back to specific situations where you have tried to persuade him or her to do something. Having reflected on that, estimate the extent to which you deployed each approach. Before looking at the connection between persuasion and change preference and at initiating change for ourselves, it is worth considering the levels of commitment to change we generate according to how we persuade someone to do something.

'Stern parent': The lowest level of commitment generated is what Eales-White calls 'stern parent.' We know the questions and we know the answers. It is up to our followers to do what we tell them to do. Because of the positional power we hold, we shall be obeyed. There can be subtlety in the way we use this approach, often not at the conscious level, as we have absorbed and automatically use the political and language skills that reflect the norms of behavior appropriate to our organizational culture. Many gurus see parent-child relationships at the heart of many western company cultures, a reality exacerbated by the recession and the need to fight for survival. It is a historic approach that is changing as the father-dominated family unit, from whence it comes, is disappearing. It can be very effective, especially in the sort run. However, as suggested previously, it may be less effective in the long run and has two fundamental drawbacks:

1. It is not very efficient. If the followers have a high need for security, they will respond but their heart won't be behind their actions, there will not be full commitment, and they won't fully understand what they are doing. If the followers are operating at higher development levels, then the response is often 'word only' and they proceed to do their own thing.

The leader finds, much to his or her annoyance, that the things that should be done are not done or are done badly. This creates a vicious circle of misconception, combined with a leader who is checking and chasing, forced to have too much of a hands-on implementation role, rather than a hands-off strategic role.

2. It is not very effective. With different roles and responsibilities appropriate to different jobs and different levels, the goals and targets need to be different. As we have discovered with the issue of change as a whole, a unidirectional approach is not appropriate. The 'stern parent' tries to force the troops, whether a small team or a whole company, to implement his or her answers. That will be ineffective.

'Strong leader': Eales-White calls the next level of commitment 'strong leader', building on 'stern parent' and adding creative and visioning skills. The 'strong leader' is the current and historic model of good leadership. We are capable of being inspired for good or ill by a strong visionary leader. History, both national and corporate, is strewn with examples of strong visionary leaders who have inspired, controlled and moved mountains. Our self-esteem is developed by identifying with the leader sharing his or her vision and values and being part of the implementation of the vision. It can be very dangerous. From the perspective of managing change, it cannot be successful in the long term, because the vision dies with the leader, and because it is unidirectional. The leader tries to define the future, while this cannot be defined in a world of change. The fundamental difference between the 'stern parent' and the 'strong leader' is that the latter can achieve what the former wants to achieve but cannot. As regards the commitment of the follower, that is given. But full understanding cannot be assumed. We can follow our own dreams better than those of someone else, even if we have borrowed them for a while. See also Nadler and Tushman (1990).

'**Questioning coach**': The deepest level of commitment is that generated by the 'questioning coach.' His or her approaches are a mixture of logic, empathy and group orientation, with few incentives. It is not an individual approach, as there is a strong team dimension. If our leader has provided us with an environment where we can explore and share, where we can create and support, where we can take risks without fear of ridicule, knowing there is a soft landing if we fall, then we can dream that we can make a reality, and be relentless in pursuit of their achievement. We shall be committed to action and shall fully understand what to do, how to do it and why we are doing it. However – and there is always a 'however' – this entire vision is predicated on both ourselves and our leader being capable of operating for sustained periods of time at growth level. This may remain a dream.

A critical concern for leaders initiating change is the environment in which individuals operate. The more we can create an environment that is positive to change, the more growth will be obtained from change. We can easily underestimate the power we have in creating the right environment, simply because we do not proactively think of the environment as a strategic tool at our disposal. If we encourage explicitly certain types of behavior, then they will take place.

CHANGING THE DIMENSIONS

Eales-White considers that by using a thoughtful, planned approach to initiating change, we are managing the dimensions of the relevant variable for growth:
1 Phasing in gradually
2 Explicitly managing our own expectations and those of others
3 Reducing the significance, by breaking the change down into its component parts
4 Providing time so that the change will not be sudden
5 Moving towards a higher development level to increase the probability of growth
6 Promoting discovery, so that when the change occurs, it will connect both to the present and to the past
7 Managing perceptions for ourselves and others to ensure that the change is perceived positively

CLOSING CASE

The task of reducing costs and running a more cost-effective organization, part of the change process for a Chinese company, gives us an idea of some of the problems associated with the management of the change process. After substantial investment in the 1990s, the day of reckoning is fast-approaching for many foreign enterprises in China, with headquarters-based executives asking tougher and tougher questions. When is our China operation going to start making money? If this is still some way off – as it is in the majority of cases – then can costs be contained or reduced? For some, the trail of red ink has already led to closure or the selling of businesses – but before it gets that far, showing that costs are at least under control is important.

Chinese staff members fear that cost-cutting may lead to cut-backs in training and cause reduced salaries, benefits and bonuses. Many are young and inexperienced, have only seen a fast-growing environment and often lack the maturity to cope with a down-turn in business and staying motivated nevertheless. Some local staff members are intimidated and even frightened by the onset of cost-cutting measures in a company – is the organization about to go bust? Will we lose our job? Even if we survive this downturn, might things get worse in the future?

Rocks and grains of sand: Some savings will be large, some will be small, but they can all add up. "It's a question of rocks and grains of sand," explained the General Manager (GM) of an Australian resources company in Beijing. "It all helps to achieve the result. The 'rocks' are the big savings, like moving your office to a cheaper office tower, or at least substantially renegotiating the rent. The grains of sand are like sending the ayi (cleaning lady) out to buy cleaning materials and stationery items in local shops, which can make a small saving. Related examples include asking the drivers to wash the cars rather than using the car wash, and using both sides of pieces of paper."

Taking control of the budget: It comes down to a question of empowerment. For example, if all department heads have budgetary control for their own department, and they are informed about current costs and given a target for possible reduction – especially when invited to suggest what kind of reduction they think they could make – then significant results can be achieved. This empowerment can also have greater implications across the board in the organization, in terms of achieving sales targets, production quality, accounts receivables collections and other performance indicators.

Centralizing for a better deal: It sounds contradictory to the concept, outlined above, of empowering department heads to make their own purchasing, to then suggest that you should centralize to get a better deal. An ideal scenario may be to empower people to see how they can reduce costs in a certain area, and then compare these to the costs that might be obtained centrally through bulk-purchase.

Take outsourced travel and accommodation services, for example. An enterprising sales manager – whose staff travel extensively and stay in hotels a great deal – may have developed good *guanxi* (or connections) with particular hotels and is already getting a good rate. In considering the whole company, though, could an even better rate be obtained if everyone stayed there, from all departments? The sales manager may then find himself getting an even better deal by discussing his current cost-saving arrangements with the administration department, and meanwhile the administration department can benefit from the shared knowledge.

One of the results of a Shanghai cost-saving seminar was an initiative from the British Chamber of Commerce to set up a travel privilege scheme, negotiating with several airlines to secure substantial airline discounts for members. This in effect offers a centralized purchasing opportunity for all British companies not just in China but throughout Asia Pacific. Basically, when negotiating for a better deal, the general principle is that the more you are buying, the cheaper the unit cost.

This worked just as well in negotiating with FESCO (the government staffing agency for foreign companies) and other staff-employing bodies, as it did with airlines. In this context, non-competing companies sharing the same building could decide to pool resources, as long as everyone could agree (see above).

Focus on saving rather than spending: It is a question of attitude. According to one of the Shanghai seminar participants, "staff members in China often make an assumption that foreign companies have an endless supply of cash to pump into their China operations. The more money frittered away on extravagances – such as hiring a specialized company for watering the plants in the office when the ayi could do it, the more some of these staff have a sort of misplaced pride that their company is so apparently wealthy."

"Some of them brag that their GM's courtyard house costs US $12,000 per month to rent. Also, they'll mention how the GM takes the car and driver just to cross the road to go to his club (which costs US $15,000 to be a member) which he visits only a few times a year. But this pride can be redirected to making economies. It is important to make clear what the rewarded behaviors are in the company."

One of the challenges here is that many Chinese staff members can have a misplaced pride in extravagance. Ordering hugely expensive banquet meals and not eating them and wasting most of the food are seen as fashionable. They often have a high regard for someone who is that conspicuously wealthy. So there is an important need for mindset change before people can be brought on board to support cost-saving initiatives. Leadership from the front will be very important.

Giving directions: To make cost-savings work, the manager in charge must give clear directions, setting the main objectives, making ball-park estimates of cost-savings which could be possible, and emphasizing the need for practicality and legality in these savings.

Within this structure, creative thinking should be encouraged. When staff members have made successful savings and everyone is sharing the benefits, then it's important to publicize the results. If the culture which created and celebrates 'salesman of the month' can be spread to 'saver of the month,' this can help in the process of recognition and encourage others to aspire to this accolade.

Examples of cost-saving initiatives: Staff members who have been successfully empowered to be cost-conscious (by whatever way) will then take it upon themselves to make cost-saving initiatives. For example, it usually falls upon the manager of the company to start the process of approaching the landlord of the office building to try to negotiate a better deal. But companies which have created a 'have a go' economizing regime find that senior staff, of their own initiative, will bargain directly to gain a substantial reduction in the rent, even in mid-lease.

Savvy staff members know better than their expatriate bosses about what is possible within current market conditions, and will not hesitate to call the bluff of landlords to see what they can get. The landlords may realize that, knowing how much the company has invested in furniture and fittings, they may not actually carry out their threat of leaving. But they can't be entirely sure. This way, rentals have been reduced by up to one-half, due to timely and informed negotiating .

Another example of a 'rock' rather than a 'grain of sand' type of saving is in the area of telecommunications costs. In one example, the company's MIS people implemented a scheme using the Internet for all phone calls and faxes, effecting a 40% reduction on telecoms outlay. An increased emphasis on sending e-mails rather than making telephone calls or sending faxes has been an effective area for saving by many companies, although of course it cannot be used all the time. The gradual and piecemeal opening-up of the China telecoms market is now offering opportunities to the cost-conscious. Using stored-value telecoms cards is one instance.

Costs run out of control when people simply just don't know how much things cost. One of the most common examples of this is the use of mobile telephones, especially long-distance. Frequent traffic jams and business trips – when users are away from land-lines – leads to indiscriminate usage. One manager found that publication of the mobile phone bills list, with each person's name next to their bill total (including his own) was a sobering experience. "People did not have to be told to reduce their bills. It then became a competition to be economical, particularly in making the other party become the caller by leaving messages for them when they were known to be unavailable."

This involves a significant mindset change for staff – having a mobile telephone was seen as a sign of status and power – the badge of "big brother." The well-known high level of expense in using a mobile telephone was part of the prestige of having one. Now, companies are asking people to reduce their mobile telephone expenses – the strategy outlined above, of encouraging a competitive, clever and smart use of mobile telephony – is one way of achieving this mindset shift.

CASE QUESTIONS:
- *Do you agree that cost-saving can be an important part of a change process?*
- *What might be the disadvantages of too much emphasis on cost reduction?*
- *Which cultural factors can be seen as an important issue here in making this initiative work?*
- *How can mindsets be turned around from "spend, spend, spend" to "save, save, save?"*
- *How can fears be abated and motivation levels maintained in this part of a change process?*
- *Which kinds of expenses impact on foreign managers in China which they may not have to face at home?*
- *How long do you think a company should go on investing before they see a return?*
- *Is the China market a special case?*

CONCLUSION

In this chapter, focusing on the process of change, we have looked in detail at several approaches to corporate transformation. Kotter's eight mistakes in change initiatives is well-known and essential reading for all students of change management, so there is a strong emphasis on this approach here. What drives change? What is the impact of competition and globalization? What are the stages we need to go through to successfully achieve change? We have also looked in detail at Eales-White's approach to initiating change, including techniques of persuasion and incentives. The roles of 'stern parent', 'strong leader' and 'questioning coach' are examined in terms of their impact on a successful change process. Eales-White's step-by-step checklist presents useful guidelines for handling change. The two cases, a continuation of the GE case and some of the processes used there, and the discussion on cost-saving attempts by foreign companies in China, show the diversity of approaches needed when taking on a change program.

REFERENCES

Beer M., Eisenstat R.A., and Spector B. 1990. Why change programs don't produce change. *Harvard Business Review. 68* (6): 158-66.

Eales-White, Rupert 1996. *Creating Growth from Change*. London: McGraw Hill

Goldstein J. 1988. A far-from-equilibrium systems approach to resistance to change. *Organizational Dynamics*. 16-26.

Jones Stephanie. 1999. *Cutting costs and incentivising staff – the route to profitability*. China Staff. September 1999

Kotter John P. 1995. Why Transformation Efforts Fail. *Harvard Business Review*. March.

Kotter John P. 1996. *Leading Change*. Boston: Harvard Business School Press

Krüger W. 1996. Implementation: the core task of change management *CEMS Business Review. 1*: 77-96.

Lawrence P.R. 1954. How to deal with resistance to change. *Harvard Business Review*. 49-57.

Maurer R. 1996. Using resistance to build support for change. *The Journal for Quality and Participation. 19* (3): 56-66.

Nadler D.A. Tushman M.L. 1990. Beyond the charismatic leader: leadership and organizational change. *California Management Review. 32* (2): 77-97.

Piderit S.K. 2000. Rethinking resistance and recognizing ambivalence: a multidimensional view of attitudes toward an organizational change. *Academy of Management Review. 25* (4): 783-94

Reichers A.E. Wanous J.P. Austin J.T. 1997. Understanding and managing cynicism about organizational change. *Academy of Management Executive. 11* (1): 48-59

Welch J. 2005. Speaker Series September 18 2002. Available from: http://mba.tuck.dartmouth.edu/cgl/downloads/JackWelch.pdf [Accessed 13 November 2006]

Welch J. 2005. *Winning* New York: HarperCollins

Welch J. 2006. Press release book tour stop February 09 2006. Available from: http://www.24-7pressrelease.com/pdf/2006/02/09/press_release_10871.pl

RECOMMENDED FURTHER READING

Ansoff I.H. 1990. *Implanting Strategic Management* London: Prentice Hall

Boeker W. 1997. Strategic change: the influence of managerial characteristics and organizational growth. *Academy of Management Journal. 40* (1): 152-70

Ghoshal S. and Bartlett C.A. 1996. Rebuilding behavioral context: a blueprint for corporate renewal. *Sloan Management Review. 37* (2): 23-36

Hannan M.T. and Freeman J. 1984. Structural inertia and organizational change. *American Sociological Review. 49* 149-64

Hutt M.D. Walker, B.A. and Frankwick G.L. 1995. Hurdle the cross-functional barriers to strategic change. *Sloan Management Review. 36* (3): 22-30

Kanter R.M. 1989. The new managerial work. *Harvard Business Review. 67* (6): 85-92

Leana C.R. and Barry B. 2000. Stability and change as simultaneous experiences in organizational life. *Academy of Management Review. 25* (4): 753-9

Levy A. 1986. Second-order planned change: definition and conceptualization. *Organizational Dynamics.* 5-20.

Morrison E.W. and Milliken F.J. 2000. Organizational silence: a barrier to change and development in a pluralistic world. *Academy of Management Review. 25* (4): 706-25

Nadler D.A. and Tushman M.L. 1989. Organizational frame bending: principles for managing reorientation. *Academy of Management Executive. 3*, 194-204

Schalk R., Campbell J.W. and Freese C. 1998. Change and employee behaviour. *Leadership & Organization Development Journal. 19* (3): 157-63

Strebel P. 1994. Choosing the right change path. *California Management Review. 3* (6): 2 29-51

Van de Ven A.H. and Poole M.S. 1995. Explaining development and change in organizations. *Academy of Management Review. 20* (3) 510-40

Waddell D. and Sohal A.S. 1998. Resistance: a constructive tool for change management. *Management Decision. 36* (8) 543-8

Zaltman G. and Duncan R. 1977. *Strategies for Planned Change.* Toronto: Wiley

CHAPTER NINE
MANAGING CHANGE
SILVIO DE BONO AND STEPHANIE JONES

OPENING CASE: GENERAL ELECTRIC (GE) (PART THREE)

How did GE achieve such radical change? It was partly due to the creation of a new culture for the firm. As it was such a large company, this culture change process was several years in the making. From being a slow and ponderous dinosaur, bureaucratic and inflexible, GE was gradually forced to espouse new business characteristics: leanness, agility, creativity, and distribution of ownership and rewards to larger numbers of employees. It also emphasized individual characteristics, having a sense of reality, offering strong leadership, openness and transparency, simplicity in its approach, integrity in all its business dealings, and supporting individual dignity in the way all people were treated. Inevitably, some areas of culture change were more successful than others. Several are still in process, as old habits die hard.

How was the culture change achieved? What were some of the techniques and approaches used by Welch to break down the old order? One was creating 'The Harvard of Corporate America', a business school within GE which became a melting pot of new ideas and a testing-ground for new targets and objectives. Everyone, from Welch downwards, had to defend their ground amidst rigorous debate at Crotonville. The concept of 'Workout' was also typical of Welch – everyone stretched themselves to the limits and felt the burn. 'Boundaryless' was a concept referring to a lack of distinctions between departments and units, between producers and customers, all part of the Welch initiative to eradicate bureaucracy and stifling management layers.

Meanwhile, 'Best Practices' were documented and emulated around the firm. These included the 'Grocery Store' concept which supported 'Just in Time' (JIT) or minimal inventory, a radical concept for a large business. GE tried very hard to be a 'Learning Organization' – the concept was new then, and was meant to aid the organization in achieving CAP – or the Change Acceleration Process. For a while, Welch saw quality initiatives as gimmicky, but once he bought into 'Six Sigma', he really believed in it. GE was not first in the field here, but they were willing to learn from others, especially Motorola. In GE, as in many other businesses, there was nothing new in their change initiatives , but they got on with the need for strong execution. GE's real change was in the doing, not in the thinking.

GE ACHIEVEMENTS, 1981-2001

The measurement of GE's transformation can be seen in the focus on specific measures:
- Sales Per Employee
  - 1981:   US$ 69,059 - 2001: US$ 382,352

- Market Capitalization
  - 1981:   US$ 13 billion   - 2001: US$ 500 billion

- Revenues
  - 1981:   US$ 28 billion   - 2001: US$ 130 billion

- Most Profitable Unit
  - 1981:   Consumer Products (TVs, Appliances, Lighting)
  - 2001:   Financial Services (Mortgages, Investments)

Welch was interested in numbers. All managers had to come to him armed with ambitious targets, and if they failed to make these, life was tough. This, he felt, was the only way to measure real change. Everything else was impressionistic or illusory. Numbers were solid and were the language of analysts and investors.

Graph 1: GE performance, 1980-1997

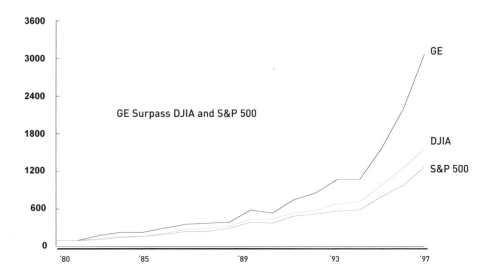

The lower, horizontal axis records the time period, of 1980 to 1997. The lines indicate what an investor can achieve in terms of growth from a US $ 100 investment. The dark line above the others indicates GE's performance, in which $ 100 could be turned into $ 3,315 in this 17 year period. The slightly lower line represents the Dow Jones Industrial Average, whereby $ 100 could be grown to $ 1,555 over the same time period. The lowest line below represents the Standard & Poor 500 average, of $ 1,300. This achievement was relevant for employees as well as for shareholders, as during this time Welch substantially increased the proportion of employees owning company stock.

LESSONS FOR CHANGE FROM THE GE CULTURE CHANGE CASE INCLUDE:

1   Put the right people in the right jobs
2   Come up with key ideas and push, push, push them until they become reality
3   Hate bureaucracy
4   Talk straight... and expect others to do the same
5   Do deals, launch initiatives...... act, act, act and don't look back
6   Always make your numbers

GE was voted the world's most admired company to work for... consecutively for five years; the World's Most Respected Company – by the *Financial Times* (1999, 2000, 2001, 2002, 2003); The *Scientific American* 50 Award (2002); the Global Most Admired Company – *Fortune* magazine (1999, 2000, 2001, 2002); the 10 Best Board of Directors — *Business Week* (2002); Sixth in the *Fortune 500*. If ranked independently, 13 GE businesses would appear on the *Fortune 500*. Finally, GE also won Best Overall Investor Relations - *Investor Relations* magazine (US Awards 2002). These accolades were an important way of measuring and providing evidence of GE's success.

Internally, Welch led many initiatives to help ensure that change would happen. The stock options provided to employees, with their impressive growth trajectory, were seen as especially attractive. The levels between the CEO and the Shop Floor were reduced from nine to a range of four to six. Whilst most companies generally believe in defend first, attack if necessary, GE in this period clearly believed "attack first, defend if necessary." The effective integration of functions and 'Accelerating Change' had their impact. Uncompromising support by the best of the best was another Welch slogan, together with the need to experience flexibility from one corner to another and the argument that size does matter! This concludes the GE case study described in these three chapters.

CASE QUESTIONS:
* *How did GE achieve the changes made in the two decades?*
* *What would you define as the three most important factors?*
* *Why was it so important to please shareholders and investors during these twenty years? Are there other factors we might consider now?*
* *Discuss the elements of the GE culture change – which were the easiest, and the most difficult, to achieve?*
* *Why did Welch choose these particular measures to produce evidence of the GE transformation?*
* *Which other measures might he have considered?*
* *For GE, why did size matter?*
* *To what extent was the GE transformation due to Welch's particular brand of leadership?*

LEARNING OBJECTIVES:

This chapter, 'Managing Change,' the third of our three chapters on the vital subject of change, aims to help you:
* To appreciate the best approaches of how to implement change;
* To acknowledge the existence and relevance of different Change Management Interventions

- To appreciate the role of change agents in managing change

In the process, this chapter will attempt to introduce you to the issues of:
- The implementation of change
- Management's role in ensuring change
- Possible change management interventions
- The organization of the future

THE IMPLEMENTATION OF CHANGE

A change management process critically includes the implementation of change. This can be the 'make or break time' for any change process. It is very clear that some (perhaps many) change management programs fail at the implementation stage. Kotter and Schlesinger (1979) argue that successful change strategies are those that are internally consistent, aligned with corporate values and objectives, and are compatible with key situational variables. In practical terms, you can often notice that change implementation does not follow any 'hard and fast' rules and consequently, different change agents may vary their approaches at different stages of the change process.

Hayes (2002) points out that there are six situational variables which are to be taken into account when implementing change:

1   The urgency of the need for change and stakes involved;
2   The clarity of viewpoint and understanding of the desired future state;
3   The extent and type of resistance that is anticipated;
4   The extent to which change managers have the required data to hand for designing and implementing the change;
5   The degree to which other stakeholders trust the change managers;
6   The degree to which the change managers have to rely on the commitment and energy of others to implement the plan.

It is very important to note that in most cases, change agents/managers adopt more than one approch. In overcoming this challenge, Hayes (2002) recommends a continuum intervention model as described in the figure shown below:

Table 1 : Abstract of continuum of intervention strategies. Hayes (2002:162)

DIRECTIVE	COLLABORATIVE

• Urgent required Change	• Non- Urgent required Change
• Desired and state clearly specified from the start	• Problem/opportunity recognised
• Little resistance anticipated	• Great resistance anticipated
• Change Agents have access to all information	• Change Agents need information from others
• Others have high trust in Change Agents	• Others have low trust in Change Agents
• Change Agents do not have to rely on others.	• Change Agents rely on others' commitment

155

The above figure shows the extreme varieties of interventions, from the most extreme directive changes to the more collaborative, involvement-promoting changes. In this light several other authors in the field, including Bologun and Hailey (1999) clearly point out that as a result, the change strategy may need to change over time. There are other factors at work, too. Zaltman and Duncan (1977) cite complexity, communicability and compatibility, relative advantage and divisibility as factors that might influence the way change agents attempt to influence others.

Hayes (2002) defined complexity and communicability as the key ingredients in ensuring that all stakeholders are on the same platform. Similarly a change that is compatible with the change target preferences and that offers relative advantage over current practice might lend itself to a persuasive strategy (Hayes. 2002). In addition where the change is divisible and where quick action is required, it might be decided to direct a part of the organization to adopt a small scale trial of the change implementation before making a decision about how to proceed.

EXERCISE: Consider a change process in which you have been involved and think about, firstly, the six situational variables outlined above. Which was most important for this organization undergoing change? Which played the biggest part in the successful implementation program? Which was neglected, and with what consequences? Then look at the continuum shown above. Was this change process directive or collaborative? What were the advantages and disadvantages of the approach adopted in this particular case? What would you recommend in a change process in which you might be involved in the future?

MANAGEMENT'S ROLE IN ENSURING SUCCESSFUL CHANGE

In view of the fact that there are no 'hard-and-fast rules' on how to adopt and implement change, several theoreticians in this field including Beckhard and Harris (1987) and Nadler (1993) have expressed different methods of adaptation to a new state of change. By looking into this literature review of change management, Hayes (2002) came up with six points which we have adapted into a flow diagram for ease of reference (see the Figure below).

In the first instance, management's role is specifically to provide a clear sense of direction to the rest of the team. This requires a high degree of leadership and communication skills. In this phase it is also imperative to set a clear vision of the future state – showing that there is a journey from the present state to the future state.

In the second instance, in order to ensure that any change program is a success, a transition manager needs to be appointed. He/she should be given the necessary power and authority to make all relatively important decisions. Through good communication, the transition manager, often referred to as the change agent, must lead the team to the desired destination.

Diagram 1: Adaptation of Hayes (2002) summary of management's role in successful change (Hayes 2002: 162, 166-171)

In the third instance, the transition plan should be clear and well communicated to all members of the team. Beckard and Harris (1987) identified seven characteristics of effective transition plans, namely:

1 Purposeful *(clear purpose of the change program)*;
2 Task-specific *(clear identifiable goals)*;
3 Integrated *(one phase leads to the other)*;
4 Adaptable *(adapting to anticipated changes)*;
5 Agreed by the top management and all staff *(shared agreement)*; and
6 Cost effective *(avoiding unnecessary waste)*.

Fourthly, the resources for the transition need to be sourced and brought together, which may take a substantial investment. By multiple and consistent leverage points for change, the process must be carried out simultaneously and in a clear and similar way. Finally, feedback mechanisms must be in place so that all involved in the change process understand what is going on and the progress they are making.

As already mentioned in previous chapters, providing the necessary resources is an essential element in the change management process. To this extent, the next phase would require the project management team to provide the necessary technical, financial and human resources to effect the necessary change. Unless these resources are adequately provided the change management program may remain ineffective.

In any change program it is also essential to ensure that all stakeholders are adequately motivated and committed to the change program. Unless people within the team are motivated, the overall result will not be optimal. Finally, it is also essential to use multiple and consistent leverage points for change. In doing so, it is essential that all components of the change program are consistently re-aligned towards the same direction. Every member of the team should not only be playing the same music but with the same tempo and style.

In meeting this task of implementing change, **the change agent or transition manager** may be advised to develop and exhibit a special series of personal competencies (abilities, skills, knowledge, motivation), which we have summarized below. The details of these recommended competencies were developed as a result of our direct experiences in change management programs in different regions, especially Europe, the Middle East and Asia. The ranking and extent of these competencies may vary by person, by the needs of the change management project itself, as well as in different countries and environments.

CHANGE MANAGEMENT COMPETENCIES REQUIRED BY THE CHANGE AGENT:

- Risk-taking
- Entrepreneurial and innovative
- Tough – in hiring and firing
- Inspirational, with charisma, leadership-oriented
- Thick-skinned – not over-sensitive
- Short-term success-oriented, project-based, change-leading
- Pushy, aggressive
- Strong impact and influence skills
- Honest and direct to the point of bluntness
- Uncompromising, revolutionary
- Savvy, street-smart, even cynical
- Maverick, unconventional

We have also noticed that in certain instances, once the change project has been completed or is on the verge of completion, a consolidator needs to be appointed. The role of this person is based on the idea of leading the team and the project to the final phase or to new directions. The Consolidator builds on what has been achieved by the Change Agent and puts it in the right framework at the right time. The changes are more likely to be sustained and accepted with the help of a qualified and competent Consolidator. The competencies required by the Consolidator may vary from those of the change agent, as shown below:

CHANGE MANAGEMENT COMPETENCIES REQUIRED BY THE CONSOLIDATOR

- Prudent, careful
- Committed to the company for the long-term
- Reasonable, perceptive, team-building
- Focused on managing resources effectively
- Sensitive, caring
- Long-term oriented, focused on steady and secure growth
- Assertive, not passive, but not so aggressive
- More discreet and subtle impact and influencing skills
- Diplomatic, culturally aware, able to play politics

- Flexible according to the needs of the business
- Focused on believing in the company, loyal, supporting company policy
- Fitting in with company culture
- Is respectful of the 'face' of another person

EXERCISE: do you see yourself as a change agent or as a consolidator? Consider these competencies and assess your own personality. Ask a close associate to reflect on his or her knowledge of you and your behavior. Then reverse the process and give the other person feedback on their perceived competencies. Emphasize the advantages and need for both in a change situation.

How can we describe **the characteristics of a change management program** in a clear and consistent way? These can influence the way an individual or an organization will react to the outcome of the change process. These characteristics can be seen as:

1 **Environment** - The environment may be defined as the context in which change occurs. In this sense the environment can be described as either stable, or one in which change has become the norm.

2 **Continuity** – A change can connect or not connect to the present and the past. It can represent a discontinuity. If it does, change is more difficult to manage since the individual or organization finds difficulty in reconciling the change event with their existing model of reality.

3 **Phasing** – How the change is phased in is also an important factor. It is generally held true that if change is phased in gradually, it is more successful than if it is suddenly implemented.

4 **Frequency** – A change can be a single discreet event or can be regularly repeated.

5 **Duration** – The actual change event can take a second or several years, and last for a short or long time. A sudden event can have permanent (positive or negative) impact. On the other hand, a change process, such as a new project for a company or change to a new job for an individual, can last much longer from beginning to end and have much less impact.

6 **Initiator** – This is one of the key factors in a successful change project. If the individual who initiates change, the change agent, is effective and credible, this can make a big difference. When initiating change for others, he or she should always try to manage perceptions in a conscious and structured strategic process.

7 **Perception** – How the individuals in a company perceive change is also very important. If he or she has been consulted and involved in the decision, then an individual tends to be more comfortable with the change than if it is imposed or announced as a 'fait accompli.' This is probably the single most important point when considering change management at any level within an organization.

8 **Expectation** – Expectations and the management of expectations are the key to successful change management. In fact, perception, expectation, continuity and phasing are closely linked factors in change. Change that is suddenly presented will represent discontinuity, if the event is unexpected.

9 **Impact** – This factor is different in nature to the others. The others are all casual factors that will determine the impact of the change event on the individual or organization. The impact can be shallow or deep, temporary or permanent or, like all other factors, somewhere in between.

CHANGE MANAGEMENT INTERVENTIONS

Change is created in an organization by making interventions – intervening in the situation in some specific way to create a new way of operating and thinking. Theoretically speaking, it can be argued that there are four main management interventions which can be considered when implementing change, namely:

*   *Human Process Interventions;*

*   *Techno-Structural Interventions;*

*   *Human Resource Management Interventions; and*

*   *Strategic Interventions*

These are explained in more detail below.

These interventions are generally applied in many management change programs at different times and for different reasons. All four interventions can be equally important depending on the circumstances.

HUMAN PROCESS INTERVENTIONS

Cummings and Worley (2001) explain that human process interventions are those activities which are carried out at a personal level, and which have a strong influence on the overall success of the change management project. The most basic human process interventions are T-Groups which "are designed to provide members with experiential learning about group dynamics, leadership and interpersonal relations" (Cummings & Worley. 2001: 216). Campbell and Dunnette (1968) listed six overall objectives or advantages which are common to most **T-Groups**:

*   Increased understanding, insight and awareness about own behavior;
*   Increased understanding of sensitivity about the behavior of others;
*   Better understanding and awareness of the group;

- Increased diagnostic skills in interpersonal and group situations;
- Increased ability to transform learning into action;
- Improvement in individuals' ability to analyze their own interpersonal behavior.

The other notable human intervention is Process Consulting, which "is a general framework for carrying out helping relationships", according to Cummings and Worley (2001: 219). In general terms this process looks into the overall processes of the department and the organization and tries to identify different ways and means of how to improve the overall processes. Schein (1998: 20) defines process consultation as "the creation of a relationship that permits the client to perceive, understand, and act on the process events that occur in (his/her) internal and external environment in order to improve the situation as defined by the client."

Basic Process Interventions can vary from Individual Interventions to Group Interventions. The former is designed to help people to be more effective or to increase the information they have about what they do not know about themselves. On the other hand, at the Group Level, these interventions are generally aimed at the process, content or structure of the group. Cummings and Worley (2001: 224) state that "process interventions sensitize the group to its own internal processes and generate interest in analyzing those processes. Interventions include comments, questions or observations." These observations concern relationships between group members, problem solving and decision-making as well as identifying and establishing the purpose of the group.

Third party interventions focus on conflicts arising between two or more people within the same organization. However, contrary to what many people may think, Third Party Interventions may not necessarily solve all interpersonal conflicts within the organization. As a result, the major advantage of Third Party Interventions is that it helps parties interact directly with each either, thus facilitating their diagnosis of the conflict and how to resolve it. The last Human Process Intervention is **Team Building**, which refers to a broad range of planned activities that help groups improve the way they accomplish tasks and help group members enhance their interpersonal and problem solving skills Cummings and Worley (2001).

TECHNO-STRUCTURAL INTERVENTIONS

Of all the different change management interventions, Techno-Structural Intervention is probably an area which provokes diverse opinions. Techno-Structural intervention describes the overall required changes in the organizational design. It involves changes in technological and structural dynamics. Unless well-managed, techno-structural change usually creates conflict between different organization members. Although there are different organizational designs, Techno-Structural Interventions usually consider a common platform when bringing about the required techno-structural change. In downsizing instances, the change agent must ensure that all members within the organization are not only adequately informed, but the eventual choice of people to lay-off from the organization is handled professionally, ethically and conscientiously.

Table 2 : Downsizing tactics. Cameron, Freeman and Mishra (1991: 62)

Downsizing Tactic	Characteristics	Examples
Workforce reduction	Aimed at headcount reduction with short term implementation. Fosters a transition rather than a transformation	• Attrition • Transfer and outplacement • Retirement incentives • Buyout packages • Layoffs
Organization re-design	Aimed at organizational change with moderate term implementation. Fosters transition and potentially transformation	• Eliminate functions • Merge units • Eliminate layers • Eliminate products • Re-design tasks
Systemic design	Aimed at culture change with longer-term implementation and fosters transformation	• Change responsibility • Involve all constituents • Fosters continuous improvement and innovation • Simplification • Downsizing a way of life.

In addition to downsizing, Techno-Structural Changes also include **re-engineering**, which can be described as being the fundamental re-thinking and radical re-design of business processes to achieve dramatic improvements in performance (Hammer & Champy. 1993).

It begins with defining the scope and objectives of your re-engineering project, then going through a learning process (with your customers, your employees, your competitors and non-competitors, and with new technology). Given this knowledge base, you can create a vision for the future and design new business processes. Given the definition of the proposed state, you can then create a plan of action based on the gap between your current processes, technologies and structures, and where you want to go. It is then a matter of implementing your solution.

Over time many derivatives of radical, breakthrough improvement and of continuous improvement have emerged that attempt to address the difficulties of implementing major change in corporations. It is difficult to find a single approach exactly matched to a particular company's needs, and the challenge is to know what method to use when, and how to pull it off successfully such that bottom-line business results are achieved.

Eales-White (1994) defines Business Process Re-engineering (BPR) as using a rigorous and disciplined methodology to identify the current state, determine the optimum future state, and design an implementation plan. Too often, however, this methodology ignores these human resistance issues and the need to address them in the implementation plan. When that happens, people who are targets of the change end up expending the majority of their time and energy figuring out how to stop the change, or change it until it looks like something they can live with, not what the engineers developed. This is how re-engineering fails. What can we do about this problem? If we are thoughtful and listen well, the targets of the change will tell us what to do.

The process steps are the activities that you and the personnel do to complete the transaction. In this simple example, we have described a business process. Imagine other business processes: ordering clothes from mail order companies, requesting a new telephone service from your telephone company, developing new products, administering the social security process, building a new home, etc.

In the extreme, re-engineering assumes that the current process is irrelevant – "it doesn't work, it's broken, so forget it. Start over." Such a 'clean slate' perspective enables the designers of business processes to disassociate themselves from today's process, and focus on a new process. It is like projecting yourself into the future and asking yourself: what should the process look like? What do my customers want it to look like? What do other employees want it to look like? How is the particular task completed by excellent companies? What might we be able to do with new technology?

In addition, probably the oldest and most common approach to **designing work** is based on engineering concepts and methods. In doing so one can make use of several approaches including the scientific approach initially proposed by Frederick Taylor or the motivational approach using research carried out by motivational gurus including Frederick Herzberg, amongst others, although the latter has been criticized because his distinguished 'hygiene factors' are difficult to operationalize.

A renowned model into how one should look into Work Design concepts was developed by Hackman and Oldham (1980) (see the figure below).

According to Cummings and Worley (2001) citing Hackman and Oldham (1980), five core dimensions of work affect three critical psychological states, which in turn produce personal job outcomes. These outcomes include high internal work motivation, high quality work performance, satisfaction with work and low absenteeism and turnover. The five job dimensions include skill, variety, task identify and significance as well as autonomy and feedback from the work itself.

In addition to the above, change agents and managers are constantly faced with the challenge of enriching the job on one hand (quality) and enlarging it on the other hand (quantity). The diagram below illustrates this ever-lasting tension between the virtually opposing dimensions.

Diagram 2: Abstract of continuum of intervention strategies
Hackman and Oldham (1980: 90)

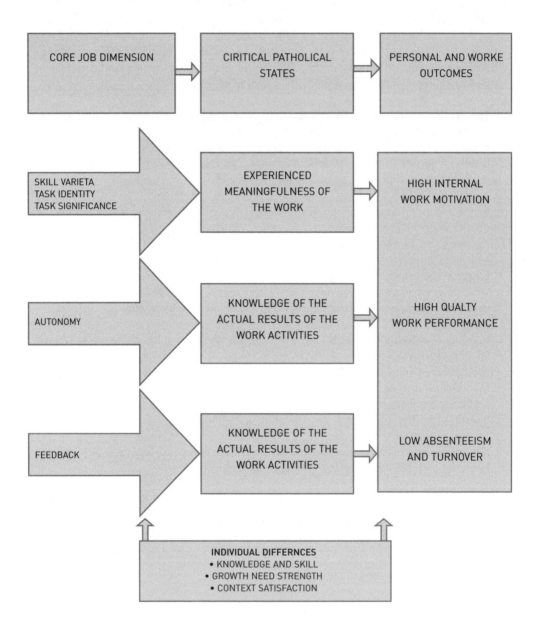

Diagram 3 : Job enrichment versus job enlargement

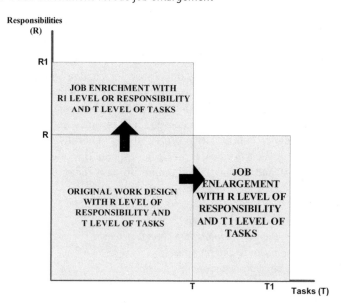

The diagram above makes the difference between job enrichment and job enlargement quite evident. In the former, the same number of tasks is maintained while the employee is given a higher set of responsibilities. Examples of this include issues like clerical and administrative staff given higher level tasks such as answering general correspondence or coordinating activities, which is higher than their normal set of duties. The likely effects of this change are generally positive provided that the employee looks forward to the opportunity. On the other hand, in job enlargement, the employee is not given any superior tasks to perform but an increase in work load. In the same vein one can cite examples where technical and administrative staff members are given extra duties of the same levels such as more papers to file or more letters to send. Generally speaking, job enlargement does not increase individual motivational level at all.

HUMAN RESOURCE MANAGEMENT INTERVENTIONS

One of the aspirations of any change agent is probably to effect the necessary changes while at the same time to maintain or even increase the level of employee commitment and employee citizenship behavior towards the organization. In meeting this outcome, it is highly important for employees to be assigned specific goals, continuously monitored and appraised, and rewarded for their efforts.

In the course of the past years, there have been several attempts to come up with a more scientific method of setting performance targets (Locke and Latham. 1990). Setting proper, measurable and specific goals ensures that the final destination is clearer to all stakeholders. However, establishing challenging goals involves managing the level of participation and the level of goal difficulty.

As a result, you can see a direct correlation between goal-setting and achieving performance. In general, goal-setting drives people forward, it encourages motivation and encourages personal behavior (O'Leary-Kelly, Martocchio, and Frink. 1994). A common form of goal-setting used in organizations is 'Management by Objectives' (MBO). This applied method is clearly an attempt to converge corporate goals with personal goals. Once the goals have been set, it is imperative for change agents to assess the performance of the employees within the organization and in particular within the change management program. Thus, it can be argued that performance appraisal represents an important link between goal-setting processes and reward systems (Peck, 1984). However, abundant evidence indicates that organizations generally do a poor job in job appraisals. In overcoming these hurdles, three Organizational Development practitioners, Mohrman, Resnick-West and Lawler (1994), came up with these steps to be used in performance appraisals:

1   Select the right people at the design stage;
2   Diagnose the current situation including the change program;
3   Establish the system's purpose and objectives;
4   Design the performance appraisal system;
5   Experiment with the implementation; and
6   Evaluate and monitor the system.

Finally, any Human Resource Intervention would not be complete if a proper reward system is not in place. In is undoubtedly true that rewards are probably the best motivational sources, since they do not only produce a high level of satisfaction but also a high level of commitment, at least for a period of time. Over the years managers and change agents have developed an array of rewards. These range from purely financial rewards including lump sum increases, performance-based pay systems, gain- or bonus-sharing to personal rewards including personal benefits and growth benefits such as career progression and development, job rotations, phased retirement, etc.

STRATEGIC INTERVENTIONS

Strategic interventions in change situations tend to address the relationship between an organization and its environment. Organizations are open systems and must relate to their environments. This includes external agents, such as suppliers, customers, regulators and competitors, as well as indirect influences in the wider cultural, political and economic context (Cummings and Worley. 2001).

The Integrated Strategic Change (ISC) is an intervention that brings change management issues across traditional strategic planning. This was developed as a response to the fact that more often than not best business strategies are not implemented (Ouchi. 1979). This process is phased in four steps namely:

1   Performing the strategic analysis, which carries out a strategic diagnosis of the current organization under study (Schein. 1985);

2   Exercising Strategic Choice, which determines what strategic change should the organization go for in order to reach its goals;

3   Designing the Strategic Change Plan, which involves a comprehending agenda for moving the organization from its current strategy to a newly developed strategy;

4   Implementing the Strategic Plan, which is the final step and draws heavily on knowledge of motivation, group dynamics and change processes.

EXERCISE: consider the above change management interventions. Which one do you think is the most difficult and time-consuming to implement? In your own experience of organizational change, which interventions were most, and least, effective? What are the barriers to implementing these interventions ? Is it largely a matter of cost, time or management control? Do consultants add value in these areas in our experience, or have management and in-house staff been able to handle many of these effectively?

THE ORGANIZATION OF THE FUTURE

According to Kotter (2002), the rate of change in the business world is not going to slow down. He predicts that competition in most industries will probably speed up over the next few decades. "Enterprises everywhere will be presented with even more terrible hazards and wonderful opportunities, driven by the globalization of the economy along with related technological and social trends", he suggests.

The typical twenty-first century organization has not operated well in a rapidly changing environment. Structure, systems, practices, and culture have often been more of a drag on change than a facilitator. If environmental volatility continues to increase, as most people now predict, the standard organization of the twentieth century will likely become a dinosaur. So what will the winning enterprise of the twenty-first century look like? Kotter (2002) suggests the importance of the characteristics of a persistent sense of urgency, teamwork at the top, the need for people who can create and communicate a vision, broad-based empowerment, delegated management for excellent short-term performance, and no unnecessary interdependence.

A persistent sense of urgency - Major change is never successful unless the complacency level is low. A high urgency rate helps enormously in completing all of the stages of a transformation process. If the rate of external change continues to climb, then the urgency rate of the winning twenty-first century organization will have to be medium to high all the time.

A higher rate of urgency does not imply ever-present panic, anxiety, or fear. It means a state in which complacency is virtually absent, in which people are always looking for both problems and opportunities, and in which the norm is 'do it now.' Maintaining urgency will require, first and foremost, performance information systems that are far superior to what we generally see today. The tradition of distributing financial accounting data to a small number of people on a monthly or quarterly basis will have to become a thing of the past. More people more often will need data on customers, competitors, employees, suppliers, shareholders, technological developments, and financial results. The systems that supply this information cannot be designed, as are some today, to make the organization or one of its units look good. They will need to be created to provide honest and unvarnished news, especially about performance.

In the past decade, a number of companies have taken important steps toward creating these new performance feedback systems. Information on customer satisfaction, in particular, is being collected more accurately, more often, and for more people. Likewise, managers are actually seeing customers, especially disgruntled ones, more often. All this is good, but we still have a long way to go. Typical employees in typical firms today still receive little data on their performance, the performance of their group or department, and the performance of the organization as a whole.

To create these systems and use their output productively, corporate cultures in the twenty-first century will have to value candid discussions far more than they do today. Norms associated with political politeness, and with the killing of the messenger of bad news, will have to change (these are not 'norms' in the sense in which we later will distinguish 'values' from 'norms,' but 'norms' in the sense of implicit norms or socially guided habits). The combination of valid data from a number of external sources, broad communication of that information inside an organization, and a willingness to deal honestly with the feedback will go a long way toward banishing complacency.

Teamwork at the top - In a slow-moving world, all an organization needs is a good executive in charge. Teamwork at the top is not essential. In a moderately paced context, teamwork is necessary to deal with periodic transformations, but much of the time the old model will still work. In a fast-moving world, teamwork is enormously helpful almost all the time. In an environment of constant change, individuals, even if supremely talented, won't have enough time or expertise to absorb rapidly competitor, customer, and technological information. They won't have enough time to communicate all of the important decisions to hundreds or thousands of others. They will rarely have the charisma or skills to single-handedly gain commitments to change from large numbers of people.

Succession in future could be a process of picking at least the core of a team. With the basic elements of a strong team in place on day one, a new CEO would be in a much stronger position to build the kind of coalition needed to handle change.

People who can create and communicate vision - In the twentieth century, the development of business professionals in the classroom and on the job focused on management. People were taught how to plan, budget, organize, staff, control, and problem-solve. Only in the last decade or so has much thought gone into developing leaders – to produce people who can create and communicate visions and strategies. Because management deals mostly with the status quo and leadership deals mostly with change, in the next century we will have to become much more skilled at creating leaders.

Development of leadership potential does not happen in a two-week course or even a four year college program, although both can help. Most complex skills emerge over decades, which is why we increasingly talk about continuous learning for your whole life. Because we spend so many of our waking hours at work, most of our development takes place – or does not take place – on the job. This simple fact has enormous implications. If our time at work encourages and helps us to develop leadership skills, we will eventually realize whatever potential we have. Conversely, if time at work does little or nothing to develop those skills, we will probably never live up to our potential.

Highly controlling organizations often destroy leadership by not allowing people to blossom, test themselves and grow. In stiff bureaucracies, young men and women with potential typically see few good role models, are not encouraged to lead, and may even be punished if they go out of bounds, challenge the status quo, and take risks. These kinds of organizations tend either to repel people with leadership potential or to homogenize those individuals by teaching them only about bureaucratic management, Kotter (2002) explains.

Successful organizations in the twenty-first century will have to become more like incubators of leadership. Wasting talent will become increasingly costly in a world of rapid change. Developing leadership will, in turn, demand flatter and leaner structures along with less controlling and more risk-taking cultures. The negative consequences of putting people with potential into small boxes and micromanaging them will only increase. People need to be encouraged to attempt to lead, at first on a small scale, both to help the organization adapt to changing circumstances and to help themselves to grow. In this way, through thousands of hours of trial and error, coaching, and encouragement, they will achieve their potential.

Broad-based empowerment - The hearts and minds of all members of the workforce are needed to cope with the fast-shifting realities of the business climate. Without sufficient empowerment, critical information about quality sits unused in workers' minds and energy to implement changes lies dormant.

Many of the same kinds of organizational attributes required to develop leadership are also needed to empower employees. Those facilitating factors would include flatter hierarchies, less bureaucracy, and a greater willingness to take risk. In addition, constant empowerment for a constantly changing world works best in organizations in which the senior managers focus on leadership and in which they delegate most managerial responsibilities to lower levels.

If we have difficulty imagining this degree of empowerment actually emerging in the workplace, Kotter (2002) suggests that we look at organizations that operate today in a sea of shifting conditions, such as high-tech companies and professional service firms that thrive in intensely competitive environments. What we will find are unusually flat hierarchies, little bureaucracy, a propensity for risk-taking, workforces that largely manage themselves, and senior level people who focus on providing leadership for client projects, technological development, or customer service. The model has already been tested. With proper leadership at the top, as well as the other required conditions, it can work well.

Delegated management for excellent short term performance - Some business futurists write as if management as we know it will disappear in the twenty-first century. Everyone of importance will become visionary and inspiring. Those boring people who worry about whether inventories are on target will no longer be needed. Yet even in a rapidly changing world, someone has to make the current system perform to expectations or those in power will lose the support of important constituencies.

Since this kind of organization delegates a great deal of authority to lower levels, excellence in management means that the empowered employees handle this responsibility well. That, in turn, means they must receive sufficient management training and be supported with appropriate systems. Today, even when we find managerially empowered employees, they often have not been given sufficient educational and other assistance. Instead, both training and systems are still designed to serve the needs of middle management. Changing this reality is usually more of an attitudinal challenge than a technical or economic issue. "No, this training is for managers," someone says, meaning that you have to have a certain minimum status in the hierarchy to deserve the educational perk. "We can't give this information out to all those people," someone else says in response to a proposal for shifting the control systems. Kotter (2002) suggests these reasons for a lack of transparency:

1   "Because of security." The real question is, whose security? If information on the poor performance of some department or some product is widely known, will this hurt the firm? Or will it embarrass a few executives and put pressure on certain people to do something?
2   "Because they won't know what to do with the information." They will if they've been trained.
3   "Because of the expense." Curious logic. By delegating management responsibility, we're getting people who typically make 20,000 to 50,000 dollars a year to do work that used to be done by people making 50,000 to 200,000 per year. The payroll savings will always outdistance any training or new system expenses, unless you retain unnecessary middle management jobs. However, organizational politics and inertia prevent these improvements being effected.

An organization with more delegation, which means a lean and flat hierarchy, is in a far superior position to maneuver than one with a big, change-resistant lump in the middle. This fact alone will force more delegation over the next few decades, despite all the excuses offered as to why that's a bad idea.

No unnecessary interdependence - All organizations have unneeded internal interconnections between people and groups. The German subsidiary can't agree to anything without checking with corporate. The controller's department in the head office sends a hundred pounds of reports per week to the plants, where the paper is largely ignored. Because of some problems back in 1965, a routine was created in which engineers make certain presentations to marketing and manufacturing people in meetings that still go on today despite the existence of information technology that can communicate the same information more quickly and easily. In some firms this is the case unless interdependence is nearly overwhelming, making major changes a hopelessly complicated affair. Although such situations may seem foolish on the outside, on the inside they can be accepted, perhaps grudgingly, and very hard to alter.

In the twenty-first century, a volatile business environment will force more organizations to manage more quickly and inexpensively. Independencies left over from an earlier era, which add no value, will be less tolerable. In this sense, the twenty-first-century organization will probably be a lot more efficient than the one we typically see today. A process of continual cleaning will certainly be encouraged in a faster-moving environment. Instead of waiting for interdependencies to reach unmanageable levels, the effective organization in the next century will re-examine linkages on a more regular basis and eliminate those that are no longer relevant.

An adaptive corporate culture - In total, all of the above practices will help an organization adapt to a rapidly changing environment. Creating those practices so they stick is an exercise in creating adaptive corporate cultures. In the twentieth century, we have found group norms and shared values in organizations mostly to be barriers to change. They don't need to be. Cultures can facilitate adaptation if they value performing well for an organization's constituencies, if they really support competent leadership and management, if they encourage teamwork at the top, and if they demand a minimum of layers, bureaucracy, and interdependencies.

Creating such cultures is an exercise in transformation: increasing the urgency rate, creating the guiding coalition, and so on. In most industries today, the pressure to change cultures is not intense, so it's easy to delay. "Let the next generation of executives do it." "Things aren't so bad; look at last quarter's net income." Keep one fact in mind as you consider this: At least one player in your industry probably isn't thinking that way.

Truly adaptive firms with adaptive cultures are awesome competitive machines. They produce superb products and services faster and better. They run circles around bloated bureaucracies. Even when they have far fewer resources and patents or less market share, they compete and win again and again.

Kotter (2002) points out that people who have been moved around in marginally effective restructurings and quality programs often worry that this ever-changing, adaptive organization will be a difficult challenge for all employees. The pace of change does require getting used to it, especially for people who have spent most of their working lives in old-fashioned bureaucracies.

SUCCESSFUL CHANGE GUIDELINES IN POINT FORM

In summary, some useful change management guidelines to take home with you include:

1　Staying the same or relying on past successes is a formula for complacency and eventual failure.

2　Quick fix solutions rarely last. Successful changes take time.

3　The change process is as important as the change itself – even the right things done the wrong way are not likely to succeed.

4   Always appoint a change agent and a change owner and, where appropriate, a change team to manage the change process and make change happen;

5   The focus of change should be on the present realities and future ideals and how to move step by step towards those ideals. Dwelling on the past is energy draining;

6   Not all situations are the same. Change strategies should be tailored to the unique characteristics of the organization and realities of the situation, level of change desired and the desired end results;

7   Involvement in the change process increases understanding, commitment and ownership. However, involving the wrong people or involvement in overkill will create resistance to change or take change in the wrong direction;

8   Positive change is more effective than negative change;

9   The incentive to change must be much greater than the incentive to stay the same. Perceived incentives must outweigh the reasons and excuses for not changing;

10 Focus on a 'few' high impact changes until they are successfully accomplished. Success builds confidence and momentum for change. Over-committing builds frustration, resistance and failure;

11 Some resistance to change can be expected. However, continued resistance must be dealt with or the change process will be undermined;

12 The more there is at stake, the greater the resistance to change and the greater the need to carefully manage the change;

13 Provide people with the skills needed to successfully adapt to change;

14 Systems, processes, values, and reward systems must be aligned to sustain change;

15 The probability for successful change can be increased by:
- Creating a clear and understandable vision of the change and change process
- Establishing accountability for change
- Valuing and reinforcing efforts to change, a willingness to innovate and experiment
- Removing obstacles
- Having reasonable consequences for continued non-compliance.

CLOSING CASE: HOW THE BANK OF VALLETTA IN MALTA FOUGHT OFF HSBC

Malta, a small independent island nation in the Mediterranean off the coast of Italy, is the home of stoical, self-reliant and self-contained people with a strong business mindset. Patriotic and familiar with looking after themselves (they have experienced being under siege from all quarters in a friendless sea) they have developed their own businesses in all sectors. The Bank of Valletta is no exception. Old-established, focusing on building friendly relationships with customers, somewhat traditional but reliable and secure, the bank enjoyed a solid customer base across the prosperous island with its population half a million.

Suddenly, the bank's comfortable existence was threatened with the arrival of HSBC. In the process of fighting off an international competitor with deep pockets and a cut-throat market share-gaining strategy, the Bank of Valletta was able to reinvent itself and move aggressively into the 21st century. The bank was 'doing OK' before, and it may have simply carried on like this. The change process the bank experienced was not necessarily planned, although some of the changes were in the more distant pipeline. The HSBC attack accelerated the pace of change, and as a result, arguably the bank is stronger and more resilient.

It was in 1997 that HSBC, the 'world's local bank,' decided to descend upon the small island state, pursuing an uncompromising strategy of discounting heavily to win market share before then pushing up prices to build profitability. Supported heavily by the HSBC headquarters in London, the bank put a huge weight of public relations and marketing strength behind the assault on Malta's banking customers. They were willing to make losses for a few years, with a view to capturing many customers, especially those from overseas who recognized and respected the HSBC brand. With thousands of branches in hundreds of countries, HSBC saw Malta – then about to join the EU and to adopt the Euro – as a good future prospect.

The Bank of Valletta then employed only seven people in the marketing department. Marketing had never been a strong point of emphasis for the bank. "But with the imminent arrival of HSBC," remembers marketer Joe Zammit, a Maltese from a traditional family on the island, "suddenly we could ask for a bigger budget and get it. It was like a battle, fighting off this invader, just like the old days." How could the bank fend off this huge attacker, in this David and Goliath scenario? Zammit had long been a keen advocate of Internet banking, mobile phone banking and other modern conveniences, but his employer had not been enthusiastic. "Now I could argue that we should adopt these facilities for our customers, so that HSBC would not have advantages over us" (as HSBC already had those services in general use), as Zammit explained. Previously cautious, the management agreed, and Bank of Valletta rolled out a state-of-the-art system in advance of its rival's. The bank was able to maintain its prices but dramatically improved its services.

The bank actually enjoyed advantages over its much bigger rivals as, making decisions quickly among their small team, they were able to approve and make changes rapidly. HSBC, meanwhile, had to wait for head office in London to make decisions for them. Their expected gain in market share over the local bank failed to materialize to the extent they had hoped to achieve. Now there are branches of HSBC in many locations on the island, and their advertisements are everywhere – especially where they might be seen by foreigners. The Bank of Valletta retains the majority market share on the island – but this is not just because the local population is patriotic. The bank offers a modern and efficient service and enjoys a loyal following. Its customers are the beneficiaries of this unplanned change – its decision to fight back in the most proactive way. And the marketing department was able to launch the newest banking products without a big fight with its own finance and management teams.

CASE QUESTIONS:
- *In what ways did the attack by HSBC accelerate change at Bank of Valletta?*
- *Can unplanned change be more rapid and gain more support than planned change?*
- *In what ways was the small local bank able to act more quickly?*
- *Why would people prefer a multinational supplier than a local one?*
- *Which alternative strategies might be adopted by HSBC? Might these have been more successful?*
- *In what ways did cultural issues impact on the behavior of the local bank and its team?*

CONCLUSION

This chapter, completing our analysis of the management of change, has examined aspects of how organizations have gone about transforming themselves. First of all, identifying change competencies in key staff is a vital step to better decide on the how of change. Business Process Engineering is a widely recognized approach to handling the mechanics of change, hence a clear emphasis here. The attitudes of people in the organization vary, yet they must be won over to make the process work. They have different interpretations of the future change, the current change, and the way to change. Management's role in this process is key, and we discuss useful guidelines for them to follow, including Kotter's 'how advice' for would-be change agents. The two cases contrast planned and unplanned change: General Electric embarking on a major transformation led from the top compared with the small Maltese bank fighting off its international aggressor, and re-inventing itself as a way to maintain its market position. Here the initiatives came from the small marketing team, who saw the attack as an opportunity to push through the changes they had long wanted to make.

REFERENCES

Antonioni. D. 1994. Improve the Performance Management Process Before Discounting Performance Appraisals. *Compensation and Benefits Review. 26* (3): 29-37.

Bologun. J. and Hailey. V.H. 1999. *Exploring Strategic Change.* London: Prentice Hall. Beckhard. R. and Harris. R.T. 1987. *Organisational Transitions: Managing Complex Change.* Reading MAS: Addison-Wesley.

Cameron. K. Freeman S. and Mishra A. 1991. The Best in White Collar Downsizing: Managing Contradictions. *Academy of Management Executive. 5*

Campbell. J. and Dunnette. M. 1968. Effectiveness of T-Group Experiences in Managerial Training and Development. *Psychological Bulletin. 70,* 73-103

Cummings. T. and Worley. C.G. 2001. *Organisation Development and Change.* Australia: South Western College Publishing.

Eales-White. R. 1994. *Creating Growth from Change. How to react. develop and grow.* London: McGraw Hill.

Hackman.. J. and Oldham. G. 1980. *Work Redesign.* London: Addision-Wesley.

Hammer. M and Champy. J. 1993. *Reengineering the Corporation.* New York: Harper Collins.

Hayes. J. 2002. *The Theory and Practice of Change Management.* London: Palgrave.

Kotter. J. and Schlesinger. L.A. 1979. Choosing Strategies for Change. Harvard Business Review. March/April.

Kotter J.P. 2002. An Integrative Model of Organizational Dynamics. in E. Porter. D. Nadler and C. Cammann eds. *Organizational Assessment*. London: Wiley.

Locke. E. and Latham. G. 1990. *A Theory of Goal Setting and Task Performance*. Englewood Cliffs, NJ: Prentice Hall.

Mohrman, A., Resnick-West, J. and Lawler, E. 1994. Designing Performance Appraisal Systems. In E. Lawler, Performance Management: the next generation. *Compensation and Benefits Review. 26* (3): 16-19.

O'Leary-Kelly. O.. Martocchio. J. Frink. D. 1994. A Review of the Influence of Group on Goals Performance. *Academy of Management Journal 37*, 1285-1301.

Ouchi. W.G. 1979. *Conceptual Framework for the Design of Organizational Control Mechanisms*. Management Science. 1979

Nadler. D.A. 1993. Concepts for the Management of Organisational Change in Mabey and B. Mayon-White eds. *Managing Change*. London: Paul Chapman.

Peck. C. 1984. Pay for Performance: The Intention of Compensation and Performance Appraisal. *Research Bulletin*. 155 New York: Conference Board.

Schein. E. 1985. Organisational Culture in Kilmann. R.. Saxton. M. & Serpa. R. eds. *Gaining Control of Corporate Governance*. San Francisco: Jossey Bass.

Schein. E. 1998. *Process Consultation Revisited*. Reading. MAS: Addison-Wesley.

Zaltman G. and Duncan R. 1977. *Strategies for Planned Change*. London: Wiley Publications.

RECOMMENDATIONS FOR FURTHER READING

Ansoff. I.H. 1990. *Implanting Strategic Management*. London: Prentice Hall.

Barr. P.S. Stimpert. J.L.. Huff. A.S. 1992. Cognitive change. strategic action. and organizational renewal. *Strategic Management Journal. 13*. 15-36

Goldstein. J. 1988.. A far-from-equilibrium systems approach to resistance to change. *Organizational Dynamics*. 16-26

Hannan. M.T. Freeman. J. 1984. Structural inertia and organizational change. *American Sociological Review. 49*. 149-64

Kanter. R.M. 1989. The new managerial work. *Harvard Business Review. 67:.6.* 85-92.

Klein. K.J. Sorra. J.S. 1996.. The challenge of innovation implementation. *Academy of Management Review. 21:* 4. 22-42

Leana. C.R.. Barry. B. 2000. Stability and change as simultaneous experiences in organizational life. *Academy of Management Review. 25* (4) 753-9

Marshak. R.J. 1993.. Managing the metaphors of change. *Organizational Dynamics. 22:*1. 44-56

Nadler. D.A.. Tushman. M.L. 1990.. Beyond the charismatic leader: leadership and organizational change. *California Management Review. 32:.2.* 77-97

Nemeth. C.J. 1997.. Managing innovation: when less is more. *California Management Review. 40* (1) 59-74

Zaltman. G.. Duncan. R. 1977. *Strategies for Planned Change*. Toronto: Wiley.

CHAPTER TEN
ETHICS AND CORPORATE SOCIAL RESPONSIBILITY
JOOP REMMÉ

LEARNING OBJECTIVES:

- To gain insight in the role of ethics in society and in management
- To become familiar with the background and reality of corporate social responsibility

INTRODUCTION

This chapter introduces ethics as an important dimension of the responsibilities of business entities, especially as a responsibility to the societies in which they operate. Business corporations are increasingly expected to recognize the role of ethics. This is the reason for including this topic in our book: Ethics is increasingly a part of business. What do we mean when we talk about 'ethics'? In order to explain this, we have to distinguish it from 'morality', with which ethics is often confused both in everyday language and in academic discourse (Boatright (2000: 22); Donaldson (1989: 10)). We can say in simple terms that the two relate as theory and practice.

Let us begin with the practice, that is, with morality. A recent and widely accepted definition regards morality as "concerned with the norms, values, and beliefs embedded in social processes which define right and wrong for an individual or a community." (Crane/Matten (2004: 11). Some other definitions emphasize the practice aspect of morality even more strongly; for instance "Morality is generally used to describe a sociological phenomenon, namely the existence in a society of rules and standards of conduct" (Boatright (2004: 22/23)). In other words, 'morality' is something that can be observed, as a sociological phenomenon. It serves as a practical guide for interpersonal behavior.

Derived from 'morality' is 'ethics', which is "concerned with the study of morality and the application of reason to elucidate specific rules and principles that determine right and wrong for any given situation." (Boatright (2000: 22). Thus, ethics is about all efforts to make sense of the sociological phenomenon guiding interpersonal behavior.

In the definitions above, we have encountered the terms 'values' and 'norms'. They are related as ethics and morality are related. With 'norms', we talk of practical rules which serve as a tool, such as traffic rules (the norm "stop when the light turns red" is of clear practical use). These norms are entwined with our behavior. Values are the notions that the norms express. For instance, behind the norm of a traffic rule we find the value of 'traffic safety'. Norms are situational, as for instance countries do not all have the same traffic rules. Norms are also subject to cultural and historical developments. For instance, in The Netherlands, the norm once was to show respect to someone by tipping your hat, but today people rarely wear hats and new norms for showing respect have developed. Values are far less situational and changeable; for instance, showing respect to other people is valued throughout the ages and in most, if not all, cultures.

The concepts mentioned above are common in organizations these days. It is recognized that there is a role for morality, for instance in one's behavior toward colleagues and clients. Employees are taught the norms of the organization, as when "a complaint has to be answered with x days", and the values that they express, as with 'client-friendliness', 'service'.

The definitions for the notions of 'corporate' and 'social' will be given further on. For now, we will focus on various traditions of ethics and morality. Then we explore the variety in moral perspectives which we may find in people we meet. The basis of ethics, throughout a variety of cultures, is the idea that people ought to treat each other and their environment in a responsible manner. The notion of responsibility also pertains to the business context, where it has become the more relevant the more entrepreneurs and business organizations have an impact on society. These days, corporations and entrepreneurs are more and more expected to honor such responsibilities. This topic, under the modern term 'corporate social responsibility', is discussed in this chapter following the discussion of traditions of ethics.

APPROACHES TO ETHICS

Since the oldest civilizations, human society has developed systems of ethical thinking. One could say that human organization has always had a moral dimension. As soon as human organization became formalized in structures of human interaction, which we call 'civilizations,' and as the principles and structures in them became formalized, the moral dimension also formally materialized. Thus ethics develops as a field of interest.

A few words have to be devoted to the status of ethics in human organizations. This is taken here in the wider sense of "how in general people cooperate in order to structure their reality". The reality of cooperating requires notions of what is important and which goals should one try to attain. This is expressed in ethics. Now ethics can have either a very strong or a much weaker status. This can be seen as the tension between 'moral absolutism' on the one hand and 'moral relativism' on the other hand. The question becomes how strongly rules and norms are imposed. The moral absolutist position is then the position of people who argue that their rules and norms are universally imperative, and more so than any other system of ethics. The problem with this position is one of legitimacy: How can someone with that position legitimize it? It is after all a point of view which regards other points of view on ethics as inferior, to say the least.

The other and opposite position, that of moral relativism, holds that every culture and every individual is entitled to have its own position on ethics and no position has a right to claim superiority over any other position. This approach, although the more appealing to many people, can also be problematic. It appears that even when we do our best to respect the uniqueness of other cultures, there are certain practices that apparently we find less than acceptable.

Both of the extreme positions come with problems. The tension between moral absolutism and moral relativism forms the horizon, against which contemporary issues of a moral nature are dealt with, also within the business world.

THE JUDEO-CHRISTIAN TRADITION

The Jewish tradition dates from some one thousand years BC. It is strongly connected with the Jewish people's experience in the ancient world. But it starts from a view of a general human reality, the creation of the world as an act of goodness of the benign Supreme Being, God. An important and especially human development is given in a description of human weakness. This called the 'fall from grace'. This is described in the very first book of the Bible, Genesis. The first man and woman lived in an ideal environment, which they could have preserved if they had only obeyed God's rule not to touch the fruit of a particular tree. However, they proved unable to withstand temptation and thus disobeyed God. The result is that they were banned from their ideal surroundings, from then on living in the realization of their own weakness.

A characteristic element is the notion of 'law,' 'torah'. This is seen as the expression of God's will towards creation. For that reason, the Jewish bible is called 'Torah.'. The most well known expression of this element is in the Ten Commandments (Exodus, 20). There are in fact 613 commandments in the Torah (Kelner, 1991: 84)). The central message behind these commandments is the motivation to follow the example of God, which is expressed in the commandments. The part of the Torah devoted to how a person is to live his or her life is called the 'Halakhah'. This literally means 'my way'. Throughout Jewish tradition the center of this way of life is seen in the charity commandment: "Thou shall love thy neighbor as thyself" (Leviticus: 19.18). The other commandments are related to this motive, as with the commandment to be unbiased in passing judgment (Leviticus: 19. 15). We recognize here a warning against discrimination; a topic, which we will discuss in the next chapter. Thus, one can discern in early Judaism a universalistic approach.

The origins of Christianity are Jewish. Christians follow the teaching and example of a Jewish religious leader, Jesus of Nazareth. Christ repeated the charity commandment: "So in everything, do to others what you would have them do to you, for this sums up the Law and the Prophets" (Matthew: 7. 12). This commandment received in the teachings of Christ a new dimension. It is directly linked to Christ as the human persona of God and as such encountering brotherly love. This notion of brotherly love is thus immediately connected to love for God (Marc: 12. 30/31). The new emphasis also means that the commandment is no longer seen as a matter of reciprocity. It does not mean "Do good to someone who does good to you, and then you both win,". The connection with the love of God means that you do not act in a certain way because of how someone else treats you, but because it is in relation to the love of God, who is regarded as treating mankind with goodness. Therefore, we can say that Christianity is even more deontological than Judaism is.

A similar selfless attitude is discernable in a text called the Sermon on the Mount (Matthew: 5.1-7.1), in which Christ blesses especially the humble and the weak. He emphasizes that especially the weak deserve brotherly love in the eyes of God and renders a particular dimension to the charity commandment, stated in this text. Calling this attitude 'selfless,' does not imply a negation of the interests of the self; indeed "love thy neighbor like thyself" implies that one does love oneself.

The diverging traditions of Christianity express different emphases in terms of ethics. The Catholic tradition has developed a tradition of confession and remorse for moral mistakes, or 'sins,' with a casuistic technique of fitting the showing of remorse to the precise nature of the mistake. This was sometimes corrupted into a practice of negotiating for the goodness of God. This brings an ego-motive into moral behavior and thus damages the selflessness preached by Christ. Traditions such as the Lutheran and Calvinist traditions sought to protect the selfless nature of correct moral behavior by denying a direct link between remorse and receiving the goodness of God.

THE VIRTUE TRADITION

This tradition starts with Aristotle, a philosopher who lived in the 5th century BC. He was a genius in the scientific breakthroughs which he accomplished. Think only of how he formulated a system of logic that we still use today, for instance in the development of software. He was at the same time practical and focused on tangible challenges. His approach to ethics testifies to this (Hutchinson. 1995). He begins from the notion that human beings, like other creatures, are characterized by growth towards the kind of perfection that is befitting them. For instance, the growth for a flower has a different goal of perfection than the growth of a human being. This is called the 'good.'

For a human being that equates with 'success'. He warns not to confuse this with potential instruments towards success, such as power and wealth. This is harder for people with ties and commitments, he adds. We see here a precursor of the later criticism of the 'company man.' The good has to mean to live life well, that is with virtue. This is an important notion in the ethics of Aristotle, and many after him, and it more or less means 'strength.' You could say that the ethics of Aristotle hinges on three notions: understanding, virtue and choice. Together they build character.

This leads us to a very important characteristic of the ethics of Aristotle: The focus is on the situations and choices of the individual. This occurs within a particular social context: the community, within one is raised and called upon to act according to virtue. The capabilities of the individual to deal with those situations and make choices can be trained, in developing a particular strength of character and relevant insights.

Unlike later theories which use the notion of 'virtue,' Aristotle is not against pleasure. For him, pleasure is justified, depending on the activity which produces the pleasure. For instance, eating and drinking, without exuberance, are entirely natural activities and objecting to the pleasure connected with them would not make sense.

But he does point to the possibility of 'vice.' What he means by this concept is the behavior where an emotion is followed without the guidance of reason. It is thereby easily out of proportion or misguided. It is thought to have a damaging effect on the development of strong character. This notion is opposed to 'virtue,' but not in such a way that every virtue has a particular vice as its particular opposite. Aristotle sees more than one vice connected to a virtue; for instance, connected to the virtue 'courage' are the vices 'cowardice' and 'harshness'. The vice consists in irrationally jumping to one of these extremes, while it is a matter of virtue to find the balance. Again, this has to be the balance for the individual and situation in question, as it is already virtuous for the individual to find the right balance for the challenge he or she is facing. This balance is sometimes more difficult than at other times, as. For instance, 'adultery' is always seen as wrong and 'abstinence' not necessarily so. With qualities like 'sex' and 'anger', one can look for a balance between too little and too much. The right balance is a matter of virtue and disbalance of vice.

In recent years, there is renewed interest into virtue ethics. This is partly due to the appearance of Robert Solomon's **Ethics and Excellence,** in 1992. He points out (103) that the Aristotelian emphasis on virtue is mirrored in today's emphasis on integrity. The bottom line of the Aristotelian message to people in today's business community, as Solomon sees it, is to question their activities as successful in the full specter of what makes a person's life successful, not just in terms of the financial bottom line. Aristotle's' approach has proven to be of interest to management development. For this, one can consider its emphasis on virtue as an individual capability and on individual development within a social context.

THE UTILITARIAN TRADITION

The utilitarians responded to the virtue tradition, which had become part of the Christian tradition (Gooding. 1995). They were struggling with two questions: 1) why would a certain course of action be considered good in cases where nothing comes of it?, and 2) if we think in terms of 'good' being the result of action we deem preferable, then how, given the vast diversity amongst humankind, can we find a criterion for what we then recognize as 'good'? Their approach is called 'consequentialist'. This means that the quality of a course of action is weighed in terms of its results. This is opposed to the approach found in the virtue tradition and in Kantianism, which is called 'deontological,' from 'deon,' which means 'duty'.

The utilitarian tradition, which is largely British, has as its two most important representatives Bentham (1748-1832) and Mill (1806-1873). Bentham is associated with 'classic utilitarianism,' which holds that utility is about promoting pleasure and avoiding pain. It is about a kind of usefulness, which all people were thought to be able to identify with. That this makes sense can be seen from the fact that those very principles were brought back a century later by Freud, in his principles for human behavior, which he called 'eros' and 'thanatos'; these are optimistic and pessimistic tendencies in human behavior.

This usefulness criterium resulted in the criticism that Bentham advocated 'hedonism', in other words: the pursuit of primarily pleasure. His approach was called 'hedonistic utilitarianism.' Still, that is not entirely correct. In fact, he did not advocate the pursuit of pleasure. What he did was to try to find a common denominator in all those things that other traditions were advocating. He asked, if, for instance, Christianity advocates brotherly love, is that not something that gives us pleasure? To avoid the misunderstanding that utilitarianism is about pleasure primarily, later utilitarianism no longer spoke of pleasure and pain, but about preference: a just solution is one in which more preferences are satisfied than in other situations. Also, with Mill (Schneewind: 153), we see the admittance that some of those preferences are deemed worthwhile also when they are not satisfied. Think, for instance, of 'love' and 'beauty' as generally considered good things, even when they are not really found.

When it comes to personal ethics, this approach does not always work well, which we saw with 'love' and 'beauty.' But people like Bentham and Mill, trained as a lawyer and an economist respectively, were primarily interested in issues in the public domain. As utilitarianism is egalitarian, and Bentham even went further and argued for 'animal rights', utilitarianism recognizes the issue of how to be just for all. Then, they would say, the 'right' way in governing would be one in which more utility is maximized than would have been the case with any of the alternatives. This does require comparability both in terms of 'utility' and in terms of people concerned, which utilitarianism has not satisfactorily solved.

A later form of utilitarianism is 'Pareto Efficiency' suggested by the economist Pareto (1848-1923): a course of action is just if at least one of those concerned benefits, while none of the others suffer. Typically this applies to choices between different courses of action. As with older forms of utilitarianism, it may not by itself offer enough justification. If, for instance, the same person is consistently better off, the other people would object, even when they are not worse off.

Thus, typically, a utilitarian approach is combined with a deontological approach. From that approach, the justification would be argued which is not sufficiently found in the utilitarian approach. If, for instance, in modern government, politicians make utilitarian judgments, such as "Which of these options give the best distribution of citizens who benefit and citizens who are negatively affected?", their choices are moderated by deontological principles. The deontological principles are, for instance, the rights found in constitutions, common law and international treaties. To use another example, managers may make such choices, while being moderated by the company strategy, prevailing laws or the company's code of conduct.

THE KANTIAN TRADITION

Immanuel Kant (1724-1804) was in his thinking a product of the Enlightenment, the cultural movement which dominated Western Europe and beyond in the second half of the 18th century. The US constitution is strongly influenced by this development. This movement is characterized by a strong belief in the potential of every human being, once given freedom as a universal right, particular in his rational capabilities. One of the results of this belief was an emphasis on democracy and a fair rule of law.

Accordingly, Kant tried to develop a system of ethics which would be recognized by all as sensible and fair. Thus, he formulated two rules.

The first is the Categorical Imperative, which Kant – a devout Christian – saw as the modern translation of the Christian charity commandment. Still, he turned it around. He did not express what one should do in order to live according to ethics, but rather what one should avoid. Hereby, he left space for what is allowed to the free individual. This had some history, as Rabbi Hillel, a contemporary of Christ, had phrased the charity commandment as "what you dislike, don't do to others"; (Kelner: 87). The Imperative holds that you have to "act only according to that maxim by which you can at the same time will that it should become a universal law."(DeGeorge: 83). This somewhat technical formula can be called Kant's 'anti-selfism rule.' What it means is that a particular course of action is ethically preferable if it would make sense, rationally speaking, for all men to do. You can see this in some old principles, such as "you shall not kill". This makes perfect sense as a rule for all to follow. You can also be more specific and think of a business case, where you decide to give your employees a bonus in accordance with what has previously been promised and by ratio of the effort put in and success achieved per employee. This course of action makes perfect sense as a general rule, and that has something to do with why people consider it as 'fair.'

The second rule holds that one should always treat other people as 'ends,' and not just as 'means.' This seems like a simple enough rule, but it is in practical life more complicated than it seems. When we look at the business organization, then we see that it is built on regarding people as means. This holds for the old bureaucratic organization, but also for newer types of organization. To treat the people in organizations also as ends is often not quite so easy to accomplish. In the business organization this would mean respecting their needs and involving them in the decisions made in the organization. This connects with stakeholder thinking, which we will discuss in chapter 12.

MUSLIM ETHICS

The ethics of Islam (Nanji. 1991) is comparable to the ethics of the other two major monotheistic religions, with which it is related: Judaism and Christianity. In Islam as well, the approach to ethics is related to the revelation of the will of God, Allah. This revelation is found in the Quran and is thought to be exemplified in the life of the Prophet Muhammad. In following this example, a person has to be wise in dealing with the limitations that are typical of human existence. Satan is thought to be the enemy of God precisely because he refuses to accept those limitations; a notion Islam shares with Christianity, in which such an attitude is called 'arrogance' and deemed the worst sin.

In Muslim ethics, the community is seen as the platform for expressing ones' observance of the divine commandments (Quran, Sutra 25), which are expressed in the Quran. It is in this setting that one is expected to develop towards a more pure life. This is comparable to Aristotle's' emphasis on growth towards excellence. Over time, the emphasis within Islam shifted from the individual responsibility to interpret the Quranic commandments to a literal observance of them. This resulted in the codification of five categories of moral acts: 1) obligatory acts, such as prayer, 2) recommended acts, such as charity, 3) neutral acts, such as nourishment, 4) acts that are discouraged, such as smoking, and 5) acts that are forbidden, such as drunkenness.

The Shi'a and Sunni traditions within Islam show some shifts of emphasis. Thus, the Shi'a Muslims place more emphasis on understanding, especially associated with the authority of wise leaders, the imams, with even less emphasis on individual choice in moral matters. The Sunni's appear to go in the other direction, emphasizing individual spiritual development.

Within Islam, the religious, the moral and the social are interwoven. Thus, social processes, such as the conduct of business, are also considered of religious interest. This results in the concern with interest as part of business, which many Muslims condemn as immoral. We will come back to this in the next chapter. Christianity saw the same concern in the late middle ages, when it too was very much entangled with the social and political fabric of society. In the next chapter, we will discuss Islamic Banking.

HINDU ETHICS

It is a bit difficult to talk of 'Hindu ethics,' as Hinduism is even more difficult to discuss in a consistent manner than other religions are (Bilimoria. 1991). One distinguishing feature, from early on, is that ethics is not a matter of human beings only. Hinduism expresses concern to all sentient beings; in other words, beings with sentience. According to Hinduism, 'good' is associated with happiness, pleasure, calmness, friendship, knowledge and truth. In aspiring to this, and do 'the right thing,' the obligation developed an emphasis on rites. Doing those is called 'dharma,' the duty to unite the cosmic and moral orders.

As in Brahmanic Hinduism a social hierarchy of castes develops, 'dharma' becomes specified in specific obligations the caste renders upon a person. What is 'dharma' to one particular person may be strictly forbidden to someone else. This also stands for a shift in emphasis from respecting the existing order to human action. Another notion that is important in this culture is 'karma,' which means that the moral quality of ones' actions translates into a particular spiritual fate. Connected to the notion of 'dharma,' is now the notion of 'purusharta,' or legitimate 'human ends.' These are distinguished into four categories: 1) material interests, 2) pleasure and affective fulfillment, 3) dharma, and 4) 'moksha' or 'liberation.' These are seen in a hierarchy with 'moksha' at the pinnacle. A comparison with the Maslow Pyramid seems relevant here.

A different approach becomes apparent within Upanishadic Hinduism. The Upanishadic Hindu is expected to have risen above emotions, inclinations and sentiments, as they are left behind in a development towards a more spiritual calling. This higher calling has sometimes been called 'self-centered' and a reason for denying that there is ethics at all in this style of Hinduism. Yet, this style of Hinduism does express the virtues of self-restraint, giving and compassion.

Interesting is also the tradition from the Bhagavad Gita, which book strongly influenced Hinduism. It allows reconciliation between various traditions in a synthesis of asceticism and duty. This is expressed in the concept of 'nishkama karma' or 'disinterested action.'

Another tradition within Hinduism is that of Jainism. This very spiritual style of Hinduism is characterized by the zeal of self-renunciation, exemplified by monastic life; hence, preferred models of social behavior are shaped after the ideal of monastic life. To this preferred way of life belong five pledges: 'ahimsa', or non-harming, 'satya', or being truthful, 'asteya', or no theft, 'brahmacharya', or sexual continence, and 'apigraha', or non-possessiveness. The most basic of these values is ahimsa, which includes a most rigorous style of vegetarianism. It also means that one has to avoid harming himself, to the extreme that where a 'white lie' could save someone's' life, one still has to refrain from it, as a lie would harm ones' own soul. In general, one could say that Jain ethics is universalistic, and thus not limited to one group or culture, and prescriptive.

A modern form of Hindu ethics is found in the approach of Mahatma Ghandi, in the 20th century. He showed a combination of adherence of old Hindu principles with a modern interpretation and application. He did not have a problem with the existing caste structure, but he did criticize the unequal distribution of privileges resulting from it. He thereby developed into a defender of the lower caste, while he remained far from the socialist ideal of surrendering power to the lower classes. He is most known for his approach of 'satyagraha', or 'non-resistance,' thus combining the old Hindu notions of 'satya', 'ahimsa' and 'tapasya'. This approach is not as passive as is often thought, as it consists in an active confrontation with perceived injustice, albeit in a non-violent manner. This approach was influential far beyond India, notably in South Africa and in the United States of America, as seen in the work of Martin Luther King.

BUDDHIST ETHICS

Buddhism (De Silva. 1991) is sometimes compared to the Jain tradition within Hinduism. It is based upon the life and example of an Indian prince, called Siddhartha, who lived in the 6th century BC. To him, morality was a way of life on a path towards liberation and away from suffering. This path started from the notion of 'dukkha,' which indicates the unsatisfying character of life. For the Buddha, ethics combines a social meaning with a personal quest. In that personal quest, the qualities of rational engagement, recommending certain conducts, social expression and character-building towards a more free state of being are combined.

The example given by the Buddha is seen as 'the middle path.' This is the way between, on the one hand, renunciation of human needs and desires, and on the other hand indulging in sensuality and material gain. Spiritual growth is seen as fed by free will and correct insight towards being freed from base emotions and vain realities.

This expected state of liberation gives Buddhism a consequentialist character, as the goodness of a course of action is measured in terms of a later outcome. This is strengthened further by the belief in reincarnation, which is determined by the quality of life one has led. But unlike utilitarian consequentialism, Buddhism is not open to just anything that will produce the desired result, but it indicates certain duties as guides towards improvement, requiring skill and dedication. This gives Buddhist ethics a deontological dimension as well.

From the deontological character, it is possible for Buddhism to indicate what is 'evil.' Buddhism distinguishes between defilements and evil actions. This is somewhat reminiscent of the Christian distinction between 'regular sins' and 'capital sins'. Defilements are things like greed, hypocrisy, envy, treachery, while the evil actions are variations on killing, stealing and giving in to defilements.

Buddhism is not necessarily vegetarian. It regards eating meat as sensible in some contexts, but restraining from killing animals is considered more righteous. This is connected with the central virtues of conscientiousness, benevolence and self-restraint.

In its social ethics, Buddhism is egalitarian, although it does appreciate the role of the family structure. The social structure does require righteousness, which at least must involve impartiality, respecting what is due and truthfulness. Thus one can organize society according to dharma; a notion borrowed from Hinduism. This furthers ones' own enlightenment.

A later strand of Buddhism is Zen, which builds upon the Buddhist tradition and shifts the emphasis more to the inner transformation of the individual.

ETHICS FROM CHINESE CULTURE

In talking about 'Chinese ethics,' we have to realize that this is not an exact notion (Hansen.1991). One complication, among others, is that Buddhism is also a part of the Chinese tradition and it later became entwined with the traditions which originated in China.

Two dimensions appear to be important in the tradition of Chinese ethics: language and convention, or 'li'. The earliest thinker, Confucius, who lived around 500 BC, described conventions as justified by their mere sturdiness. Language served as the primary source of solidity, as the conventions had to be expressed in language in precisely the right manner, in the way in which a musician studies scales. It is then the expression of 'ren', or 'humanity' / 'benevolence'. Confucius had a rule that is comparable to the Christian charity commandment, although reversed in negative terms: "What you do not desire, do not effect on another." However, his approach to ethics is not egalitarian. As a consequence of his emphasis on convention, Confucius saw rights and duties as related to roles in society.

Mozi (Mo Tzu), who lived a few generations after Confucius, stepped away from accepting conventions per se. He pointed out that some conventions can not be considered right and therefore can not serve as guide. He asked the same question that the utilitarians in Europe would ask 2000 years later: "How then are we to determine what is a guide and what is not?" and arrived at the same answer: 'utility.' But that notion needs to be explained further. Unlike the later European utilitarians, he referred to nature, or 'tian', which is also connected to a notion of 'heaven' or an all-encompassing order. Thus a balance is sought between 'according to nature' and 'not according to nature.' He saw nature to be the source for the preference material well-being, which is the content of utility. He did not only criticize Confucius in this respect. He also saw the right course of action for the individual to be connected to the universal quality of nature, thus stepping away from Confucius' emphasis on differences in social role.

Mencius (Meng Tzu) lived around 300 BC,. He also pointed at the importance of 'tian', but sought it primarily within the individual human being. According to him, nature had placed in every human being certain seeds, which can be developed to become virtues. Those are humanity, or sympathy for other human beings, the inclination to feel shame, or morality, respect, and the ability to distinguish right. or 'shi', from wrong, or 'fei'. Thus, human beings are to be seen, according to him, with benevolence. This also creates expectations towards government, in the sense that if a ruler does not act from benevolence revolt is legitimate. We see here a comparison with the 'regicide' teachings of the 14th century English philosopher William of Ockam. Mencius is, unlike Confucius, skeptical about language, in the sense that it expresses a supra-individual order, and he insists on linking morality to individual virtue.

The skeptical attitude towards language is shared by Laozi who lived in the same era. He launched the tradition of Taoism. This started with his emphasis on the proper path, or 'Tao', given by the universe. Thus places nature again in a universal reality. The 'tao' is not so fixed that language can be unambiguous, hence his skepticism concerning language. Opposite to Confucius, he looked for virtue in those qualities which escape conventions. Where conventions emphasize things like fortitude, wisdom, action, control, he emphasized weakness, questioning, passiveness, abandoning, and such. A comparison with Christ can be made here.

Zhuangzi, who lived in the same era, belongs to the tradition of Taoism. He criticized looking for direction in nature, as any understanding of nature requires a starting-point in human reality. An important insight was that something like objective language would be impossible, as it is impossible to apprehend the unlimited from the perspective of what is limited.

Xunzi, in the third century BC, brought new life to the teachings of Confucius. He continued Confucius' appreciation of language and of conventions, while he did admit that both needed justification. He thought a fixed social pattern could make language unambiguous. Thus, language and convention reinforce each other. But convention needs more than language to be based on. Therefore Xunzi emphasized and developed the role of rituals. He is different from Confucius, in that he saw language and rituals as accessible to all people. Therefore, like Mencius, he saw in all people the capacity to live an exemplary life.

Thus, we see some themes which have continued in Chinese culture. They are pursued with a pragmatic attitude, thinking rather in terms of norms than in terms of abstract values. They have in later ages been combined with influences from new cultures, primarily Buddhism.

OTHER CULTURES

The traditions which were discussed above comprise the vast majority of the world's population, but there are other cultures as well. We could look at the Masai culture in Africa, the cultures of indigenous Americans and the Aboriginal culture in Australia, as they show their own traditions in ethics. It is only because of lack of space that we could not discuss those cultures here, not because those cultures would not offer us much of interest.

This can only be expected. After all, we can safely state that all societies develop some kind of system to regulate interpersonal behavior. Such a system becomes strengthened throughout the tradition of its civilization. Also, the system contributes to the consistency and productivity. This is combined in modern times with ways in which organizations deal with their responsibilities, in their own effort to achieve consistency and to validate their role in society.

Questions
- *Is respect for human life shared by various traditions in ethics?*
- *Do you see points of understanding between the traditions?*
- *Are the various traditions equally appreciative of change?*

Case: *Competitive Retail in China*

The two largest retail companies in the world, Wal Mart and Carrefour, are both interested in expanding within the Chinese market, as can be expected. Of these, Wal Mart is the biggest and also the first to enter China. Still, it looks very much as if Carrefour is doing much better in terms of profitability and the number of opened stores. What could be behind this success?

Both Wal Mart and Carrefour entered the Chinese retail market in 1995, Carrefour just a few months after Wal Mart. Both companies' activities in China could grow only slowly, due to restrictions imposed by the Chinese government. In September 2001, China joined the World Trade Organization. As a result, it had to ease the restrictions on foreign investment within three years, which it did. This allowed Wal Mart and Carrefour to intensify their investments in China and thereby their mutual competition within the Chinese market.

Could national cultures play a role in the lead for Carrefour? Wal Mart and Carrefour have come from the US and French cultures respectively and entered the realm of another culture, the Chinese. They had different starting points, in terms of culture. Let us briefly compare the two cultures. Of course, the generalizations below have to be understood as just that. They are made for the sake of being brief.

The French are formal and hierarchical, in the sense that they not only respect hierarchy, but also tolerate emphasizing one's role in a hierarchy. They are intellectual and appreciate sophisticated culture. Control is less relevant and time is flexible, although this may depend on someone's place the in hierarchy. The French are not as universalistic as Anglo-Saxon cultures are. They show more appreciation for relationships and flexibility. Still, they are clearly individualistic, to the extent that they are often not good team members.

A US citizen is informal in behavior, but formal in respecting procedures and the rule of law, from a universalistic attitude. He or she respects power, not hierarchy, in the sense that someone is respected not because of a certain role in a hierarchy, but because of the ability to acquire and use power. Control is appreciated and sought. Time is treated with precision. Also in the US, the attitude is largely individualistic, although they are often good team members.

Chinese culture is formal, but also flexible. It understands rules, but also honors relationships. Hierarchy is considered important, but the collectivistic mentality keeps the Chinese from emphasizing their individual role in a hierarchy too strongly.

Possibly we can conclude from this that the French culture would be more understandable to the Chinese than the US culture. The French appreciate relationships more than US citizens do, they are formalistic, while at the same time somewhat flexible; characteristics which bring them closer to Chinese culture than do US characteristics. The French appreciation for cultural sophistication contributes to this as well. Also, less than ideal team-player skills of the French are more appreciated by the Chinese than the proficiency in that matter which is found with US citizens. Both French and Chinese appear to have a certain disdain of the US and are reluctant to take US citizens seriously.

What about company strategies? Wal Mart and Carrefour are very different in this respect; differences which may be related to their national cultures. The main difference is that Wal Mart is centralized, where Carrefour is largely decentralized. When Wal Mart could expand its activities in China, it had a delay of several years, because it focused on expanding in Beijing. Carrefour, on the other hand, focused on opening stores in the provinces and negotiated with provincial governments, which took far less time. It appeared to be treated more favorably by the Chinese authorities, but this could perhaps also be the result of its strategy to negotiate on a regional level, and not on a national level, as Wal Mart did. In distribution, you see the same difference: Wal Mart is building an enormous central distribution facility in Kenzian, while Carrefour has organized its logistical processes in a much more decentralized and local manner.

Probably, the Carrefour approach worked better in China so far than the Wal Mart approach. At least, one can say that Carrefour's expansion has gone more rapidly and in a more profitable manner than Wal Mart's. Culture may not explain everything, but it might well be a factor in this case. Another factor may well be that French products are seen by the Chinese as posh, unlike US products.

A few issues may shed light on the comparison between the two companies. One such issue is product recalls in 2007, which appeared to afflict Wal Mart much more than Carrefour. Another issue is bribery, as accusations of bribery have been uttered regarding Carrefour. Could it be that product recalls are more likely to take place with a centralized logistical structure? Could it be that a decentralized strategy and negotiating with local authorities put a company more at risk of engaging in corruption? It is at least food for thought.

Questions with the case:
- *Which aspects of US culture and of French culture may be closest to the Chinese?*
- *Which aspects of US culture and of French culture may have been difficult to deal with for the Chinese?*
- *What would you recommend Wal Mart to do in the future to compete more effectively against Carrefour in China?*

HOW DOES A CORPORATION CARRY RESPONSIBILITY?

For the definition of 'corporate,' we can use the definition of Daft (2002: 181) provides: "A corporation is an artificial entity created by the state and existing apart from its owners." Crane and Matten (2004:38) concur: "A corporation is essentially defined in terms of legal status and the ownership of assets." In order to understand this notion, we have to recognize first that the corporation is an artificially created entity, a construct. Secondly, it is set up in order to better manage assets, business processes and, not to forget, risks.

In the recent past, two apparently conflicting approaches to organizations have developed side by side. On the one hand, corporations were seen as faceless and dehumanized machines. On the other hand, they were discussed as if they were human, in talk about 'organizational learning,' the 'organizational soul,' the 'spirit of the organization,' and so on. Apparently, we are somewhat accustomed to attributing human characteristics to organizations. What this means is that we recognize those human qualities in the relationships between people, resulting in what we call the 'company culture.' One aspect of company culture is the degree to which it is made explicit. It is the result of commitment.

In general, human beings who are united in some social structure build their own culture, whether they want to or not, and often the people who lead such structures also have a certain impact on the nature of the company culture. But those cultures vary in the degree to which they are consciously and willingly shaped into what they are. How responsibilities are seen and the values from which they are accepted, says much about the culture and leadership of the organization. More on the culture of companies will be said in another volume of this same series (see: *People, Teams and Culture*, by Jones et al.) It is from its own company culture that an organization, or rather the people who belong to it, deal with the responsibilities which follow from their roles in the organization.

It is relevant to make a distinction between the organization as a legal entity and the organization as a social entity, although the two are connected. One could say that the responsibilities of the organization as a legal entity form the bottom line. At the very least you could say that the company has those responsibilities which are prescribed by law. More difficult are the other responsibilities, as they are less clear and less documented. Those other responsibilities are largely derived from social expectations; although less clearly documented, they also have a strong force and are to be taken into account.

APPROACHES TO CORPORATE SOCIAL RESPONSIBILITY

Corporate social responsibility, or CSR, is still widely debated (Vogel. 2006), both with an eye on its very legitimacy as well as with an eye on what it means in practical terms. In this debate two opposite positions can be discerned. On the one hand, there are the critics of CSR. Their most well known representative is Milton Friedman. In a newspaper-article (New York Times. September 13. 1970), he defended the point of view that the main responsibility of a corporation is to satisfy the interests of its owners. This has become known in the classical phrase: "The business of business is business." The argument is that the corporation which serves the interests of its owners is the best suited to create and exchange value. This is in the interest of all involved, including society in a wider sense. There is an argument that can be brought in against this point of view. It holds that apparently many corporations have thrived after having taken into account the interests of several major stakeholders, not just the owners.

On the other side in the debate is a variety of academics, activists and also business people. They give several arguments for associating corporations with much wider responsibilities than Friedman would allow. They argue for a much stronger role of companies in dealing with national and international social problems. An example of this approach can be found in the Millennium Goals project, in which the United Nations, countries, Non-Governmental Organizations, or NGOs, and business organizations work together to address the most serious social problems on the globe. An ethical argument in support of this approach is known in the tradition of ethics as 'might gives plight': someone who has more opportunity to help other people is especially called upon to in fact do so (Dower. N. in: Singer. 1991:.279). One could, for instance, say that if someone is apparently drowning in a canal and there are two bystanders, but of these two only one is an experienced swimmer, then this experienced swimmer is more morally bound to act than the other one who can perhaps only call to other bystanders, or who can offer some other less direct form of support. In the business context, you could say that in addressing the problem of AIDS, some pharmaceutical companies have more options in offering help than other companies, and many governments, and that therefore those companies especially could be called upon to offer some kind of assistance. An argument that is brought in against this is that this approach might lead a business organization into activities which surpass the interests of its primary stakeholders; not only the shareholders, but also, for instance, the employees: Is it in their interest to use the organization's resources in such a way?

One of the more important models to structure the various approaches to CSR is the four-level pyramid (Carroll. 2000). In it, four levels are distinguished, which, as is the case with a pyramid, become smaller as they approach the top, and which are from below to top: 1) economic responsibilities required by society, 2) legal responsibilities likewise required by society, 3) ethical responsibilities as expected by society, and 4) philanthropic responsibilities as desired by society.

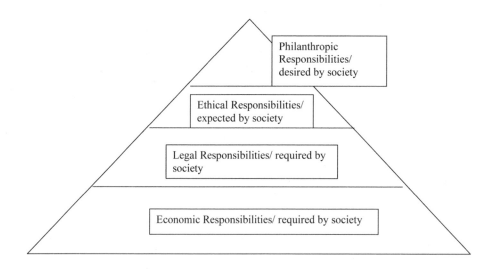

Source: Crane/Matten (2004: 43)

One problem with this structure is that it can be regarded as meaning, as is the case with the Maslow pyramid (Hellriegel. 1995: 140/141), that the 'higher' level is only relevant once the 'lower' levels have been satisfied. This is not in fact the case even with the Maslow pyramid: people often do look for self-actualization even when material needs have not been fully addressed. The Carroll pyramid (Carroll, 2000; Crane and Matten, 2004: 43) also does not mean that the higher levels are only relevant once the lower levels have been satisfied. This would mean, for example, that ethical responsibilities are only addressed once economic and legal responsibilities are fully satisfied. Although this is not what Carroll advocates, his model can be understood in this way.

Also, Crane and Matten (2004) point out that the model does not address the problem of what to do when responsibilities conflict. One could say that the discussions regarding CSR largely are found within the top two levels of the pyramid. Most critics of CSR typically advocate the relevance of economic and legal responsibilities, which business organizations hold toward the societies in which they operate. Those two rungs appear to be the home of the sense-making, which is CSR. What is meant by this is the way in which CSR relates to how people give meaning to their lives through their work. On the other hand, CSR also finds a place in the lower two rungs. After all, it is a matter of responsibility to pay taxes and follow safety laws, to give some examples.

A recent attempt at structuring the CSR debate can be found in The Economist (28. 2005. pp.73-75), in a contribution by Ian Davis, worldwide managing director of McKinsey and

Co. In this contribution, Ian Davis tries to rescue the issue of CSR from a polarized debate. On the one side, he sees the Friedman school of criticism. On the other side, he sees a CSR movement consisting of NGOs trying to influence businesses. Businesses he sees acting defensively as a result of the actions of the NGOs, afraid to be accused of offering 'window-dressing' CSR initiatives. He criticizes both positions.

Davis rejects the Friedman position of 'the business of business is business' by pointing out that it ignores the important role played by social factors in determining business success. His criticism of Friedman also includes pointing out, that questions of ethics and organizational legitimacy cannot be left to legal systems, especially where companies have to do business in countries where such systems are inadequate.

This does not mean that Davis agrees with the other side in the debate, although he appears to be somewhat less critical regarding that side. He criticizes companies for having allowed NGOs and governments to determine the CSR agenda. He claims that in this way they were forced into a defensive position. The alternative, and arguably a middle position, is that companies need to both have a wider perspective than the 'business of business is business' approach would give them, and a better understanding of the role that social issues play in their strategies, and of the related responsibilities and opportunities. Davis calls this the company's 'social contract.' His recommendation is to see CSR in terms of a contract between the company and society.

Davis criticizes the 'business of business is business' approach in terms that it is not aware of the contextual and social aspects behind organizational behavior. He also criticizes the opposed CSR approach by arguing that companies do not construct their own genuine processes of how to make sense with their responsibilities when they merely adopt what comes out of influences from NGOs and governments.

CORPORATE CODES

In the past decades, more and more business corporations have developed a code of ethics. Many professional organizations, such as organizations of accountants, lawyers and journalists, have also developed their own codes. This has regulated the morality within their professional communities. For the sake of the focus of this book, we can forgo discussing them in detail. We therefore focus on the codes within business organizations. The number of those codes has increased in recent years. This is especially the case in the United States of America, but also outside of the United States the number of companies with a code is rapidly increasing.

These codes can be grouped into the following types: 1) border code, 2) aspiration code, 3) statement of corporate values, and 4) a combination of the above.

A border code is a code which states clearly which behaviors are disapproved by the organization. This goes often with an indication of the connected response by the organization, such as dismissal. Such a code is practical. It gives management, for instance the HRM department, tools and guidelines for management development, promotions and, if there is a need to, dismissal. The downside can be that it is not a document which people like to read and have available; often, employees may try to dismiss the code because of this dislike.

An example of an aspiration code can be found in 'The HP Way,' of Hewlett-Packard, or HP. When we look at the statements on diversity in this code, you see that rather than forbidding undesired behaviors, they encourage desired behaviors. It does that by building on the very motivation which the employees of the company have in common in working for that company. This motivation is part of the core of the company culture. Obviously, this is a much more stimulating text to read. However, it lacks the clarity of the border code and thus has less of an instrumental value in management.

For an example of a corporate values statement, we can look at the former ABN AMRO Bank, which during the writing of this book was acquired and ceased to exist as an independent bank. Its brief statement lists the four corporate values of ABN AMRO bank: integrity, teamwork, respect and professionalism. The statement explains how these values were seen by the organization. An indication that this was intended to go well beyond public relations is seen in the link made with the organization's business principles. This was a key component of its strategy. What this means is that the business plans of the business units are also judged on how they express the core values. This core values require to be linked with the business principles, next to other criteria, such as financial and market criteria. The business principles express how at ABN AMRO one is supposed to do business; in other words, what do integrity, respect, teamwork and professionalism mean in terms of the bank's core processes.

The fourth type of code consists of a combination of the above-mentioned types, usually of the border type and the aspiration types. An example of such a code is the Code of Conduct of Shell. This code even combines all three types, as it starts with a statement of the Shell values. It contains certain rules which are clearly of a 'border' type, such as "Don't proceed with an import if there is any doubt about its legality or propriety." It also contains statements which rather have the 'aspiration' quality, such as "Shell is committed to achieving excellence in all its business activities, including health, safety, and environmental performance."

Having a code is for an organization not enough. The code needs to be a part of an ethics program. That means that the organization has to use the code in its HRM processes. For instance, it is of no use to state in your code that integrity is paramount, when you keep hiring untrustworthy people. The signal has to be given to all staff that the code is an instrument that they will have to adhere to and use. For instance, the Shell Code has a section, entitled "How can the code help you?" Such a signal may well come from the CEO, as with the Shell Code, which has a preface by the Chairman. A strong signal is also send by regularly inspecting compliance with the code. Such a program would need to be carefully managed, with equity and the possibility of appeals to unfavorable decisions, as one thing that will strongly undermine the effect of a code of conduct is the appearance of exceptions being made.

Specific attention goes these days to the role of the United Nations' Declaration of Human Rights (see: references). More and more multinational business organizations refer to this document from 1948, although some are also having some difficulty with it. For instance, the Boeing Corporation had an issue with this in 2003, when some shareholders asked the company to adopt a human right policy, especially with an eye on dealing with regimes that are suspected of violating human rights, while the Board of Boeing Corporation advised the shareholders against it, stating that it would unduly limit its opportunities for business. The reason why business organizations refer to the document is that it gives some guidance, especially to their managers and other employees, in dealing with moral dilemmas throughout the many cultures in which the organization operates and has to receive legitimacy.

We have explored in the first part of this chapter that managing across cultures can lead to many misunderstandings and confusing situations (see: Jones, DeBono, Van der Heijden). Company codes can then help in giving guidance, but what grounds do companies have to legitimize the values and rules expressed therein? Referring to the UN Declaration may provide such legitimization. This does require that this aspect of the company code is given attention to in management development programs and other HR processes, so it actually becomes a reality in the culture and day to day life of the organization.

Still, it is sometimes also understandable when companies hesitate to work with the UN Declaration. Often, managers are afraid that referring to the UN Declaration raises expectations among various stakeholders and then opens the company up to litigation and protests. Still, more and more Boards of companies overcome such hesitation. This is an indication of the role that will be played by the UN Declaration of Human Rights in the future.

Questions
- *How do you think representatives of the religious-ethical traditions described above approach a corporate code program?*
- *Would referring to the UN Declaration of Human Rights make a company code stronger? If so, why?*

CONCLUSION

We have seen in this text that various cultural traditions have developed various approaches to expected behavior and responsibility. At the same time, the traditions show certain similarities, which offer platforms for mutual understanding.

Within business organizations, such platforms are increasingly incorporated into codes of ethics or statements of corporate values. They are tools, not eternal answers, which allow managers and leaders to find their way through often confusing situations, enabling them to be productive in those very situations.

REFERENCES

Bilimoria.P. *Indian Ethics*. in: Singer. 1991. pp.43-47

Daft. R.L. 2002 *Management*. South Western College

Davis. Ian. 'The Biggest Contract'. *The Economist*. 2005. n.28. pp.73-75

DeGeorge. R.T. 1999; 1=1982. *Business Ethics*, New Jersey: Prentice Hall

De Silva. P. *Buddhist Ethics*. in Singer. 1991. pp.59-69

Gooding.R. Utility and the Good. in: Singer. 1991

Hansen. Ch. Classical Chinese Ethics. in: Singer. 1991. pp.69-81 *Harvard Business Review on Corporate Responsibility.* 2003. Boston: Harvard Business School Press

Hellriegel. D. and Slocum Jr.,J.W. 2004. *Organizational Behavior*.10th Ed.. Thomson Learning/South-Western

Hutchinson. D.S. Ethics. in: Barnes, J. 1995. *Aristotle*. Cambridge. pp.233-258.

Jones. Stephanie. DeBono. Silvio. Vander Heijden. Beate. *People. Teams. Culture.* Aachen (2008). Meyer Verlag

Kelner. M. Jewish Ethics. in: Singer. 1991, p.82-90

Kotler. Ph. 2005. *Corporate Social Responsibility – doing the most good for your company and your cause*. Hoboken

Nanji.A. Islamic Ethics. in: Singer. 1991. pp.106-118

Schneewind. J.R. Modern Moral Philosophy. in: Singer 1991. pp.147-160

Singer. P. 1991. *A Companion to Ethics*. Oxford: Blackwell

Solomon. R.C. 1992. *Ethics and Excellence – cooperation and integrity in Business.* New York/ Oxford: Oxford University Press

Vogel. D. 2005. *The market for Virtue – The Potential and Limits of Corporate Social Responsibility*. Washington: The Brookings Institution

CODES OF CONDUCT (GENERAL)

ABNAMRO: http://www.abnamro.com/com/about/corp_values.jsp (November. 2007)

HP: http://www.hp.com/hpinfo/abouthp/diversity/?jumpid=reg_R1002 (November. 2007)

Shell:
http://www.shell.com/home/content/aboutshellen/who_we_are/our_values/honesty_int egrity_respect/honesty_integrity_respect_09112006.html (November. 2007)

CODES OF CONDUCT REFERRING TO THE UN DECLARATION OF HUMAN RIGHTS:

The United Nations Declaration of Human Rights:
http://www.un.org/Overview/rights.html (October. 2007)

The United Nations Millennium Goals:
http://www.un.org/millenniumgoals/ (November 2007)

General Electric:
http://www.ge.com/company/citizenship/downloads/pdf/chapters/human_rights_cit07.p df (July 26, 2007

Shell:
http://www.shell.com/home/content/envirosocen/society/human_rights/our_approach_t
o_human_rights/our_approach_to_human_rights_16042007.html (July 26, 2007)
Unilever:
http://www.unilever.com/ourvalues/environment-society/sus-dev-
report/employees/respecting-rights.asp (July 26, 2007)
Boeing:
http://www.boeing.com/companyoffices/financial/finreports/annual/03proxy/item5.html
(July 26, 2007)

RECOMMENDED FURTHER READING

Boatright. J. R.. 2006; 1st = 1993. *Ethics and the Conduct of Business*. Upper Saddle River: Prentice Hall

Crane. A. and Matten. D. 2004. *Business Ethics – A European Perspective*. New York/ Oxford: Oxford University Press

Daft. R.L. 2002 *Management*. South Western College

Donaldson, Th.. 1989. *The Ethics of International Business*. New York/ Oxford: Oxford University Press

Donnelly, J. 2003. *Universal Human Rights in Theory and Practice*. Ithaca/London: Cornell Univsersity Press

DeGeorge. R.T. 1999; 1=1982. *Business Ethics*. New Jersey: Prentice Hall *Harvard Business Review on Corporate Responsibility*. 2003. Boston: Harvard Business School Press

Hellriegel. D. and Slocum Jr.,J.W. 2004. *Organizational Behavior*. 10th Ed. Thomson Learning/South-Western

Jones. St, et al. *People. Teams. Culture*. Aachen (2008) Myer Verlag

Jonsen. Albert R,/ Toulmin. Stephen. 1988. *The Abuse of Casuistry. A History of Moral Reasoning*. Berkeley. University of California Press

Kotler. Ph. Lee. N. 2005. *Corporate Social Responsibility – doing the most good for your company and your cause*. Hoboken: Wiley

Tulder. R. van and Zwart. A. van der. 2006. *International Business-Society Management – Linking corporate responsibility and globalization*. London/ New York: Routledge

Wines. W. A. Napier. N. K. 1992. Toward an understanding of cross-cultural ethics: A tentative model. *Journal of Business Ethics*. Dordrecht. 11: 11. 831-841

CHAPTER ELEVEN
ISSUES WITHIN CORPORATE SOCIAL RESPONSIBILITY – NEW CHALLENGES AND REALITIES
JOOP REMMÉ

LEARNING OBJECTIVES:

- To attain a working insight in some of the most important challenges in CSR
- To acquire some practical ideas on how to deal with those challenges

INTRODUCTION

The meaning of corporate social responsibility, or CSR, can be found in morality. A CSR orientation makes the members of an organization aware of moral issues that were before not so evident. As business organizations increasingly become influential in the societies in which they operate, they face new issues of this kind.

CSR cuts across the traditional boundaries of academic teaching and research. You can see this from the backgrounds of the people who write about the subject: Carroll (1991) is an economist, Crane (2004) a philosopher and Kotler (2005) a marketer, to mention but a few. The issues that we discuss here also reflect the role of CSR in varied business functions. In the following pages, we draw your attention to such multifaceted issues, as they nowadays present themselves in managerial reality.

CORRUPTION

Corruption is defined by Transparency International, a worldwide anti-corruption organization supported by the World Bank, as "the misuse of entrusted power for private gain." (see: references). This definition highlights several elements which are essential to properly understanding corruption: the element of power and its legitimization, the improper use of power and the ego-motive of those who corrupt others and those who allow others to corrupt them. The definition also extends corruption to include more than bribe-paying. It equates corruption with bribe-paying is a common misconception. Forms of nepotism or blackmail are also corruption, as they are ways in which officials and managers deviate from the proper execution of their duties.

But essential to understanding corruption, and thus for doing something about corruption, is not so much whether a bribe is paid or influence is used in some other way. Essential is rather that illegitimate influence is exerted on someone whose correct or incorrect use of entrusted power has value to the person from whom the influence is coming.

A distinction is often made between 'small corruption' and 'big corruption.' This means there is on the one hand the corruption of, often underpaid, civil servants for relatively simple services, such as dealing with a traffic fine, and speeding up a building application. On the other hand there is the corruption of more senior officials/managers, from whom the services bought are of a much larger scale. Typically, the consequences of the first type of corruption stay within the personal sphere of life. The consequences of the second type of corruption reach much further than that.

MYTHS CONCERNING CORRUPTION AND THEIR COUNTERARGUMENTS

The first myth we can look into states "corruption is part of the culture." This myth is heard from people who judge about other people's culture, but also sometimes from members of the culture concerned. Are there in fact corrupt cultures? Apparently, it sometimes seems so. But one caution is that if a country with a particular culture is suffering from a high degree of corruption, this does not necessarily mean that the culture is causing the corruption.

The perception of a link between culture and corruption is also fed by a misunderstanding of other cultures than ones' own. Those cultures may have elements which in some form remind one of corruption, but are these elements indeed indicators of corruption? For instance, several cultures, such as the Arabic, Japanese and Chinese, have rituals of gift giving to establish and solidify relationships. Thus, it is a custom in the Japanese culture to exchange gifts between business contacts. However, that element of gift giving is codified in the culture. The gift needs to be proportionate to the rank of the recipient, it can never be extravagant, it has to express some balance in the relationship, and needs to be announced and given a proper ceremony, to celebrate what it is supposed to express: the quality of the relationship. Does this look like corruption? Would corruption not need to go beyond what is expected to be practical, and thus violate what is prescribed in the culture? Still, sometimes 'corrupt' individuals try to hind behind their culture, benefiting from other peoples' ignorance of that culture.

A myth that is related to the culture myth says: "corruption honors relationships." But a regular business relationship is characterized by the exchange of value and a transparent communication regarding that exchange. When business relationships are solidified, especially as business increasingly consists of repeat business, this is done by establishing trust, whether it is trust in a cosigned contract or trust in a hand shake. In the corrupt relationship, there is only limited trust. Neither party can really rely on the other, not is there some sort of appeal if the arrangement is not met. And are you 'honoring' a relationship with someone if you stimulate that person to deviate from duties and engage in an illegal activity?

Regularly, you can hear the excuse "everyone is doing it." It seems plausible. After all, if indeed everyone is involved in it, then two things can be said: 1) it can not be that bad, and 2) a single person can hardly be expected to deviate from such a common practice. Still, is this in fact true? Perception plays a crucial role here. For instance, according to a 2006 survey held in the Netherlands (see: references), the Netherlands population thinks that 17.5% of public officials are corrupt. The available information indicates that this is in reality between

1% and 3%. But even if the public perception were correct, this would leave us to conclude that in fact the overwhelming majority is not corrupt. When you go to the Transparency International findings, you see that even in countries where corruption is reported to be a serious problem, plenty of respondents indicate that they can stay out of it (see: references). There is also another way of looking at this. Imagine that some state agency indeed is riddled with corruption, would it then for a public official be excusable to take part, given what that official is supposed to do from his or her responsibilities and in service of the public?

Have we not we all heard about the myth that "corruption is a victimless crime?" It refers to the assumption that two people facilitating a deal, perhaps by exchanging money or something else, do not have an impact on other people, outside of that deal. "Business deals are made every day and what is the harm in this one just going a bit more smoothly?" is often the thought. But typically, the checks it tries to bypass are there for a reason. Those checks are there to see to it that public money is spent adequately, and they are there to protect the public from harm. Consider the case where, as reported by the World Bank in **The Economist**, February 8, 2007 (see: references), money is spent on the construction of a road and the construction company representative bribed the official who was to oversee the project, so that he or she would not report that the road had been made 20 centimeters narrower. The result then was that the public received a bad deal for its money. The result was also that the public will have a road which is narrower than standard and accidents may be the result. Or what to think about the case where the owner of an apartment building influences an official not to bother with permits and inspections, after which the owner adds three floors to the building without strengthening the basement structure? It is doubtful if the survivors of that collapsing building, lucky not to have been home at the time of the collapse, will consider corruption to be victimless.

Two related myths are "corruption facilitates business" and "corruption is part of the capitalist way of doing business." To talk about the second of these first, there could be some truth to it. Within the everyday reality of international business, which is predominantly a market reality, corruption does take place. The figures from Transparency International demonstrate this. However, what the myth apparently hints at is that corruption is essentially linked to the market system type of business. We see something similar to what we already saw when talking about the culture myth: A certain characteristic, for example the cultural tradition of gift giving, is perverted and then thought to typify the whole phenomenon. With capitalism this is about business deals, which in the non-perverted form are nothing like corrupt deals, but open and accountable, respecting mutual interests. The "business facilitating" myth has a limited perspective: pertaining to the transaction per se it could be true for a specific instance, but pertaining to business as an ongoing process, it is not.

THE EFFECTS OF CORRUPTION

It is hard to speak of the effects of corruption, on society and on the organization, as corruption typically occurs in secret. When a building or bridge collapses, to mention only two, yet serious, possibilities, it is often hard to determine whether corruption was involved.

Still, more and more is known about the occurrence of corruption and about its consequences. There is sufficient evidence from economics to state that corruption can be linked to a lower level of prosperity, by discouraging investment, increasing the costs of supervision, increasing the waste of resources and other effects, as research by the World Bank indicates (see: references). This would explain the strong correlation between corruption and poverty. Prosperity is also damaged by the other effects, which are identified as lower levels of security/safety and the repairing of damages caused by corruption, lower trust in institutions and a worsened image of a company, industry or country. Corruption also decreases prosperity in that it usually constitutes the abuse of resources, which could have been used in a more productive and prosperity-generating manner. In more general terms, corruption leads to higher costs for doing business. This decreases the competitive force of business and thus in turn leads to other negative consequences.

Special mention has to be given to governance. Corruption damages the trust in governance. Thus it damages its efficiency. But it is also apparently the case that corruption can be stimulated by governance, in an unintended way. Sometimes, laws and regulations are so complicated or conflicting, that some entrepreneurs resort to corruption to circumvent them. It may even happen that this is intentional, as when the elite in a certain country stimulates laws that invite certain people to offer them bribes. Of course, all this damages the trust of the general public and of the business community in government. That lowering of trust has again damaging consequences. This does not mean that corruption always involves government officials. It also occurs in business to business transactions. Still, one could argue that the expectations towards government officials are of a different quality from the expectations towards members of the business world.

Corruption reduces safety in a direct sense, as when a bridge is built without proper supervision and the bridge collapses, probably with loss of human lives. This happened after the government inspector had been bribed. It can also be less direct, in the sense that the public knows that certain safety procedures are not lived up to, so that all kinds of accidents might occur.

WHAT TO DO ABOUT CORRUPTION

Often, people wonder what to do about corruption, especially when they give credence to one of the myths described above. There are no easy solutions. But steps towards improvement are certainly feasible. To begin with, education and public information, doing away with the myths, already have a positive effect. Another step could be to analyze the organizational structures and procedures of organizations. Then one can determine if perhaps some officials are placed in positions which make it tempting to some people to influence them. When, for instance, in procurement, certain decisions have to be approved by several people, instead of by only one, corruption becomes less likely. A more strategic approach is to develop and nourish a culture within the organization in which integrity is promoted and deviating from integrity, as with cases of corruption, is prevented. This has implications for HR and management in general. A code that can be used by management and that can be linked to the organizational culture is the right tool, as a part of an 'ethics program.'

A common factor in the methods to diminish corruption is transparency. This does not mean that everything should be in the open. Both government organizations and business organizations have good reasons to be discrete about certain decisions and certain information. For instance, one reason that comes to mind is protecting the privacy of the individual. Transparency does mean that managers, businessmen and government employees have to be able to be open to the appropriate people. For instance, if a hotel manager and an airline representative make a deal about lodgings for cabin crew, which usually is attractive business for hotels, both of them can be held accountable by their own organizations on how the deal was made and they are obligated to be transparent to their own companies.

This does not completely rule out corruption, as one of them may well represent an organization where corruption is seen as a 'legitimate' way to do business. To give an indication, in some European countries, it is only recently that engaging in corruption in other countries is against the law. Thus, a representative of a Dutch company could well think that corruption in another country was acceptable, considering that his own legal system did not punish the corrupt acts. But if both sides are held to such accountability, corruption has become far less likely. After all, would you bribe someone if you have reason to think that that person will be forced to disclose it?

The World Bank has a vested interest in fighting corruption, as it is an obstacle to economic development. The bank's approach consists mainly in:

- Increasing political accountability;
- Strengthening civil society participation;
- Creating a competitive private sector;
- Institutional restraints on power;
- Improving public sector management.

This confirms the idea that accountability goes a long way in diminishing corruption and protecting development. It requires transparency, and a more professional way of organizing, thus also having an impact on market processes The World Bank's many anti-corruption projects have offered abundant proof of the value of accountability.

Questions:
- *How do you distinguish corrupt deals from legitimate business deals?*
- *How can you notice the effects of corruption?*
- *Is corruption something 'to get used to?'*

BOTTOM OF THE PYRAMID

In 2005, the Indian management theorist C.K. Prahalad published his book *The Fortune at the Bottom of the pyramid – eradicating poverty through profits.* In this book he expresses his amazement that for most business organizations the poor, constituting the overwhelming majority of the world's population, do not constitute a market of interest. He did see that NGOs, national - and international organizations were doing the utmost to help those people, who collectively are called "Bottom of the Pyramid," or BOP, markets. That help was not with overwhelming success. Thus, he came with a novel approach: we have to stop thinking of the poor as victims, but rather as resilient consumers and entrepreneurs. He points out that it is confusing to see the large number of poor people on the planet as 'the poor,' as if they are all determined by that same characteristic. In reality, Prahalad points out, they have needs and offerings like anyone else and they have those in a great variety. This requires a multitude of innovative approaches. He also points out that it is not necessarily relevant to determine how poor 'the poor' precisely are, in terms of income. It is much more interesting to look at the question, how rich or poor they are in terms of the opportunities which they present.

This is at the heart of Prahalads' defense against critics, who have argued that it is causing a waste to offer services and goods to the poor through market processes, as Prahalad suggests.

Prahalad answers to this twofold: 1) poverty is primarily a poverty of choice and giving people choices helps them to reduce their own poverty, and 2) through market processes 'the poor' can be turned into a 'developing market potential' and poverty can be reduced in a more durable manner. Therefore, he speaks of 'inclusive capitalism': a market system which works through and for all. Those who want to shield the poor from a market mechanism do not realize, according to Prahalad, that in fact the poor already organize in intricate informal economies. Connecting with those economies can work in everyones' interests, including the interests of people in the developing world. The very innovations which can be used in developing Bottom of the Pyramid markets are also making the world as a whole more sustainable.

Prahalad gives some twelve principles of innovation that are relevant to become successful in, what he calls, 'bottom of the pyramid markets.' These are:

1   Focus on price performance, with quantum jumps; a bar of soap, in itself, a very simple product, in a supermarket in the Netherlands costs on average 2 euros, while a typical bar of soap in a supermarket in Rwanda lasts much longer and costs the equivalent of half a euro. The Rwandan bar of soap does not have the creamy feel neither the perfume smell; it is just soap. Also, it does not require a fortune in advertising. Thus, it can be much cheaper. Another example is jeans. In India, the average price of jeans is between $40 and $60, and to most people beyond reach. This changed when a company, Ruf and Tuf, started selling "make your own jeans kits" at $6; clearly much more affordable.
2   Hybrid solutions, blending old and new technology. This reacts to how in the developed world 'better' has started to imply 'high tech.' This trend has negative consequences in the developed world, where many people are now stigmatized as not technically sophisticated, while it certainly has negative consequences in the developing world as well. Alternatively, high-tech and low-tech can be combined. For instance, when in Rwanda a modern grid-based telephone network is combined with a community-based system of communication, a single telephone can give an entire shantytown access to telecommunication. A similar system exists in India.

3   Scaleable and transportable operations across countries, cultures and languages. Transportation does not have to mean the same thing in every country. A transportation system that makes perfect sense in Europe would probably be dependent on an infrastructure which in other countries is not available or not reliable. It then makes perfect sense to rethink logistics fundamentally.

4   Reduced resource intensity: eco-friendly products. This is something that is in the interest of both the developing and the developed world. For the developing world, this will make products and services less expensive and thus more accessible. At the same time, this has value for both the developed world and the developing world, in terms of reducing the rate of depletion of the earth's resources.

5   Radical product redesign from the beginning. This is a radical call to producing companies to do their job better. Instead of developing a product and then looking for a market where it can be sold, a producer offers more value if he or she develops the product in the market where he or she wants to sell it and in close connection with the needs that his or her product could satisfy.

6   Building logistical and manufacturing infrastructure. Sometimes infrastructure is not present because the perspective that is used is based upon the model that was developed in developing countries and then considered not to be feasible in developing countries. However, if you develop it without that model much more may well be possible.

7   De-skill work in services. Many services within the developing world have become more efficient, but also burdened with technology. If a helpdesk employee in a developing country does not have sophisticated IT at his or her disposal, service may be slower, but still very feasible.

8   Educate customers to product usage. Some years ago, Nestlé exported, from Switzerland, its baby formula to African countries. The product had to be mixed with water. However, it was developed in a country where you can safely drink water from any tap. In Africa, this is not typically the case. This resulted in serious problems once the Nestlé product was introduced. The solution proved to be to educate women at community level in how to safely use the product.

9   Products must work in hostile environments. Where infrastructure and organizational structures are not yet fully developed, products must be developed, produced and packaged with that in mind. For instance, when products can be packaged in Europe in simple card board boxes, they need a different way of packaging in a country with mud roads and an extreme climate. This may also lead to new opportunities in developed and developing countries alike.

10   Adapt user interfaces to heterogeneous consumer bases. Not all people in developing countries are alike – not even within the same market. Companies therefore have to accommodate their clients in their diversity, both in developing and in developed countries.

11   Design distribution methods to reach both rural and urban areas. The poorest people on the planet live predominantly in either remote rural areas or in urban shanty towns. Connecting to their informal economies means being able to emplace logistics and communication processes which reach both environments.

12   Focus on broad architecture, enabling quick and easy incorporation of new features. Markets and opportunities have become more diverse with the development of BOP markets, and companies which can be the more flexible in that new reality will have greater chances of success.

The aspects mentioned above are intertwined. For instance, logistical infrastructure is poor or absent, and other aspects, such as educating customers or distributing the re-designed products, may well be difficult. This leaves the people in those markets dependent on products and services that do not sufficiently honor their needs.

The book by Prahalad stimulated the already existing movement, in which companies, NGOs and individuals find each other and start such processes as 'BOP Finance' and 'BOP Development.'

Questions:
- *Why do some companies think that the BOP population does not constitute a market for them?*
- *What is the primary challenge for companies in trying to connect to the BOP population?*
- *Why does developing BOP business not mean developing more high tech solutions?*
- *Does the BOP approach require new approaches in finance?*

THE MORALITY OF FINANCE

Islamic banking was developed in the last decades of the last century in Egypt. It spread to other countries in the Middle East, in response to practices in the international financial industry. Within Islamic banking, interest is seen as immoral, partly because it is supposed to stimulate greed in the individual. The objections within Islam against interest are in fact a repetition of the discussion within Christianity in the 13th and 14th centuries, in which the Christian church objected to interest as sinful. At the same time, the development of cities and trade indicated a growing need for financial services. This gave the church the challenge to design ways in which financial services could be offered. They had to be offered in such a way that it would not jeopardize the spiritual well-being of those concerned.

The other main characteristic of Islamic banking is the sharing of profit and loss. This gives Islamic banking institutions the challenge of product redesign, as they have to design their products without interest. An exception to this is 'hibah,' a gift, which is some interest paid by the bank to its clients as a reward for a savings account balance.

Observing the principle of avoiding interest, various products fall under the heading of 'Islamic banking.' For instance, a mortgage works in a different way. Instead of the loan structure which is traditionally the case with a mortgage, in Islamic banking the bank buys the item, typically a piece of real estate, and then sells it to the client in installments at a profit and against the certainty of some collateral. Unlike interest, profit is allowed in Islamic banking. Another approach to mortgage is 'Ijara wa Iqtina,' which comes down to leasing. In the leasing approach, the property is in the name of the bank, rather than in the name of the client, which is also possible as 'Ijara wa Iqtina'. And in another example, 'Mudaraba,' or venture capital, is arranged without interest and in such a way that bank and entrepreneur share profit and risk. Other banking products, comparable to products in the mainstream financial industry, are set up in similar ways.

Another approach to criticizing finance comes from a movement of which Bernhard Lietaer (2002) is the most outspoken representative. He too warns that the mainstream financial system may well stimulate greed. Unlike Islamic Banking's emphasis on the individual transaction, Lietaer emphasizes banking's impact on the international financial system. He also holds that a system of cultivating scarcity predicts that increasingly the monetary system will include local and unofficial currencies. Those currencies will complement the existing national currencies, much like the Islamic and Micro Credit systems complement mainstream finance. As an example he points to the French 'Grain de Sel', or 'grain of salt', network of consumers and entrepreneurs, in which people exchange in goods and services without any of the official currencies. His criticism of the financial systems is that he sees a wide disparity between economic developments and financial developments. For instance, the success of a company in terms of its core processes may have little to do with the development of its stock price, and the same goes for national systems. This has to do, so he argues, with the characteristic that the monetary system is built on short term gain, which makes it very hard to invest in something which is in the not short term profitable. The implications of this will become apparent when we discuss sustainability, in the next chapter.

The Micro Credit movement forms another source of criticism of the mainstream financial industry, which is linked to the BOP movement, discussed above. As recognized by the World Bank (see: references), a large part of the world's population would have no access to financial services if it were not for micro credit institutions. Typically, loans for modest sums are not worthwhile for banks to offer, due to the banks' cost structure. Also, often those who apply for such modest loans do not have any collateral, and the banks do not accept the risk of offering a loan without collateral. Often, those turned down by the banks for these reasons have only loan sharks to turn to, and face impossible interest rates.

To meet these issues, a micro finance industry has slowly developed since the middle of the last century, although a precursor can be seen in the village bank movement led by Wilhelm Raiffeissen in Germany in the second half of the 19th century. Both Raiffeissen and his Canadian colleague Desjardins started their movement from concern over excessive interests asked for loans. In the last decades of the 20th century, several micro finance institutions have developed on the basis of radically new loan products and new processes. For Instance, Grameen Bank requires, instead of collateral, that the loan is supported by five members of the applicants' community, not being relatives. Notable is also the fact that the founder of Grameen Bank, Muhammed Yunus, received the Nobel Prize for Economics in 2006 for his work on micro finance. Still there is also criticism, as some wonder whether microfinance is sustainable as an industry given doubts about the repayment rate, justified or not, and other flaws.

Questions:
- *What is the main moral issue that is addressed in Islamic Banking?*
- *Is there a moral issue within the mainstream financial industry? If so, what is the issue or what are the issues?*
- *What is the use of micro-credit? Why would it be a matter of CSR?*
- *Are the new approaches in finance, such as micro credit and Islamic banking, more or less vulnerable to corruption than existing practices in finance?*

DISCRIMINATION

For as long as we can recall, discrimination has existed. It has also for quite some time been criticized as unjust. The concern stems from the idea that all people deserve to be treated justly. All major cultures and religions know this notion, although it sometimes becomes complicated through the impact of other notions and customs. Increasingly this came to mean "the same as other people under similar circumstances." In other words, different people should not be treated differently when they find themselves in the same situation.

In itself, discrimination is necessarily a problem. It merely means 'to distinguish' and this is something we do all the time. But in practice it came to stand for 'to distinguish negatively.' This means that after having made a distinction between people, you then favor some over others for no other reason than that you think more highly of some people than you do of others. In an extreme, and unfortunately all but rare, form, this results in racism and sometimes even genocide. Racism means that you think of people as divided into specific ethnic groups – races – and then consider some ethnic groups as markedly inferior to others. In other words, first there is a generalization and then a value judgment.

History has shown many examples of this. One is the slave trade, in particularly the 17th, 18th and 19th centuries, in which European slave traders brought millions of African slaves to the Americas. The racism that spurred this slave trade was the idea that the indigenous population of Latin and Central America was not fit to do manual labor. Thus, the colonialists started to look for other and more suitable people to do their labor. Those people they still regarded as 'inferior' to their own ethnic group. Those people they found in Africa. They bought slaves from African slave traders and brought them to the Americas, often in cruel and demeaning ways. The racist attitude towards African people has tarnished Western culture until deep into the 20th century. Unfortunately, we can still find examples these days. The Moulin Rouge case, described below, gives but one example.

A variation on this racist attitude can be found in the system of 'apartheid,' which existed in South Africa from at least 1919, when the term was first used, until 1994. It consisted in political control by a Caucasian minority, which had come from Europe, primarily the UK and the Netherlands. It led to a segregation of society along ethnic lines. This was segregation in two senses. The first was geographical segregation, in that certain parts of South Africa were considered 'thuislanden', or 'home territories', for the indigenous African population, with some degree of self rule. The other was segregation by law in that there were different rules for citizens of different ethnic backgrounds. In other words, the ethnic background of a citizen determined how the state would treat that citizen. Law forbade marriages, or even romantic encounters, between members of different ethnic groups. Facilities such as buses, restaurants and toilets had to be separate. The better jobs were reserved for people of European descent. Thus, racism had been institutionalized in South African society.

A less extreme form of apartheid, but apartheid nonetheless, took place in parts of the United States of America in the 20th century. In the United States of America, slavery was abolished after the civil war of 1860-1865. After the period of slavery, racial relations were regulated in the so called 'Jim Crow laws.' According to those laws, the separate ethnic groups, primarily those of European background and those of African background, were to enjoy 'separate but equal' facilities. This was established in the court case Plessy v. Ferguson (see: references). The laws were specifically aimed at transportation, but soon also included restaurants, theatres and schools. In practicality, 'separate but equal' was rarely equal. What it amounted to was that US citizens of African descent received lesser quality facilities and services. Many US citizens of European descent felt justified in their discriminatory practices by the official policies.

How institutionalized this was became apparent in the 1960s, when after a wide civil rights movement the segregation laws were for the most part changed, it appeared that the school districts were designed so that ethnic separation in education would persist. In response to that, the authorities ordered 'busing'. This meant that schools were ordered to be more integrated and many children would be transported by bus to schools even if these were not the nearest schools. Apparently, institutionalized segregation required an institutional solution.

Other institutionalized forms of discrimination have existed and some still exist today. The above are examples of discrimination on the basis of ethnic background, and such institutionalized discrimination still exists, but there are also other kinds of institutionalized discrimination. As an example, we can look at countries where women do not have the same rights, officially or in practice, as men do. To give an example, it is only a few decades ago that women in the Netherlands could only buy real estate if a man cosigned.

Racism does not only exist in the relationships between people of European and people of African descent. It is unfortunately a global concern, which is why it plays a role in the CSR considerations of business organizations. For instance, Korean migrant workers in Japan often complain about a racist attitude on the part of Japanese people. And within Africa, there are in many countries tensions of a racist nature between people of different ethnic or cultural background. And racism is not the only kind of discrimination, as we can also see sexism, ageism and other kinds.

What causes racism is probably complicated, and several factors may well be involved. There may be an ideology which deems certain people as inferior to other people. For instance, the now illegal caste system in India can be regarded as such an ideology. There can also be the effect of geological circumstances. We can think of the traditionally negative attitude of Japanese people towards Chinese and Koreans can partly be explained through the Japanese island background and the xenophobia which resulted from it. There is often the element of fear. In the United States of America, for instance, racism on the part of the Caucasian working class has to do with the fear of losing jobs to African-Americans, Hispanics or yet others. Another cause may be governmental. For instance, in some African countries, the erstwhile colonial powers relied on certain ethnic groups, thus, willingly or unwillingly, fueling tension between that ethnic group and other ethnic groups in the country.

More clear is what to do about racism: communicate and educate. Studies, for instance on the white-supremacist Ku Klux Klan in the United States of America, have shown that when such a movement is growing, the actual growth takes place in areas where the local population has not really been much in contact with people of a different ethnic background or culture. It has also been shown that once such contact has taken place, the tendency towards racism declines. Racism and discrimination typically go hand in hand with cultivating stereotypes.

A stereotype is both a normal phenomenon and a dangerous one. To give an example of the normality of it: when a small dog stays away from big dogs, possible motivated by a nasty occurrence or taught to do so by other small dogs, it cultivates the stereotype 'big dogs are trouble.' This stereotype may work well for the small dog. Still, it is sometimes a bit unjust, as when the small dogs treat a very friendly big dog from that same stereotype. This is an example from the world of pets, but surely we can all think of comparable stories within the human domain.

This stereotyping can turn out to be unjust, even to the point of being blatantly racist and a source of discrimination. Then we see stereotypes such as 'Hispanics are lazy,' and 'women are weak.' Three remarks have to be made on this: Firstly, what would make such statements racist, or sexist, is that they can only be true if the qualification is part of the definition. This means that the statements would only be true, if it is essential for a Hispanic to be lazy, and for a woman to be weak. One answer to that is to point at examples to the contrary, which are abundantly available.

Secondly, even when a stereotype rings true, as someone may well have met people who appear to fit the stereotype, there is injustice. This is at least in terms of how it is often perceived, in that someone is identified with a group, completely apart from how that particular individual himself behaves. For example, especially when it is true that Dutch people are perceived to be rather blunt, for someone to be called a 'typical Dutchman' is neither always justified nor in all cases pleasant. The answer to this would be to use the stereotype for as far as it applies to the individual and the best way to discover its meaning is to communicate with that individual.

Thirdly, stereotypes themselves can be rather innocent. Someone who states that Africans have 'a terrific sense of rhythm' may well intend this statement with respect. Still, such statements are often accompanied with a value judgment, indicating that some people are inferior in some way to other people. To continue the example just given, one may well consider ones' own group inferior, as in 'we do not have the sense of rhythm Africans have,' but does that make much of a difference?

But the problem is: How can you have the authority to make such statements about other people, especially when it concerns people who are different from you and who you might for that reason not fully understand? The assumption of such authority is called 'moral absolutist.' It is often the cause of intolerance and discrimination. A reply to this could be to establish the legitimacy of value statements, and downplay those that are not legitimate.

Discrimination is the more problematic against the background of a growing international consensus on treating people as equal, as expressed in the UN Declaration on Human

Rights (see: references). The first part of the very first article of this declaration, dating from 1948, reads *"All human beings are born free and equal in dignity and rights."* A proper understanding of this first article should prevent many of the misunderstandings that occur. What we are not talking about is that all people are the same or should be the same. On the contrary, the article continues with *"They are endowed with reason and conscience and should act towards one another in a spirit of brotherhood."* This means that each person has the right and the responsibility to make personal choices, and should in principle be seen as equipped to do so. We all know that some people are more able to do so than other people, but that is not the point. Rather, all people are in principle regarded as entitled to make their very own choices.

The undeniable differences between people do not diminish this principle. To underscore this point, the Declaration adds in the second article *"Everyone is entitled to all the rights and freedoms set forth in this Declaration, without distinction of any kind, such as race, color, sex, language, religion, political or other opinion, national or social origin, property, birth or other status. Furthermore, no distinction shall be made on the basis of the political, jurisdictional or international status of the country or territory to which a person belongs, whether it be independent, trust, non-self-governing or under any other limitation of sovereignty."* In other words, no difference that can be discerned between people takes away the principle that is stated in the first article, that all people have the right to be treated as equals.

Case *"The Moulin Rouge"*

One of the most famous French institutions is the Moulin Rouge nightclub in Paris. It is best known for its shows, but it is also a restaurant of some standing in French society. This institution had put an advertisement in the French newspapers in 2000 for new waiters. One of the persons who applied for these jobs, Abdelouye Marega, was very qualified, as a person and in having a certificate as a waiter. The manager of Moulin Rouge initially responded favorably to his application, until he noticed that the applicant was originally from Senegal. Then the application was turned down.

The waiter went to a social worker, who called the Moulin Rouge and asked for an explication. The answer he received was clear: "At the Moulin Rouge, we only employ foreigners if they are European and not colored, while we do employ colored people in the kitchen". The social worker did not find this acceptable and contacted SOS Racisme, a French anti-discrimination watchdog. This organization then decided to send several other applicants to Moulin Rouge, by way of test, and found the statement to reflect standing policy. It appeared that all of the low skilled jobs in the kitchen were filled with employees of African background, while all the waiters were European.

SOS Racisme compared this with Apartheid and filed a complaint with the courts.

The case was decided in November 2002 in favor of Mr. Marega and both the establishment and the HRM executive were fined. This was confirmed in appeal, although the fines were lowered. The Moulin Rouge executive had argued in court that the establishment had never in its 112 year old history hired a non-European as a waiter. This was not accepted by the courts. Also, arguments of a more managerial nature – "hiring an African as a waiter would damage the team spirit amongst the waiters" – were not deemed acceptable by the courts.

Still, treating people as equals is not always easy, even when one has the most respectful intentions. As we have seen, the UN Declaration does recognize that people have many ways in which they are different. And, what has not even been mentioned, people find themselves in very different circumstances. Those different circumstances can pertain to their work life, their housing situation, their professional development, their social life. But the question is, whether those differences are relevant. The UN Declaration states that in terms of the various rights, which are spelled out in the 28 articles which follow the two just given, no distinction has any impact on how human beings are entitled to those rights. For instance, article 6 states that every person has the right to be considered as a person before the law, completely independently from how one can be characterized in terms of the features mentioned in the second article. This means that a poor person is in principle as much a person before the law as is a rich person, a woman as much as a man, a Muslim as much as a Christian, etc. Discrimination constitutes the opposite of these principles, laid out in the UN Declaration. With discrimination, some people are allowed fewer opportunities than people with different characteristics.

The value behind the first articles of the UN Declaration is 'respect.' This term is derived from the Latin word 'respicere,' which means as much as 'to take someone in regard.' In other words: the other person is deemed worthy of being taken into consideration. This is within most cultures recognized as functional and desirable. The problem, however, with respect is that it is the more difficult where it is the most needed. To take someone else into consideration is the more relevant where the other person is different from you and then it is also more difficult than when the other person has much in common with you. The more someone else differs from you, the more you are likely to have some difficulty in showing the other person respect, even when you do intend to do so.

With differences becoming wider, chances for misunderstanding increase and so do problems in communicating. Probably 'respect' means not so much understanding each other, which might indeed be difficult, but rather that one deems someone else worth the effort of trying to understand him or her. An example within the business reality is to be found in teamwork. As we know, what distinguishes a team is that its members offer value to each other and to their joint project from their unique backgrounds, personalities and roles. What is important for the success of a team is that its members respect each other, in the sense that they deem each other and the quality of their cooperation worthy to invest energy in.

Sometimes discrimination is done with what are claimed to be 'good intentions.' What if someone from his religious beliefs, for instance, holds the point of view that women need to be protected and that for that reason he keeps his wife as much as possible in the confines of the house? He may well have the best intentions towards his wife, as he is trying to protect her. And what about the attitude that could be found in the past with certain colonialists, who kept the population of 'their' colonial territories away from political power, because they did not want to 'trouble them with the concerns of government'. They may have meant this well, although probably not all did. But it is still discrimination.

The core of the matter is that people are kept from making their own choices and from benefiting from opportunities as they arise. Allocating those freedoms and opportunities on the basis of race, gender, age, political beliefs, sexual preference, language and religion is deemed unjustified discrimination.

Another form of well intended discrimination is 'affirmative action.' This is the case where the perception exists that certain groups of people are disadvantaged in society and deserve extra support. The consequence is that in public or governmental organizations in hiring new staff or awarding business-contracts preference is given to members of the disadvantaged groups, sometimes also by using quotas. This does merit discussion. On the one side, there are those who claim that this places political considerations above quality, in finding the very best applicant for the job, and there are also people from perceived disadvantaged backgrounds who object to the policy as underestimating their individual abilities to seize opportunities by themselves. One the other side, there are those who claim that it should be possible to find suitable applicants from the disadvantaged group, so affirmative action would not diminish quality. They claim that affirmative action does not have any disadvantages and helps those who need a bit of support. Applying affirmative action is in some cases regulated by law and in other cases a result of an organization's initiative, strategy and culture.

The issue of (non-) discrimination is typically found within human resource processes as 'equity principle.' This principle acknowledges that every person is entitled to 'equal treatment with respect to employment.' The important term here is 'treatment,' as the equality does not pertain to the outcome of HR processes, but to their unbiased nature. It means that the rules which a company has set for its HR processes apply equally to all employees and, in the case of hiring, potential employees. If, for instance, an organization has a rule that states that a bonus is given of a certain amount for all achievement above a certain defined norm, then the equity principle would imply that this applies to all employees equally, unless it is stated in the rule that it only applies to certain categories of employees, such as. Sales-representatives, but then too it has to be applied equally within those categories.

Questions:
- *What constitutes the negative connotation in the concept of 'discrimination?'*
- *Describe five lines along which discrimination can take place.*
- *When would it be legitimate within a business context to discriminate?*
- *Describe the causes of racism. Do they imply ways of preventing or limiting the problem?*
- *How can discrimination have an impact on the success of business and/or the organization?*
- *What is meant by the notion of 'glass ceiling?'*
- *What is behind 'affirmative action' and how does it work?*

HUMAN RIGHTS AND CULTURE

Regarding human rights, the question is often raised, whether human rights equally relate to specific cultural contexts. Specifically, the fact that human rights are individual, in the sense that every human being can individually claim these rights, may link them closer to cultures with an individualistic tendency and not so much to cultures with a more collectivistic tendency. Thus, treating ethics and human rights from the point of view of the individual may perhaps be confusing to people from cultures which have seen great benefit from emphasizing the group, rather than the individual.

Officially, we can say that human rights are inalienable rights of every single human being, as per several international treaties. Those treaties are signed by the overwhelming majority of countries. It can also be remarked that human rights have a basis in the major cultural traditions.

The principle of human rights is meant to protect all human beings, regardless of cultures and national preferences. In reality, of course, the people who have these rights, in other words: all people, live in a cultural context; sometimes in a clear national context, increasingly in a multicultural context.

How to deal with this? For a start, a distinction can be made between having individual rights and the use of human rights. What this means is that from diverging cultural traditions - diverging also in the degree of individualism/ collectivism -, people are inclined in different ways to how they use their rights, while they al possess those rights individually. After all, the UN Declaration of Human Rights is written in a way which allows for such different applications, while keeping the same core. For instance, the economic rights can be used to support the clan or extended family, but also to provide for the dependants in the nuclear family of just for the individual.

The Indian Noble Prize winner Amartya Sen argued in one of his latest books, *Identity and Violence: The Illusion of Destiny (Issues of Our Time)* (1999), that international conflict can best be dealt with not by pointing at cultural differences, but by downplaying cultural identities and emphasizing individual rights and interests. He advocates thinking in terms of what any individual would need for a worthy life. He also described extensively the roots of personal freedoms in various Asian cultural traditions (1999: 227-248). A similar argument was given by Stephen Toulmin, some 20 years ago, in his *The Abuse of Casuistry* (1988), who described the abortion debate in the US and pointed out that seemingly unbridgeable differences could still be bridged once the discussion focused on individual circumstances and interests. These contributions appear to emphasize the value of thinking in terms of human rights.

At the same time, it would also be valuable to engage in thought-experiments, in terms of "how would you use your individual human rights given your cultural background and the cultural backgrounds of those around you?" And also "how do you expect someone with a specific different cultural background to go about this?"

Of course, individualism is not the same as egotism; far from it, as rights come with obligations as well. Certain countries with supposedly individualistic cultures also show a high degree of community work/ volunteer work. On the other hand, countries with supposedly collectivistic cultures often show a high degree of ego drive. The difference is perhaps mainly one of starting-point: in both types of culture, the individual and the group are important, but either the individual is regarded from the perspective of the group or the other way around. Also, conferring rights to individuals does not exclude their right to exercise their rights in service of their group. Thus you see certain differences in emphasis.

Regarding ethics, we have seen in chapter 10 that the major cultural traditions, including those which have originated from Asia, ethics is seen as pertaining to the behavior of the individual. Of course, you see that some cultures that this behavior is strongly seen in a group context, as with Confucianism, while with other cultures it is strongly focused on the individual, even as possibly transcending a group context, as with Buddhism. But, again, this is not an either/or distinction, but rather a shift in emphasis.

Questions:
- *What does it mean that human rights are the rights of all humans?*
- *What does the distinction between having rights and using rights mean in practical terms?*
- *What would the thought experiment, mentioned in the text, offer you?*

HEALTH

Especially multinational organizations are increasingly sensitive to issues within the sphere that is called 'HSA,' or 'Health and Safety Affairs.' Of course, health issues signify one of the ways in which a company can have an impact upon the lives of its stakeholders. It also signifies the ways in which the individual lives of employees can have an impact on the companies in which they work. Thus it affects the responsibilities of companies regarding their stakeholders. It may even become part of the company culture. Shell, for instance, prides itself on its HAS-record.

Increasingly companies accept this responsibility and even distinguish themselves in how they do so. Here too we can see a shift from responsibility towards primary stakeholders to responsibility also to secondary stakeholders. In terms of primary stakeholders, we especially speak of responsibility towards consumers and employees, and the responsibility of the organization is generally recognized as a direct consequence of how the organization conducts its core processes. It is typically regarded to be a central responsibility of an organization to ascertain that its products are safe for its consumers and that its production processes are safe for its employees.

But increasingly this responsibility is extended to secondary stakeholders, partly as the result of incidents which have demonstrated the relevance of this issue. Production processes are not only expected to be safe for employees. They also have to be safe for people, and other creatures, living nearby. This development also comes from the other direction – from society at large to the organization – in the form of health issues which affect the organization and require its responsiveness. Primarily, we can think here of infectious diseases, such as HIV and malaria, which can have an enormous impact on an organization's processes and lead to the acceptance of new responsibilities.

Case *"Heineken: Cool @ Work"*
The beverages company Heineken, best known for its Heineken beer, has to deal with health in three sometimes connected contexts. The first is connected with its beers (besides Heineken, the company has a variety of other brands of beer), which contain

alcohol (of course I am excluding here its non-alcoholic beer) and alcohol may affect a person's health. The second context is about the potential hygiene and overall health risks in its facilities. The third context has to do with some of the countries in which it operates, as those countries have populations which are seriously hurt by life-threatening diseases, such as malaria and HIV.

The first two contexts are addressed in Heineken's Cool @ Work program. It starts from the recognition that "as an alcohol producing company, Heineken has a special responsibility towards helping to prevent abuse and misuse of alcohol and promoting responsible consumption." This appears to limit responsibility to the organization's primary stakeholders, but in fact it goes beyond that, as "abuse and misuse of alcohol" also pertains to consumption of alcohol by those who should not be consumers, such as minors and pregnant women. This extension beyond primary stakeholders is recognized. It is also stated that the organization aims to be 'socially acceptable.'

But the basis is formed by the two groups of primary stakeholders, the consumers and the employees. Regarding the consumers, this means that Heineken is careful in how it markets its alcoholic products, for instance in not targeting vulnerable groups of potential consumers. It is also careful in advocating a responsible way of consuming alcohol in its advertisements and other communications. The employees are divided within human resource management into three groups: green or responsible drinkers, including non-drinkers, amber or drinkers at risk, and red or problem drinkers. Remarkable here is that Heineken hereby also takes the private lives of the employees into account. The green employees are seen as not causing problems, although educational programs will still be designed for them. They constitute what Heineken likes to call its 'ambassadors': employees who show a responsible attitude towards the consumption of alcohol.

Each Heineken company is expected to identify the members of each group of employees. Typically most fall in the green category. Certain groups of employees, such as sales staff, may fall in the amber category. Those in the red category have to be identified by name, known only to those it concerns, so that counseling and other forms of support can be provided for them.

Each Heineken company is expected to have tools and programs available to promote the responsible use of alcohol, which include education, 'employee assistance programs,' codes and checks. Top management decided that Heineken companies must have these in place and functioning. It is the responsibility of central departments, such as health services, to offer expertise, while at the same time the management of each Heineken company has to develop those services in the form best fitting local circumstances.

[Source: Heineken]

Questions:
- *How is health the responsibility of a business organization?*
- *To what extent is health the responsibility of a business organization?*

CONCLUSION

The term 'corporate social responsibility' covers a wide range of concepts and issues. In general, it refers to the various responsibilities which business organizations may have toward their stakeholders; in short, toward all members of society, including the future members of society. Those responsibilities include integrity in doing business, the absence of which will result in corruption and cause damage; the just treatment of employees, which is at stake in issues of discrimination; and how stakeholders are serviced or made dependent financially and in terms of their health. This list is not exhaustive, but it gives a good idea of the most pressing issues within CSR at the start of the 21st century.

REFERENCES

Carroll, A.B. 1991. The pyramid of corporate social responsibility: toward the moral management of organizational stakeholders. *Business Horizons*. July-August. 39-48.

Crane. A. and Matten. D. 2004. *Business Ethics – A European Perspective*. New York/ Oxford: Oxford University Press

The Economist. 2001. *Business Ethics – facing up to the issues*. January 20. London: Economist Newspaper.

The Economist 2005. The Good Company- A sceptical look at corporate social responsibility. January 22. London: Economist Newspaper.

Donaldson. Th. 1989. *The ethics of international business*. New York/ Oxford: Oxford University Press

Kotler. Ph. 2005. *Corporate Social Responsibility – doing the most good for your company and your cause*. Hoboken

Lietaer. B. 2002; 1st =1999. *The Future of Money: creating new wealth, work and a wiser world*. London: London

Microfinance. http://www.microfinancegateway.org/ (July 26, 2007)

Prahalad. C.K. 2005. *The Bottom of the Pyramid – Eradicating Poverty through Profits*. Upper Saddle River: Wharton School Publishing

Sen. Amartya. 2007. *Identity and Violence: The Illusion of Destiny (Issues of Our Time)* New York. W.W. Norton and Company

Toulmin. Stephen and Jonsen. Albert R. *The Abuse of Casuistry – A History of Moral Reasoning*. Berkeley/ Los Angeles/ London (1988) University of California Press

WEBSITES

Bottom of the Pyramid:

http://www.12manage.com/methods_prahalad_bottom_of_the_pyramid.html (July 26, 2007)

http://www1.World Bank.org/sp/safetynets/Micro%20Finance.asp (July 26. 2007)

Corruption:

Transparency International. www.transparency.org (July 26, 2007)

http://www.transparency.org/news_room/faq/corruption_faq#faqcorr1 (November 29, 2007) (on the definition of 'corruption')

http://www.transparency.org/news_room/latest_news/press_releases/2006/en_2006_10
_04_bpi_2006 (July 26. 2007) (on corruption perception)
http://www.overheidsinformatie.nl/?orgidt=Org_018445 (July 26, 2007; in Dutch) (on
survey in The Netherlands)
http://www.economist.com/research/articlesBySubject/displaystory.cfm?subjectid=5263
58&story_id=8675326 (November 29, 2007) (on the World Bank and corruption)
http://econ.World Bank.org/external (July 27. 2007) (on corruption and prosperity)
Discrimination:
Plessy vs. Ferguson. 1896. (Ruling by the US Supreme Court. 1896)
http://caselaw.lp.findlaw.com/scripts/getcase.pl?court=USandvol=163andinvol=537 (July
26, 2007)
http://www.un.org/Overview/rights.html (December 2, 2007)
Lietaer:
http://www.transaction.net/money/book/ (November 29, 2007)

RECOMMENDED FURTHER READING

Bardhan. P. 1997. Corruption and Development: A Review of Issues. *Journal of Economic
Literature. 35*:3. 1320-1346

Becker, G.S. 1971. *The Economics of Discrimination.* Chicago: The University of Chicago
Press

Donaldson. Th. 1989. *The ethics of international business.* New York/ Oxford: Oxford
University Press.

Hort. Stuart I. *Capitalism at the Crossroads – Aligning Business, Earth and Humanity.* 2007
Upper Saddle River

Maurer. W. Anthropological and accounting knowledge in Islamic banking and finance:
rethinking critical accounts. *Journal of the Royal Anthropological Institute.* London 8 (4),
645–667.

Plous, S. 2002. *Understanding Prejudice and Discrimination.* Columbus: McGraw-Hill

Mauro. P. Corruption and Growth. *The Quarterly Journal of Economics. 110:* 3: 681-712

Strauss. J. Thomas. D. Health, Nutrition, and Economic Development. *Journal of Economic
Literature. 36:* 2. 766-817

CHAPTER TWELVE
CORPORATE SOCIAL RESPONSIBILITY AND SUSTAINABILITY – THE GLOBAL CHALLENGE
JOOP REMMÉ

LEARNING OBJECTIVES:

- To become familiar with two emerging realities in management: CSR and sustainability
- To become familiar with some of the challenges that have resulted from those realities
- To be able to work with some practical points for being successful within those new realities

INTRODUCTION

These days, there is a tendency to have high expectations of the moral quality of a company's actions. This appears to be a universal trend. You could say that this trend is fed from two sources. One source is societal concern about the behavior of organizations. This tradition acheived renewed momentum in the '70s, when pollution of the environment, scarcity of resources and involvement of companies in systems that were deemed unjust, such as with apartheid, caused many people to look more critically at business organizations. The other source is international attention to global concerns which have such an impact on society that business organizations are increasingly affected by them and even called upon to act upon them. Important examples of such concerns are global warming and terrorism.

STAKEHOLDERS AND STAKEHOLDER MANAGEMENT

Thinking in terms of 'stakeholder management' started with Freeman's famous book *Strategic Management – A Stakeholder Approach*, in 1984. In Freeman's approach, a stakeholder is anyone who is affected by the actions of a company or has an impact on the company. Thus, we are talking here about relationships. A stakeholder is anyone who has a relationship with a company or a branch of government, NGO, church, etc. Those are in most cases relationships in which the company has an impact on people's lives. This occurs both where people did not themselves choose this relationship, such as is the case with people who live near a company's facilities, and where there is a more or less conscious choice.

At the same time, the people concerned may not necessarily choose to be affected by the decisions and actions of a particular company. This we see, for instance, with consumers, who by buying the products of a particular company are affected by that company. They may ask "Are those products safe?", "Do they deliver the quality which is promised?", "Are they produced through undesirable activities, such as child labor?".

Some stakeholders seek those relationships actively, as is the case with job applicants and suppliers. This concerns people who are from there on closely affected by the decisions and actions of the company. We can illustrate such relationships as follows: as an employee, your labor contract may well contain many pages of obligations on your part, reinforced by the obligations which your manager will put on you. The supplier may in his own processes be very dependent on the precise organizations of the company's processes, to mention only one aspect.

Other relationships no one actively seeks, while they have to be taken into consideration just the same. A good example can be found in the relationships of the company with various regulatory agencies that are part of the government structure. Look, for instance, at the situation in The Netherlands, where any company can be visited by a health inspector, a labor inspector, an environmental inspector, a building inspector, a tax auditor, to mention but a few. Those government employees will insist on respecting the relationship throughout the year. In many countries we also perceive relationships between companies and representatives of civil society, such as NGO's and churches. And the simplest example is perhaps the relationships between a company and the immediate neighbors of its facilities. Those relationships all point to the existence of stakeholders: individuals or groups who are affected by the company.

As is the case with all relationships, relationships with stakeholders are characterized by responsibilities. The people who did not choose the relationships, such as neighbors, may still, once they are reminded of the relationship, have certain expectations. Those expectations may include the expectation that the company's facilities do not blow up or cause any other kind of danger. The consumer definitely has expectations about what he or she can expect from the products and increasingly also from their makers. The same goes for the job applicant and the supplier.

Relationships with government-officials are a bit different, as they are usually formal in nature and prescribed by law. But then also the expectations which the government has regarding companies are laid down in laws and regulations. Next to that, governments have relationships with companies of a more market-based nature. For instance, where negotiations between a company and a government result in a license to drill for oil in a particular area, or where a government out-sources some of its operational responsibilities.

More complicated can be the relationships with representatives of civil society. Those relationships are less regulated and less clear. What adds to the complications is that often the representatives of civil society seek the relationship precisely because of the responsibilities of the company, as they see them. For instance, this is the case when the management of an oil refinery can approach the people in the nearby village, who they know to be stakeholders. They are more aware than those neighbors that an accident in their refinery could have an impact on them. Representatives of civil society could be unknown to them until the moment those representatives announce themselves, often at a time of crisis.

Those representatives could appear in the form of an environmental group, whose members may well live further away, while representing the neighbors and/or the environment in a more general sense. A complication is often that it is not always clear to which extent those representatives are actually representative of the people they say they represent. The legitimacy of representing the ecosystem, for instance, becomes even more unclear.

Traditionally, we distinguish between primary and secondary stakeholders, or between narrow and wide stakeholders. This refers to the persons and groups/organizations which play a role in the primary processes of the company: owners/stockholders, suppliers, employees, competitors and most importantly, consumers/clients. There are all the entities which companies have traditionally taken into consideration. They do this as they do have to find the capital to operate with, the suppliers for their resources, the employees to do their operations with and especially the clients who keep them in business. And they typically do this in a situation where they find themselves amongst competitors. In a monopoly situation, stakeholder management becomes a whole different story, as one can imagine. It becomes a bit more difficult with the secondary stakeholders. Some of them are known, such as the government, which, as a regulator; as a client, is a primary stakeholder.

At the same time, others may well surprise a company. They are the secondary stakeholders. To give an indication, the spokespeople for civil society can vary, from the chairman of a cooperative in one country to a priest in another country, from a union leader to a local mayor. Most companies can expect to meet representatives from environmental organizations, while it is not always obvious which ones to expect.

In short, the secondary stakeholders offer increased complexity. At the same time, they also offer opportunities, so do the primary stakeholders, who have traditionally received attention when it comes to business opportunities.

There are no standard approaches to how to do stakeholder management, but a few things can be said nonetheless. One insight to keep in mind is that stakeholders have certain interests, which make them in fact stakeholders in what the organization is doing. This means that when you check your understanding of stakeholder's interests, this allows you to see, whether a putative stakeholder is indeed to be regarded as a stakeholder and with the importance ascribed to it. Also, mapping the interests of stakeholders allows one to design a stakeholder hierarchy. It makes clear which stakeholders are more important at a particular moment than others.

The need for a stakeholder hierarchy quickly arises once the organization realizes the multitude of stakeholders it has to respond to. Obviously, not all of those stakeholders require immediate attention. Thus, it works best to decide per issue and moment, which stakeholders require more and which less attention. This is what results in a 'stakeholder hierarchy'. Some of the stakeholders may always be in the top of the stakeholder hierarchy and some only in the case at hand. It is the skill of the managers concerned to decide on this case by case.

An issue within stakeholder management is one of legitimacy. Typically, an organization deals with stakeholders through their representatives. For instance, if a company expands a production facility, the people living near that facility will be relevant stakeholders. They will be high in the stakeholder hierarchy. It will not in all cases be feasible or even desirable, to communicate with all neighbors directly, as sometimes happens in the form of town hall meetings. In many cases it is most efficient for all parties concerned to let the stakeholders be represented in communicating with the organization. In the case of the production facility, those representatives could be a neighborhood council, the board of the local soccer club and a regional environmental group.

Who do you choose to communicate with, the groups that are most likely to represent the local community, the groups that are likely to present the most difficulty when ignored or the groups that consist of the most reasonable individuals? Or do you prefer the group which most effectively represents local interests and sentiments?

Of course, one way in which this takes place is through communication of the organization with appropriate political bodies. In the case of the production facility, this might be the local city council. But that body may not adequately represent the neighbors of your facility. What if the city council is dominated by party X, while the people near your facility happened to have preferred party Y? One approach in dealing with this could be to involve more than one group, thus increasing the odds of including enough local interests and viewpoints. Another approach could be to be open to other stakeholders than the ones you have organized communication with, for instance through a website forum.

In the context of stakeholder management, there is great use of dialogue. This is a widely used and also abused notion. What is meant by it is a communication process, whereby meaning is exchanged and created. Thus people and their interests are brought together.

Figure 1: Phases of Dialogue

Phase 4	Phase 3
Flow	Inquiry
• Focus on what is new	• Beyond defensiveness
• Reconciliation of differences	• Creative
• Trust	• Conditional trust

Phase 1	Phase 2
Politeness	
• Lacks reflection	• Breakdown
• Exchange of monologues	• (potential) conflict
• Superficial 'trust'	• Instability
	• distrust

[Source: Williams Isaacs (1999). p.261]

The model given in the box above has practical applications to stakeholder management. It shows four quadrants, which Isaacs calls 'phases,' as he describes the possibility of an improvement in communication from the first to the fourth quadrant.

When you apply this model of dialogue to stakeholder management, you can see that the first phase, of politeness, applies to stakeholder management in terms of not more than public relations. It amounts to exchanging the acceptable terminology, but not daring to go beyond that. The move from the first to the second phase is often one of crisis. Stakeholder management has seen such crises. It is the context of conflict and obviously it is not stable. One can speak of successful stakeholder management when the communication between the organization and its stakeholders is according to phase 3, and enough trust is established to work together in furthering each other's interests. The style of communication of the fourth quadrant involves abandoning ones' own interest, with a focus on what one shares with other.

Although this may not seem obvious within an organizational context, some of this may take place and feed into what is happening according to phase 3. It has to be realized that the phases are not stable, as an incident might throw communication back into phase 2, for instance. These phases illustrate that trust has to be build within stakeholder management. The first phase, which is obviously one of superficiality, will not typically create much trust. The second phase destroys trust, but it might clarify where one stands and this can be used in overcoming the crisis and developing into phase 3.

Questions:
- *What is a 'stakeholder?'*
- *What is the difference between primary stakeholders and secondary stakeholders?*
- *Why is it in the interest of a business organization to take the interests of stakeholders into account?*
- *What is meant by the issue of legitimacy?*
- *How is dialogue relevant to stakeholder management?*

Case: "Shell and Stakeholder Engagement in Oman"
Oman is a country where respect for the existing power hierarchy and the prevailing norms is very important. Shell operates for many years now in Oman and tries to respect local values and traditions and has developed a social investment program. A social investment committee was established based on local traditions, called the Sur Forum. However, groups such as fishermen and youths did not feel represented in this committee. The fishermen started to complain that Shell affected their livelihoods because Shell needed a safety exclusion zone of 500 meter in width for their operations including their fishing areas. Consultation with fishermen revealed that this exclusion zone represented almost a third of one of the community's fishing areas. Therefore, Oman LNG, in which 'LNG' stands for 'Liquefied Natural Gas', developed a series of compensation-related measures.

Also, the youths started to complain that Shell did not provide them with jobs. The youths threatened to start a demonstration. However, demonstrating is not permitted in Oman.

As television and Internet influence the youths in Oman, and as they develop their own opinions and views, they become much more outspoken than the older generation. The government protected LNGs (joint venture of Shell) operations against demonstrations. The site manager and the 'wali,' a local mayor, then went to a hotel where the youth had gathered, to engage with them.

Source: Schouten and Remmé (2006)

Questions:
- *Which corporate values of Shell are in conflict in this case?*
- *What was the problem which Shell encountered?*
- *What were the risks for Shell in resolving this issue?*
- *How would you have dealt with this issue?*

EXTENDING RESPONSIBILITY FURTHER INTO THE FUTURE: SUSTAINABILITY

The notion of 'sustainability' goes back to the World Commission on Environment and Development, convened by the United Nations and chaired by Mrs. Brundtland, a former Norwegian prime minister. This commission was gathered in the 80s, when as the result of environmental concerns and the oil crisis of the mid seventies, concern grew on the way the developed world production, transportation and consumption were developing. The commission pleaded for an approach that would be responsible not just in terms of the present, but also towards the future. This approach was called 'sustainability,' which was defined as "meeting the needs of the present generation without compromising the ability of future generations to meet their own needs."

One could say that the basis for responsibility in an ethical sense consists in the assumption that other people, and in the eyes of many people, other creatures in general, are worthy of ones' consideration. This means consideration in an active sense, in that one adjusts ones' behavior accordingly. This principle is extended much further these days. We accept responsibility for other people we have not met and will in all likelihood never meet, but who nevertheless are affected by our actions. This is the globalized reality we increasingly have to deal with. In other words, this is the reality in which we have to be successful and responsible.

With sustainability, the notion of 'responsibility' becomes more-dimensional. What is meant here is that the other people or other creatures that one has to involve actively into ones' considerations may not be born yet. Those stakeholders are future co-inhabitants of our planet. This means that the people who are dependent on the quality of moral consideration in our actions are not only difficult for us to communicate with. They are in different cultures and on other parts of the globe. They are also not even present for us to communicate with.

In terms of ethics, this means extending the Kantian perspective. As we have seen in Chapter 10, the core of Kantian ethics is to consider something as just, only if it makes sense for everyone and respects the right of every human being to make a similar choice in meeting his or her legitimate needs. Now, with sustainability, what this has come to mean is to extend the consideration which in Kantian ethics is given to every human being, also to human beings who are members of future generations.

NEW PERSPECTIVES: THINKING IN BOTH SHORT AND LONG TERM, AND IN A WIDER SCOPE

Most managers are trained to deliver results in the short term; an impulse reinforced by the financial markets and accounting systems. There are several understandable reasons and backgrounds for this emphasis. One of them is to be found in the traditional way of organizing. In that bureaucratic model of the organization, each member of the organization had a very specialized job description. This stimulated that he or she felt discouraged, or at least not stimulated, to think outside of it, both in terms of scope as well as in terms of time horizon.

Developments towards sustainability tie in with other developments in international business and politics. The once-successful bureaucratic type of business organization, with its specialisms, job divisions and strict procedures, discouraged its members to look beyond what was considered a part of 'their job.' Usually they also did not need to. Decisions were made far away and change was seen as a disturbance to a dependable routine. The average employee had a very limited perspective of what his or her organization did and responsibility was largely a matter of ones' 'head office.' This type of organization has largely become unattractive.

These days, organizations need to be much more responsive to change. They often even need to change before a response is required. This involves much more innovating and decision-making at the local level, using a much wider perspective. These organizational developments tie in with the need to involve other considerations than those that were traditionally regarded as part of business into business decisions. Thus, the very approach that is required for sustainability also has various other sources in the organization's reality.

Systems thinking (Flood. 1999) has as a starting-point the idea that reality must be approached as a whole and not in a fragmented manner. It has relevance to the individual, who derives a connection to a larger whole from this approach. It is also relevant to the society and organization, which derive increased consistency from it. Systems thinking may involve complicated theory, where reality can best be understood through a sophisticated model. It may also involve combining otherwise diverse aspects of life, such as the financial, the moral, the managerial, the physiological, the humorous, political and other aspects. It also involves seeing life itself as a system, and no longer divided in 'work life' and 'private life,' or 'personal life' or 'family life.'

The relevance to sustainability is manifold. A challenge to working in the sense of sustainability is fragmentation. This is the case when one individual takes charge of a small aspect, which could be improving the specifications of the blades of a windmill, for instance, while another works on another, specified aspect. On the opposite side, one can also be so overwhelmed by the immensity of the sustainability perspective that one is discouraged from acting. Increasing the ability to think and act in terms of systems helps to change this for the better. From a moral perspective, it makes it possible to act in terms of respecting the interests of all of mankind. After all, that challenge is not much more than a nice statement, until it has become possible to include 'the big picture.'

Over the years sustainability has become an increasingly varied and complex part of reality, consisting of ideas, tools, organizations and international as well as national networks. Still, certain themes have arisen as a constant factor in its development. These themes can be divided into concerns and preferences.

To begin with the concerns, a preliminary, but probably not exhaustive, list will give a fair idea of the starting point of the sustainability movement. They are at least:

- Pollution;
- Depletion of resources and wasteful use of resources;
- Reduction of natural species;
- Climate change;
- Unhealthy ways of life;
- Unfair distribution of resources and of risks;
- Conflict, as resulting from some of the above.

The preferences of the, in number growing, people who think and work on sustainability are perhaps less clear and consistent, but a minimal overview would consist of:
- Efficient use of resources, comprising both natural resources as well as human capital;
- Integrating social, human and environmental considerations in all decisions that have an impact on the natural environment, which includes valuation of natural factors;
- Cooperation rather than competition, overcoming traditional distinctions, such as between NGO's and business organizations, or between competitors;
- Fair distribution of resources and opportunities;
- Equity, both in the present and towards new generations;
- Bio diversity;
- Animal well-being.

Questions:
- *How do you see thinking in terms of sustainability differ from traditional ways of thinking about business?*
- *Why does thinking in terms of sustainability require systems thinking?*
- *Why does sustainability require a vision for the longer term? How does managing with an eye on sustainability relate to stakeholder management?*

Case: *"The Brent Spar case: meeting international societal concerns"*

All over the world, Shell is one of the most well-known brands. It is supposed to stand for one of the largest companies in the world. In fact it is not one company. The company was created by a merger, in 1907, between Koninklijke Nederlandse Petroleum Maatschappij NV, or Royal Dutch Petroleum Company. Inc., and The Shell Transport and Trading Company. They shared ownership in a 60/40 relationship. These companies share ownership over a large number of companies which have operational responsibilities. This dual structure was solidified into a single structure in 2005, partly because of the lessons from the Brent Spar crisis.

The Brent oil field lies in the middle of the North Sea and produces a high quality of crude oil. The field is littered with oil industry installations, of which quite a few are owned and operated by Shell. The Brent Spar was one of those, half owned by Exxon, while Shell UK had operational management of the facility. As Shell decommissioned one of those installations in 1995, problems arose.

The installation was a kind of huge buoy, located between drilling installations and serving as a storage facility. This worked in that the drilling stations would be pumping oil into tanker ships, which would then transport the oil to the storage facility. From there it would later be pumped into larger tanker ships for transport to Aberdeen. This constituted a laborious and dangerous process. Therefore, early on, plans had been made by the oil companies involved and the governments of the UK and Norway to build a pipeline from Aberdeen (Scotland) to Bergen (Norway). The drilling stations would then be connected to this pipeline. After completion of the pipeline, the Brent Spar facility would be decommissioned.

The planning and preparation for the decommissioning of the Brent Spar took some 10 years. This process went parallel with the planning and constructing of the pipeline. In fact, when the pipeline was finished and the Brent Spar taken out of use, in 1991, the preparation for the discarding went on for four more years. In that time, various options for dealing with the installation were considered and weighed, judging technical, legal, environmental, financial and managerial considerations.

The conclusion arrived at by the specialists from Aberdeen University, working for Shell UK, was that the best solution would be to tow the installation to a very deep trough in the middle of the Atlantic Ocean. The specialists had advised against the alternative of dismantling the installation on land, because of the costs and also because of the environmental risks involved. As a result, Shell UK applied to the British government for a license to tow and dump the Brent Spar. It received this license in December 1994, and the British government announced its decision in February 1995, honoring a 60 day period for stakeholders to submit objections.

On April 30, 1995, thirty activists from Greenpeace occupied the installation, which by then had been without permanent staff presence. They did so in order to prevent that the installation would be towed away. Greenpeace alerted the media, stipulating that Shell had left a sizeable quantity of toxic substances in the buoy, to be dumped with it. It pointed out that some 400 other structures were to be decommissioned in the North Sea, and that allowing Shell to dump the Brent Spar would open the way to dumping all of them. Greenpeace started a campaign with the slogan "The ocean is not a rubbish dump." A conflict between Greenpeace and Shell ensued, which was viewed by the media as similar to the biblical battle of David against Goliath.

The media did not have reporters on site and relied on information from Greenpeace. The matter quickly received much attention in the media, primarily in Europe. As a result, the reporting led to severe criticism of Shell from leading politicians, such as the German Chancellor, Kohl. On June 10th, Shell tugboats connected with the Brent Spar and proceeded to tow it away. By then four Greenpeace activists had chained themselves to the structure. In the meantime, public criticism increased, including actions from politicians, a range of sabotage actions against Shell gas stations, and a significant decrease in sales. The arguments brought in by Shell in the media, stressing the scientific evidence backing its decision, were to no avail. Finally, at the end of June 1995, the Board of Shell decided to have the structure towed back to the North Sea and to look for a solution more acceptable to the public.

As part of the search for a solution, Shell hired an independent agency, Det Norske Veritas, to determine the amount and nature of toxic substances left in the Brent Spar. The findings of Det Norske Veritas indicated that the Greenpeace claim had been grossly exaggerated. It also came out that the Greenpeace activists who Greenpeace claimed had been run over by Shell boats had in fact been saved by them. Greenpeace felt forced to offer Shell an apology and admit that it had misrepresented the facts.

From the Brent Spar case some lessons can be drawn, for all those concerned. A simple lesson drawn by the media was to no longer rely on just one source. This is so even when it is complicated for a newspaper to send a boat or helicopter to a location like the Brent Spars', and it is much easier to hop on board a means of transportation provided by one of the parties in the conflict, in this case Greenpeace. It does jeopardize the quality and trustworthiness of journalism to rely on only one source. It was embarrassing to journalists to report on "massive amounts of toxic materials," on the basis of a report provided by Greenpeace, only to later have to report that this had been exaggerated by a factor of 100 and that Greenpeace had knowingly distributed falsehoods.

Several lessons were pertinent to Shell. To begin with, a discussion started within Shell about the Shell structure. After all, one complicating factor had been that the Brent Spar had been owned and operated by Shell UK, with licenses issued by the British government, while much of the public concern took place in Germany, in the Netherlands and in Scandinavian countries. The more important of the two Shell head offices was located in The Hague and outrage was noticeable among both the Dutch public and Dutch politics, while the decisions were made in the UK.

Also, within the Shell culture, it was highly unusual for the chairman of the Board to interfere with a decision made within one of the operating companies. The discussion within Shell, fed also by other developments, led to some changes in the corporate structure, resulting in the head office being concentrated in The Hague and tighter lines of coordination between the Board and the operating companies.

Another lesson had to do with stakeholder management. Although Shell had suffered some loss of sales, it also suffered the influence of people who were not its clients, and often did not even drive a car or otherwise frequent a gas station. In other words, Shell was surprised by the impact of secondary stakeholders. Already earlier on, and especially during the Brent Spar crisis, Shell management had noticed that there were several websites which were dedicated to criticizing Shell. Although initially responding defensively to this, it later decided to give room to such criticism on the Shell website itself: the Tell Shell pages, containing a well-visited forum. The forum soon collected strong criticism and detailed advice. In this forum on the Shell website anyone can send any type of feedback to Shell and is taken seriously in doing so. The content of the feedback is used within Shell to improve its operations.

In connection with that, it learned that communication to the outside is communication to the inside. In terms of actual communication, this was not new. But at Shell they speak of 'license to operate.' This means to be respected in a given society to the extent that it can successfully operate there. With this in mind, they learned at Shell that the image the company has in society has an impact on the attitude of people within the company, who typically belong to that society. In other words, when the company wants from society a 'license to operate,' it needs to realize that part of society is within the company in the form of employees. With the Brent Spar case, the average Shell employee, for instance, in The Netherlands or Germany, did not have any knowledge about the issue other than what the newspapers wrote, and the newspapers printed stories based on the Greenpeace reports,. The result was a certain discomfort amongst many Shell employees and quite a few even felt ashamed of being part of Shell.

For obvious reasons, Shell tries to avoid repeating such situations in the future. It has implemented several changes, ranging from a new edition of its code of conduct to new processes in management development. One remarkable development was on its website, with the development of the Tell Shell forum. It gave criticism a place within Shell. . This criticism and advice was taken seriously within the organization and benefited from, to the advantage of Shell operations. It also works to the advantage of what in Shell is called 'license to operate', acceptance by society to the extent that the organization can successfully operate in that society.

Questions:
- *What was the issue Shell had to solve with the Brent Spar problem?*
- *Was Shell thorough (enough) in planning the decommissioning of the Brent Spar?*
- *Where did Shell make a mistake?*
- *What were the experiences connected with communication processes?*
- *What do you think Shell and other companies have learned from this episode?*

JOHN ELKINGTON AND THE TRIPLE P MODEL

Some of the issues that need to be addressed have been raised by one of the leaders in this field, John Elkington.

In 1997, John Elkington's *Cannibals with Forks* was published. This book would have a far-reaching impact on the thinking about the responsibilities of business organizations towards the long term survival of the planet. Indeed, a far reaching topic. Elkington wrote this book from his experiences as CEO of a consultancy which focuses on environmental issues, SustainAbility, based in the UK. He points out in his book that in modern society, the ways in which production, transportation and many other business processes were dealt with created in the longer term more problems than it solved. For instance, if a profit is generated in a way which creates social unrest or environmental pollution, then an improvement in terms of economics leads to deterioration in other spheres of life. In answer to that, he launched his 'Triple P model'. This model holds that responsibility towards the planet has three dimensions: people, planet and profit, and that all three have to be honored. If you only honor the profit motive, you may notice the consequences in the other two dimensions. The same goes for honoring only the planet motive and forgetting about the people, e. g. jobs, and about the profit motive; if you do that, you may not be able to maintain this for very long. The same goes for when you only honor the people motive. Therefore, Elkington's book is an attempt at establishing a kind of economy which does not eat itself ('Cannibals'), but in fact has sufficient resilience to be meaningful in the long term.

As we have seen above, systems' thinking is highly relevant to developments towards sustainability. We see this in Elkington's vision of necessary changes. They are described as revolutions along seven dimensions.

Table 2   The Triple Bottom Line Revolutions of John Elkington

Focus	Old Paradigm	New Paradigm
1) Markets	Compliance	Competition

This means that sustainability is an issue in markets through compliance with national and international regulations, but will lead into a new source of opportunities.

2) Values	Hard	Soft

This means that the values which inspire decisions within the organization will increasingly be motivated by human concerns, instead of non-human concerns.

3) Transparency	Closed	Open

This means that increasingly stakeholders will be included in the motives for and backgrounds of decision-making.

4) Life-cycle Technology	Product	Function

This means that producers will be increasingly focused on meeting needs, for which a product is only a means and not the end in itself.

5) Partnerships	Subversion	Symbiosis

This means that groups and organizations that were before seen as antagonistic to the organizations processes and interests, and which often behaved as such, will be increasingly met in new partnership where common interests are explored.

6) Time	Wider	Longer

This means that awareness of time will shift from "everything that is happening right now" to "everything that is happening between now and the future".

7) Corporate Governance	Exclusive	Inclusive

This means that the governance of business organizations will no longer be restricted to representatives of the owners, but will include a wider range of stakeholders and thus will take a wide range of interests into account.

[Source: Elkington (1997: 3)]

Elkington sees it as crucial to the sustainability agenda to recognize the value of three dimensions, also known as the 'three P's'. They are People, Planet and Profit. These terms stand for the social dimension, the environmental dimension and the economics/financial dimension. In other words, decisions in business organizations, and also within governmental structures, should take these three dimensions into account in order for those decisions to contribute to a more sustainable future.

It is important to stress that the three notions interlock and have to be seen as a system. One way in which this happens is through 'triple bottom line accounting.' Elkington expects that in the future the financial records of companies will express not only the costs and benefits of the core processes. Also the costs of 'externalities' will count: costs of cleaning up pollution, costs and benefits of how the organization is received by society, costs and benefits of how the organization's products and services work out in the lives of its clients, and so on. Once all those factors are expressed in the accounting of business organizations, the right stimuli will be in place for organizing toward a sustainable future.

Questions:
- *What is meant by 'the Triple Bottom Line?'*
- *How do the three elements in the Triple Bottom Line relate?*
- *What is the thinking behind the title of John Elkingtons' book "Cannibals with Forks?"*
- *Is it possible, according to Elkington, to ignore one of the elements and still work in a sustainable manner?*
- *In your view, which part of the 'revolution' described by Elkington will be the hardest for managers to implement?*

THE BUSINESS CASE FOR SUSTAINABILITY

There is a relationship between business and sustainability. This relationship is widely disputed. There are those who argue against this link and they can both be found inside and outside of business organizations. Often, inside business organizations the argument is voiced that it is not up to a business organization to bear responsibility for such a far-reaching issue as the very survival of the human race. Connected with that criticism is often the argument that business organizations can not afford the investments that are necessary for change towards sustainability.

Both arguments are certainly plausible. As societies are increasingly critical regarding the power of especially the larger business organizations, it can be seen as understandable when business leaders hesitate to accept a wider role than strictly necessary. This is especially the case within highly legalistic countries, such as the United States of America. In such countries, the behaviors and the assuming of particular roles have immediate legal consequences. Also the financial argument has merit, as radically changing the ways in which an organization operates, ranging from producing, arranging housing and transportation to how it organizes marketing and HR, will in all likelihood involve sizeable investments. And connected to that argument is a governance issue: Is it not the shareholder's money that is involved in all this?

From outside of the business organization the link between business and sustainability is given by opinion leaders. One of them is Bernhard Lietaer – discussed in the previous chapter – who argues that the modern financial world operates in a way which makes sustainability unlikely. The opinion leaders point at a structural tension between the dynamics of the business world and the dynamics which are developing toward sustainability. We have seen in the discussion of the Triple Bottom Line approach, suggested by John Elkington, that there is also another possible approach.

This approach leads to what is called 'the business case for sustainability.' You could say that this challenge is very similar to Prahalads', discussed in the previous chapter. Here too a clear need, or set of needs, is recognized and the answer to that is sought in the dynamic of international business. One assumption in this approach is that international business needs its own dynamic in order to meet people's needs and create prosperity. As approaches that run counter to that dynamic may be less effective, it may be much more efficient to look for solutions that work on the dynamic of international business. For as long as history has been documented, people have been exchanging goods and services in the effort to satisfy their needs and the needs of their loved ones. Would it not be more natural to accept this dynamic as extending into the future?

Two questions connected to this issue are "Can we afford sustainability?", raised by those who worry about the expenses of new ways of producing, organizing, transporting, land use, to name only a few, and "Can we afford not to be sustainable?", raised by those who worry about the consequences of unsustainable ways of the same. Of course, these questions may well be raised by the very same people. The first question may be manageable in theory: It is often possible to organize and operate in such a way that the changes which are needed make good business sense. This is especially so if you look at it with more than a short-term perspective. But in real life it is more difficult. In most business circumstances, the question reads: "Can we afford sustainability, given the current market situation?"

Answering the question will be a matter of perspective and courage. To begin, it will be a matter of perspective. It makes much difference whether one sees the question as primarily pertaining to the costs involved, or if one sees the question as primarily pertaining to the opportunities offered by expected new market conditions. It is also a matter of courage, as it may well involve moving ahead of current market forces, in expectation of what meets the needs expressed by future market forces. This is reminiscent of what Collins and Porras (1994) describe, after they studied major companies and distinguished market leaders from companies very close to market leaders, noticing in the cultures of market leaders an element of courage. That courage enabled them to act in terms of expected market, not so much in terms of existing markets. Typically, leadership characterized by courage is more focused on the opportunities than on costs and more innovative.

This brings us to the meaning of sustainability for 'the average manager.' Although predicting the future is beyond what can be expected, there is reason to believe that managers will increasingly be expected to be more creative, with an eye on innovation and learning. They will also be more inclusive in how decisions are reached and on whose interests are taken into account, and more capable to think and act from an awareness of the systems they belong to.

Questions:
- *What will be the most important managerial skills for managing in terms of sustainability?*
- *How would you reply to a manager who asks you "Can I afford to be sustainable?"*
- *Why is systems' thinking relevant to managing for sustainability?*
- *What would be the consequences for leadership of managing with an eye on sustainability?*
- *Why does managing in line with sustainability call for innovation? How does this compare with the BOP call for sustainability, discussed in the previous chapter?*
- *Why does managing for sustainability call for leadership?*
- *How could markets respond to the call for sustainability?*

CONCLUSION

The topics discussed in the previous chapters are all relevant within the context of what was discussed in this chapter. Sustainability is a term that is highly relevant for the immense challenges facing business, politics and societies in general at the start of the 21st century. In this new reality, success for organizations will presumably involve the ability to respond adequately, perhaps even better than others, to those challenges.

REFERENCES

Collins. J. and Porras. J.L. 1994. *Built to Last – Successful Habits of Visionary Companies*. Los Angeles: Collins

Dresner. S. 2002. *The Principles of Sustainability*. Earthscan Publications. London

Dunphy, D. and Griffiths, A. R..2007. *Organizational Change for Corporate Sustainability second edition: A Guide for Leaders and Change Agents of the Future - Understanding Organizational Change*. London: Routledge

Edwards. A. R. 2005. *The Sustainability Revolution: Portrait of a Paradigm Shift*. Gabriola: New Society Publishers

Elkington, J. 1997. *Cannibals with Forks – The Triple Bottom Line of 21st century Business*. Oxford: Capstone Publishing

Flood. R. L.. 1999. *Rethinking the Fifth Discipline – Learning within the unknowable*. London/New York: Routledge

Isaacs. W. 1999. *Dialogue and the Art of Thinking Together – a pioneering approach to communications in business and in life*. New York: Doubleday

Schouten. E. and Remmé. J.H.M. "Making Sense of Corporate Social Responsibility in international business: experiences from Shell". in: *Business Ethics – A European Review*. 15:4. October 2006

http://www.shell.com/home/Framework?siteId=aboutshellenandFC2=andFC3=/abou tshell-en/html/iwgen/dialogues/about_shell_dialogues/tell_shell_02052007.html (July 26, 2007)

RECOMMENDED FURTHER READING

Donaldson. D. Preston. Lee E. 1995. The Stakeholder Theory of the Corporation: Concepts, Evidence, and Implications. *The Academy of Management Review. 20*: 1. 65-91

Dresner. S. 2002. *The Principles of Sustainability*. London: Earthscan Publications

Dunphy, D. and Griffiths, A. R..2007. *Organizational Change for Corporate Sustainability second edition: A Guide for Leaders and Change Agents of the Future - Understanding Organizational Change*. London: Routledge

Edwards. A. R. 2005. *The Sustainability Revolution: Portrait of a Paradigm Shift*. Gabriola: New Society Publishers

Flood. R. L.and Romm. N. R.A. 1997. *Critical Systems Thinking*. New York: Springer

Harrison. J.S. Freeman. E. R. Stakeholders, Social Responsibility, and Performance: Empirical Evidence and Theoretical Perspectives. *The Academy of Management Journal. 42*: 5. 479-485

Hitchcock. D. and Willard. M. 2006. *The Business Guide to Sustainability: Practical Strategies and Tools for Organizations*. London: Earthscan Publications

Senge. P. M.. Laur. J. Schley, S. and Smith. B. 2006. *Learning for Sustainability*. Boston

Willard, R., 2005. *The Next Sustainability Wave: Building Boardroom Buy-in - Conscientious Commerce*. Gabriola: New Society Publishers

CHAPTER THIRTEEN
CONNECTING WHAT HAS PRECEDED
JOOP REMMÉ

LEARNING OBJECTIVES:

- To have developed a working knowledge of the themes discussed in the previous chapters
- To understand the connections among the themes which have been discussed, in terms of their practical consequences for management.

INTRODUCTION

In this textbook, we have dwelled on a wide range of topics: leadership, organization, change, business culture, business responsibility, and national culture. Academically speaking, each of these topics could fill a separate course and a separate book, or even a range of books. But this book, although based on state-of-the-art academic research, is written with an eye on the real life of a manager. Students reading this book primarily have an interest in becoming better managers, and so this textbook has presented summarized, need-to-know information.

In the first chapter, we discussed the historical background of modern business organizations, at least in Europe and the USA. In doing so, we noticed flaws in the ways of organizing and managing in that past era, which still trouble us today. Let us now look for a moment at what it means to be a better manager in the modern business reality.

For one thing, the line between manager and leader will blur further, as increasingly all managers, and employees in general, will be expected to show characteristics of leadership in their professional behavior.

Another changing dimension of managerial life has to do with 'globalization.' This concept no longer refers only to multinational corporations. These days tools and processes are available that allow any single individual and any small company to be active in the international arena. That means that markets are becoming more diversified and more dynamic.

Among other new issues coming to the fore is dealing with cultural differences. This complication has only been touched upon in this book, because it is treated extensively in Jones, DeBono and van der Heijden. But we do note here that globalization offers challenges in how to organize for strategy formulation and implementation.

This means that the human element within organizations, which has become more and more important over the past decades, will become even more central for the success of organizations. At the same time, many organizations are still organized around assumptions that were prevalent in a time when the human element was less crucial.

This relates to another reasonable expectation: Change will happen. It is not only that change is more and more likely to take place. It is also that change is increasingly no longer a project, but an ongoing process. Therefore, the ability to manage change productively will increasingly be expected from managers, and managers have to realize that they are expected to manage especially the human dimension of change. Changing behaviors related to the performances defined in the strategy will be part of the manager's job. And a strategy will only be successful after it translates successfully into new behaviors on the part of members of the organization.

LEARNING

What has been learned from the content, questions and cases in the chapters before us is of diverse nature. One element of this diverse nature is that we have looked both at theories, on leadership, change and responsibility, and at stories of actual events, in all their practicality. Another element of it is in the variety of geographical locations from which issues and stories were brought to us. This book has been written from the awareness that managerial reality will become increasingly diverse in many ways. It will become diverse both in challenges and in opportunities, and diverse in context. This new diverse reality opens up new markets, new responsibilities and new risks.

The new challenges are not beyond the scope of human possibilities. They may even form a theater for personal development. The development of the organization is increasingly seen in terms of the personal development of its members. This has been demonstrated in the chapters on leadership. We saw there how leadership depends both on the characteristics and capabilities of professional members of organizations and on the qualities of the relationships between those individuals and the organizations to which they belong. But we have also seen in the chapters on change how this depends on the ability of people to lead and conduct change. Perhaps it can even be said that while once people were seen as the element that makes the change work, it now increasingly is the case that it is the other way around: change is the way in which people work.

RELEVANCE

The relevance of the discussed topics for emerging economies has been the background for the book. Emerging economies are not themselves a topic for this book, but the topics that are discussed in this book do have strong relevance to the challenges facing emerging economies. That applies to leadership, to ways of organizing, to ways of changing and answering resistance to change, to stakeholder management and the issues of CSR. These are increasingly global issues, but they affect emerging economies in a special way. In emerging economies, we often see that corruption (see chapter 11) undermines attempts at leadership. We also see in several emerging economies growth rates which surpass the growth rates that were familiar in the economies in which most of the books on change management were written. And we see sustainability issues pose a greater risk in emerging economies than in established economies. Those issues prompt managers on a global scale to rethink how they are organizing their structures and processes.

RECAP

Let us revisit what we discussed in the preceding chapters:

It stands to reason that in chapter 1 there is an introduction of the topics discussed in this book and of their importance in determining managerial and company success. They are discussed with an awareness of the most current research, but with an eye on managerial reality. In that reality, these topics – organizational design, change management, leadership and corporate social responsibility – typically do not receive attention in isolation. They are connected and even interdependent phenomena. They are also discussed and in terms of their historical development. It is the manager's challenge to deal with these topics in a systematic way, as the reality in which he or she will have to be successful has those topics as parts of the same system. It is explained in this chapter how a loss of a systematic approach became one of the persisting problems in old-style organizing. Therefore, these topics are brought together here in one book.

In chapters 2 and 3 attention went to the topic of leadership. As everyone has notions about leadership, it is relevant first, in chapter 2, to discuss the traditional ways and theories which explain leadership. Then we show how thinking on leadership has evolved and offer tools to promote it. This also includes important leadership competencies and traits. The traditional approaches have shown a gradual shift in emphasis. This shift went from treating leadership as the impact of what 'great men' are able to accomplish to how leaders relate to the groups and organizations that they inspire to extraordinary achievement.

Attention is also paid to behaviorist approaches to leadership. Having established the relationship between leader and organization, we have to recognize the impact of new structures and new attitudes towards organizing on leadership, resulting in new models of leadership. This we discussed in chapter 3. The new models include the perspectives of 'soft management' and leadership as seen from the various roles which leaders are associated with.

Chapter 4 discussed the relationships between strategy and structure. In discussing these two notions, it brought attention to two kinds of relationships: 1) the relationships between organizational configuration and strategic options, and 2) the relationships between organizations and their environments. The strategic options lead to specific types of organizations, which were broadly grouped as mechanistic and organic. Each of these types developed from clearly different strategic starting points. In each type the purpose is to achieve excellence in facing the challenges that the strategy has identified and which the environment has confronted the organization with. This has to build on an optimal interaction between strategy and structure.

In the early chapters, structure was treated as a given, but chapters 5 and 6 start from recognizing that structure is designed. Thus, in Chapter 5, the emphasis moved from strategy to structure. Then organizational design is discussed, with a focus on key questions and design options. Notions that are important in organizing are: division of labor and how to organize control, how tight control is arranged, how formal roles and relationships are organized, to what degree the organization is centralized and what precisely is centralized, and from what kind of paradigm the organizing is done, including a particular understanding of the nature of people concerned. Factors which influence this, such as the organization's environment, the chosen strategy, and technological development were discussed in the context of the organizational life cycle. The possible structures that result were the subject of Chapter 6. The possible choices in developing strategy were connected with different ways of designing the organizational structure. Alternatives in design were discussed. A structure can be simple, divisional, product based, geographical, a matrix or in some other way a combination, traditionally speaking,. It is also noted that new types of organizing, typically more dynamic, are being developed. New types of organization, notably the network organization and the virtual organization, were discussed in this context.

The dynamic which was introduced in Chapter 6 was developed further in Chapters 7, 8 and 9, as we looked into organizational development and change. These chapters can be characterized as answering 'the why,' 'the what,' and 'the how' of change. In discussing the 'why', attention has been paid both to incremental change, or growth, as well as to the readiness of the employees of the organization to conduct change successfully. The 'what' became apparent in discussing the most important models for change. This leads to the 'how', as it also clarified the roles of the various players within the organization as well as the impact of external players and factors. As said readiness may not always be found, resistance is a potential part of change processes, and this means that being able to deal with resistance to change is a vital part of managing change.

What that further entails was clarified in Chapter 8. Interpersonal, team and organizational methods for conducting change effectively were discussed there. Also discussed were methods for planning and organizing the change process. It is recognized that there is no clear recipe for change. Still, certain warnings can be given and they were discussed in this chapter. There is not a single best way for managing change, this chapter warned, but several options can be shown which highlight various possibilities. From these warnings, some advice on how to go about implementing change has become possible, as described in this chapter. The chapter built on the preceding chapter, for the reason that the 'why' of change has proven to be of influence on the 'what' of change. Thus, attention has been paid to the factors which drive change and the ways in which to initiate change, showing a diversity of approaches.

This was continued in Chapter 9, where the focus moved to how to do change. Methods for managing change were discussed there in more detail. Chapter 9 starts the discussion of the 'how' with an explanation of business process re-engineering. This tool and similar tools have become more needed, it is argued in the chapter, because the need for fast change, and drastic change, has dramatically increased over the past years. This has consequences in terms of the human side of change, including the leadership of change. This is the reason to go back to the discussion, raised earlier in Chapter 7, on resistance to change. The discussion in chapter 8, about guidelines for change, was also continued. Thus, change is explained as a continuous characteristic of flexible organizations. It is a capacity for transformation, of which successful companies are capable.

Chapters 10 and 11 were dedicated to ethics and corporate social responsibility. These subjects were reason to first visit the most prominent traditions on ethics. Those traditions express themselves as influences on managers and their companies in their decision-making. Those traditions are also relevant to Corporate Social Responsibility and stakeholder management, as the people involved have been influenced by such traditions. Those people will at least in part act from their backgrounds in their demands on managers and companies. Those traditions have become more relevant as societies and business organizations have become more entwined and as business organizations increasingly accept that entwinement and the responsibilities which result from it. This entwinement was illustrated with a discussion of current issues, which have arisen out of the acceptance of social responsibility by companies. Those issues are notably discrimination and corruption. The Bottom of the Pyramid movement and new developments in finance and health are also worthy of attention.

Chapter 12 resumed the discussion of corporate social responsibility, from its basis in stakeholder management. We are brought back to the topics of structure and change, as stakeholder management questions the traditional ways of leading and organizing, discussed in Chapter 1. The chapter directs the discussion of stakeholder management further to the challenge of working according to principles of sustainability. Given that the interaction between business organizations and the societies in which they operate has intensified and will probably continue to intensify, major issues which internationally have a profound impact on societies are expected to have an equally profound impact on the companies in them. Sustainability is the umbrella notion which covers all the issues concerning the future well-being of the world's population. It will in all likelihood be the horizon against which a future manager will measure his or her success and that of his or her company.

CONNECTIONS

Our discussion of sustainability strongly suggested that systems thinking is increasingly important to managers, and it is from this perspective that this book has been designed and written. Throughout, we treated leadership, structure, change and responsibility as intrinsically connected within today's organizational life.

That is why we have decided to depart from the traditional approach of MBA education, which involved treating those subjects in separate courses. Instead, we have brought issues together which also come together in the realities of manager's lives, and will increasingly do so. We did this in accordance with our view of developments in management. From our point of view, the manager is increasingly confronted with complex challenges. It does not help him or her to discuss elements of those challenges piecemeal. Rather, the manager deserves to receive assistance with those challenges precisely in their complexity, showing ways through the inter-wovenness of the elements of those challenges and helping the manager decide which elements to attend to first in precisely the situation he or she is in. This has been the original thought motivating this book and it has to be on our minds in concluding it.

EPILOGUE

This chapter concludes a book in which the topics of leadership, organization, change and corporate responsibility were discussed in their inter-wovenness and with an eye on current developments. Much more can be said on these topics than we have room for in this book. Still, we have managed to address the essentials of these topics, both in terms of background and in terms of ongoing developments. After having studied this book, it is up to the manager to do the rest.

REFERENCES

Jones. S. and De Bono. S. 2007. *Managing Cultural Differences*. Oxford: Meyer and Meyer Media.
Green to Gold. http://csr.blogs.mcdonalds.com/default.asp?item=208112 (November 17. 2007)

PRACTICAL MANAGEMENT GUIDES

Maastricht School of
Management Vol. 1
Jones, Wahba, van der Heijden
How to Write Your MBA Thesis

Students of MBA programs who are
preparing for the research, writing
and defense of their MBA thesis will
find this book especially useful.
Nine chapters give detailed
examples of how students all over
the world have managed the
problems that the MBA thesis
project has thrown at them. The
appendices include examples of
everything one needs to complete
the thesis – proposal, abstract,
contents page, introduction,
literature review, research
methodology, data analysis,
conclusions and recommendations,
and suggested areas for future
research.

Maastricht School of
Management Vol. 3
DeBono, van der Heijden and
Jones
Managing Cultural Diversity

This practical, interactive
course textbook is divided into
three parts: looking at the way
teams work, how people are
managed in organizations, and
how we can understand the
impact of organizational and
national cultures. A diverse
range of topics with a clear
international flavor are introduced,
ranging from team dynamics
to managing human resources
and intercultural diversity.
Students of MBA programs will
find this book especially useful.

320 pages
11 photos, 5 charts
Paperback, 6^1/2" x 9^1/4"
ISBN: 978-1-84126-231-4
$ 34.00 US
£ 16.95 UK/€ 24.95

c. 300 pages
Paperback, 6^1/2" x 9^1/4"
ISBN: 978-1-84126-239-0
$ 34.00 US
£ 16.95 UK/€ 24.95

The Series

This series makes excellent, affordable textbooks for students worldwide. By emphasizing
the international, multicultural, sustainability, and social responsibility dimensions of
management, and by giving special attention to change issues in transitional
economies, these volumes aim to define the way management subjects should be
taught to multicultural audiences. It provides students all over the world with essential
advise for successful studies.

Editors of the Series:
Ronald Tuninga and Fred Philipps

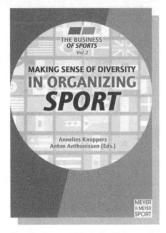

The Business of Sports, Volume 1
James Skinner and Allan Edwards
The Sport Empire

The book critiquies the globalisation of sport from a Autonomist Marxist perspective. This analysis is supported by numerous international sport examples that highlight how sport is being governed by a select group of sport organisations, multinational companies and media conglomerates. This domination of the sport industry is marginalising disadvantaged groups and is subsequently being challenged by new methods of protest and resistance. "The Sport Empire" provides compelling reading for those interested in the effects of globalisation of sport.

192 pages, 3 charts
Paperback, $6^1/2$" x $9^1/4$"
ISBN: 978-1-84126-168-3
$ 19.95 US/$ 29.95 CDN
£ 14.95 UK/€ 18.95

The Business of Sports, Volume 2
Annelies Knoppers and
Anton Anthonissen (Eds.)
Making Sense of Diversity in Organizing Sport

This book is about the way otherness can be suppressed by dominant meanings. The purpose of the book is to focus on organizational consequences of processes of sense making and assigning meanings to diversity in sport organizations. There is a dominant European perspective on sense making of diversity and a more American approach. The conclusion is that scholars and researchers who work in the area of diversity need to pay attention to both ways of looking at diversity.

120 pages, 2 charts
Paperback, $6^1/2$" x $9^1/4$"
ISBN: 978-1-84126-203-1
$ 19.95 US
£ 14.95 UK/€ 18.95

The Business of Sports

This Sport Management Book Series aims to incorporate cutting edge work which is designed to transcend the boun-daries between business and sport.
The series will be used as a forum for research and scholarly insight surrounding the major issues of importance for those concerned with sport management and sport marketing.
The series will provide an opportunity to illustrate and highlight the ways in which the business of sport has expanded to become a global industry.

Editors of the Series:
Dr. James Skinner, Griffith University, Queensland, Australia
Prof. Paul De Knop, Free University Brussels, Belgium

MEYER
&MEYER
MEDIA